OFF THE GRID

Histories of Belgian graphic design

Edited by Sara De Bondt

p.5 **Foreword**
Sara De Bondt

p.7 **CONTEXT**

p.8 **Design strategies of modernist graphic designers in Belgium**
Katrien Van Haute

p.24 **Typo Belgiëque**
Jo De Baerdemaeker

p.34 **La Cambre and graphic design: The early years**
Richard Hollis

p.40 **Graphic design and the colonisation of Congo**
Sara De Bondt

p.60 **The Belgian Chamber of Graphic Designers**
Sara De Bondt

p.74 **Practices in the margins of design history: Club culture and graphic design in Belgium**
Katarina Serulus

p.89 **IN THEIR OWN WORDS**

p.90 **Sophie Alouf-Bertot**
p.95 **Rob Buytaert**
p.98 **Boudewijn Delaere**
p.104 **Paul Ibou**
p.109 **Herman Lampaert**

p.113 **PLATES**

p.161 **DESIGNERS**

p.162 **Jeanine Behaeghel**
Sara De Bondt

p.172 **Marleen Deceukelier**
Belgian Institute Graphic Design

p.174 **Anne Delcoigne**
Belgian Institute Graphic Design

p.176 **Gilles Fiszman: The power of nuance**
Hugo Puttaert

p.182 **Corneille Hannoset, Constantin Brodzki and Marcel Broodthaers**
Jan Ceuleers

p.198 **Luk Mestdagh: An amiable troublemaker**
Hugo Puttaert

p.204 **Multi-Art by Liliane-Emma Staal and Paul Ibou**
Sara De Bondt

p.224 **Michel Olyff: Image as effigy**
Hugo Puttaert

p.230 **Lucien De Roeck**
Jean-Michel Meyers

p.240 **Frie Soomers**
Belgian Institute Graphic Design

p.242 **Jean-Jacques Stiefenhofer: In design we trust**
Hilde Pauwels

p.256 Graphic design archives in Belgian public institutions
p.258 Bibliography
p.265 Photographers
p.266 Image credits
p.267 Acknowledgements
p.268 Index
p.272 Colophon

Foreword

The history of Belgian graphic design remains largely uncharted – a blind spot this book seeks to address. Despite the significant contributions of Belgium-based graphic designers, it is scarcely written about, even in Belgium. The last and only historical overview was published nearly 25 years ago.

While *Off the Grid* focuses on graphic design produced in Belgium in the twentieth century – with an emphasis on the period from the 1950s to the 1980s – it is not intended to celebrate a national style. As the Brussels-based Hungarian graphic designer Charles Rohonyi wrote in 1971, 'Belgium is undoubtedly the one European country with the highest number of foreigners per square mile. This has equally made it a country "without graphic frontiers".'

The ubiquity of graphic design often renders it invisible. This is particularly the case in Belgium, where, to date, there is not a single public institution dedicated to collecting and preserving graphic design. One of the aims of this publication, illustrated with works gathered from over 50 private and public archives, is to draw attention to the enormous value of graphic design traces and to highlight their precarity if their preservation and study is not pursued.

The Design Museum Gent stands out as a rare supporter of graphic design in the country. It was there that I was fortunate to organise an exhibition on Belgian printed matter from the 1960s and 1970s, as part of my doctoral research on Belgian graphic design history. The exhibition gave this book its title and impetus, by revealing the extraordinary and largely overlooked diversity of material produced in Belgium in the second half of the twentieth century.

As the starting point of this research project, the exhibition allowed historical shortcuts and personal visual connections which are more difficult to present in book form. Nevertheless, I hope this collection of essays and points of views, the plates and 'In their own words' section convey the exhibition's original sense of profusion and multiplicity. Inspired by Martha Scotford's call for a 'messy history,' it is not a single-authored tome in neat chronology, but rather a condensation of conversations and exchanges with fellow designers, teachers, students, historians, family members and former assistants of some of the featured protagonists, and archivists.

This book will have reached its goal if it can reveal how much more work remains in excavating graphic design made in Belgium. Let us not wait another quarter century for the next title on Belgian graphic design to appear, but instead keep multiplying the perspectives on this – as I hope *Off the Grid* will prove – fascinating and rich field of inquiry.

Sara De Bondt

CONTEXT

This chapter presents research into the histories of Belgian graphic design by scholars active in the field today. Several of the essays were first presented during the *This is...* lecture series at Design Museum Gent (2019–20).

Katrien Van Haute

DESIGN STRATEGIES OF MODERNIST GRAPHIC DESIGNERS IN BELGIUM

Katrien Van Haute (1977) holds a PhD on the genesis of graphic design and modern typography in Belgium at the beginning of the twentieth century. She teaches at LUCA School of Arts (campus Sint-Lucas Ghent) on the history of typography and other graphic design-related subjects.

There was such a tactile power to the posters and other ephemera included in the exhibition *Off the Grid* at Design Museum Gent (2019–20). They were so much more colourful than the image I previously had of Belgium at that time. I realised how much more immediate print can be when it is not printed digitally. The intensity of the colours of a screenprint is unparalleled.

The technique that is used to create graphic design is never an afterthought. Today, the influence of technology on creation is stronger than it ever has been. In an age dominated by computer-mediated communication, the tangible has become highly appreciated. When printing is no longer evident, many designs remain forever in a kind of digital limbo, never becoming objects. They circulate on platforms such as Instagram as digital promises, like frozen embryos in a laboratory.

Preliminary studies in the form of sketches or scribbles on paper have also become rare. That is a shame, because they can tell us so much about the creative process and testify to the strategies that the designer employed. Today, that sketching and brainstorming is mainly done digitally, and we no longer have any illusions about the durability of the devices we need for this. As a result of the gradual replacement of paper with digital matter, there may come a day when it will be clear that we can consult the work processes of the twentieth century more easily than those of the twenty-first century.

In my art-historical research into graphic design, I am always curious about the practical side of things. In what way, and with what materials, did the designer get to work? And how did the design manifest itself? Sketches, preliminary studies, and proofs – preferably annotated – are particularly interesting primary sources. They form the basis of this text, in which I discuss the design strategies of the pioneers of Belgian graphic design, the generation that preceded the designers of the 1960s and 1970s.

The birth of a new discipline

The field of graphic design is roughly as old as abstract art in the West, dating back to the early twentieth century. And that is no coincidence: graphic design and abstract art are related. When painters such as Wassily Kandinsky, Piet Mondriaan, or Kazimir Malevich were no longer interested in the identifiable rendering of nature, they began to experiment with their basic tools: colour, composition, and form. At the same time, printers freed themselves from old, symmetrical printing schemes. For centuries, it had been the custom to set the text directly onto the printing press, composing stick in hand. Typography was purely manual work, which had been increasingly taken over by automatic typesetting machines since the late nineteenth century. Just as in the visual arts, traditional printing models were being questioned, graphic designers began to experiment with the tools available in print shops: fonts, ink, colour, and paper. Both in the visual arts and in printing, image makers were fascinated by abstract composition.

A Belgian example of this kind of experiment is the book *Beeldekens uit het leven van Sint-Franciskus van Assisi* (*Images from the Life of St Francis of Assisi*, 1927, fig. 1) by Michel de Ghelderode, designed by Victor Servranckx. The layout has liberated itself from the traditional axial scheme. Arranging graphic elements on a page was no longer a routine operation, but became an artistic act. It became graphic design.

 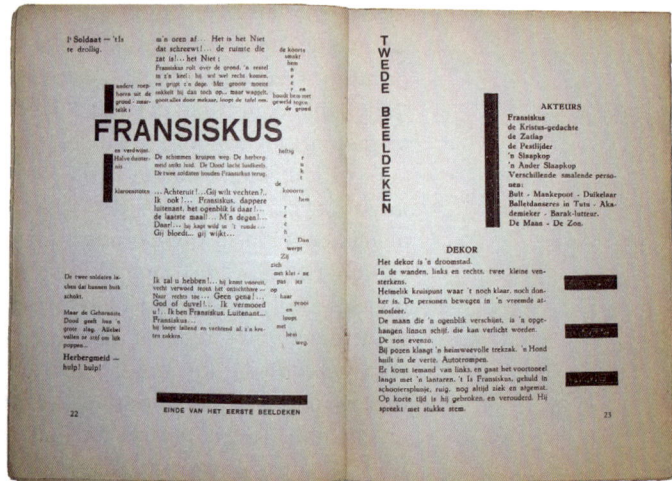

fig. 1
Victor Servranckx
Cover and book design for Michel de Ghelderode, *Beeldekens uit het leven van Sint-Franciskus van Assisi* (Images from the Life of St Francis of Assisi), 1927

Asymmetry

In order to create more dynamism and contrast, graphic designers abandoned the static layout and embraced asymmetry, which meant that it was no longer possible to typeset directly in the print shop. A plan had to be made beforehand and a new tool was introduced: the pencil. Graphic designer Jos Léonard made at least six sketches with his pencil for the poster of the exhibition *Belgische kunstenaars van heden* (*Belgian Artists of Today*, 1940, fig. 2) at the Rijksmuseum in Amsterdam. He composed the typography of one of them quite classically, around a central axis of symmetry, but this meant that there was little room for variations. The five other sketches are asymmetrical, offering endless possibilities. The designer's job is to investigate with the pencil and to decide which composition is the most exciting and can best visualise the message.

I came across many such sketches during my doctoral research on Léonard.[1] I found a pile of preliminary studies in Namur, where the Moretus Plantin University Library hosts the Godenne Foundation. The foundation is named after Willy Godenne, Léonard's regular printer. In 1926, they decided to work together; Léonard took on the role of 'advertisement artist'. He was one of the first abstract artists in Belgium. Godenne must have been very proud of this collaboration, since he kept just about everything that he had made with Léonard, right down to his sketches.

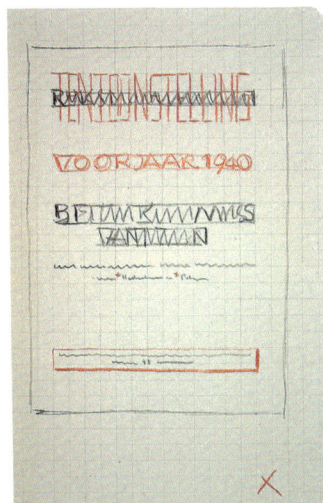
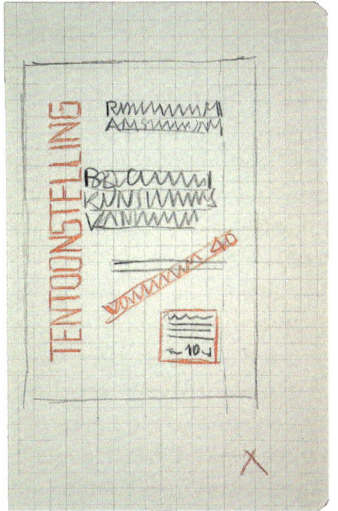
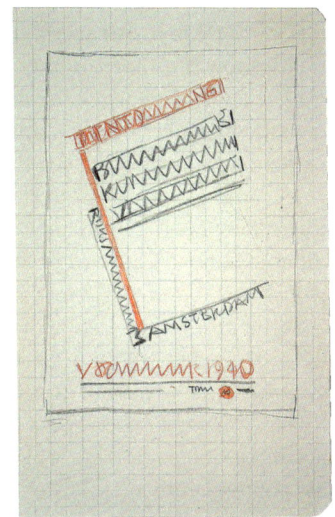

fig. 2
Jos Léonard
Sketches for the poster of *Belgische kunstenaars van heden (Belgian Artists of Today)*, 1940

On some of the design sketches, both Léonard and Godenne have written something, each in his own recognisable handwriting, making it possible to reconstruct their dialogue. Godenne often made technical notes about the choice of paper or the font size. On the sketch for an advert for the Flemish bookshop Gudrun (1926, fig. 3), Léonard made a suggestion about copywriting. If you compare this sketch with the printed design, you can see that all his proposals were accepted.

In any case, this advertisement is a remarkable design. As an adherent of the Vlaamse Beweging (the movement for Flemish independence), Léonard probably did not hesitate when opting for yellow and black, the colours of the Flemish flag. Viewed through contemporary eyes, the incorporation of these colours in a Constructivist design together with the Flemish-minded text seems strange. The heavy capitals and the almost aggressive arrows are reminiscent of 1920s Russian advertising propaganda. As a young artist, Léonard called himself a Constructivist, which would appear difficult to reconcile with his political convictions. The Constructivists strove for internationalism and universalism, which seems to be at odds with regionalist Flemish nationalism. Such paradoxes, however, appear frequently in Belgian design from those years.[2]

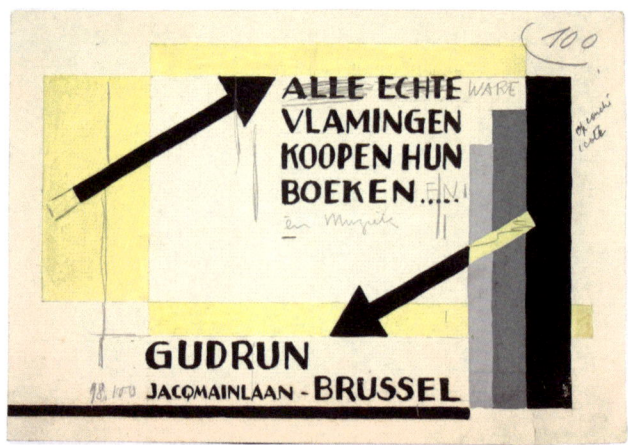

fig. 3
Jos Léonard
Leaflet for
Gudrun bookshop, 1926
Sketch (top)
Printed copy (bottom)

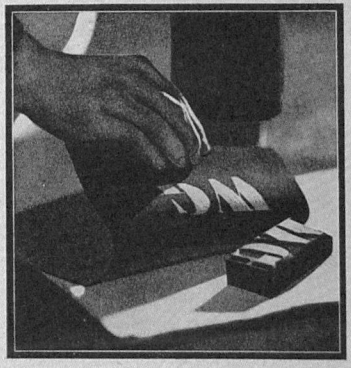

fig. 4
Jos Léonard and Willy Godenne
Poster for solo exhibition, 1928

Some forty years later, it was much more unusual for a graphic designer to include his or her political preference in a graphic design. After World War II, 'neutrality' had become the norm. This explains why Herman Lampaert emphatically avoided the colours yellow and black for his poster for the exhibition *Facetten van de jonge Vlaamse kunst (Facets of Young Flemish Art*, 1969, see p.139): he feared that the design would otherwise have become 'too nationalistic'.[3] Hence he preferred to use the full spectrum of colours. What was obvious for a graphic designer in 1926 would have been inappropriate 40 years later.

The pencil as a trophy

In his writings, Jan Tschichold, an important German theorist of modernist graphic design, strongly emphasised the use of the pencil. This was proof that designing printed matter was indeed an artistic activity. As a professional – he was classically trained as a calligrapher, and the son of a sign maker – he viewed the pencil as a trophy, as proof of the equal status of designers and artists.

This is probably why the hand and the pencil feature so prominently in the exhibition poster for Studio Novio (fig. 4), Léonard's and Godenne's design studio. The photograph depicting Léonard's work focuses on the pencil and the hand that is holding it. In an almost didactic way, it is shown that graphic design is an artistic act. Similarly, the photograph in the bottom right captures the essence of the printing craft: the magical moment when the ink is transferred onto the paper.

The fact that the duo produced an exhibition after just two years of collaboration was a statement in itself. The commercial printed matter that they had created together apparently deserved to be exhibited in the historical museum of the Plantin-Moretus printing family in Antwerp, a choice that suggests that Godenne wanted to measure himself against the old masters in his field.

Collaboration between printer and designer

Léonard and Godenne based their model of cooperation on the Arts and Crafts idea that art and craft should form a unity – the principle on which, later, Bauhaus' pedagogical project was founded. The work of the printer was just as important as that of the artist.

This idea is also reflected in Studio Novio's logo (fig. 5), a black-and-white drawing that, at first glance, looks abstract, but is not. On the left is a white person, that is the artist. He passes his drawing to the printer on the right. The printer is black, a reference to the dirty black hands that printing sometimes entails and to the fact that, for centuries, the art of printing was called 'the black art'. The craft was surrounded by secrecy and mystery. It was given a pseudo-magical status, comparable to that of alchemists.

One might assume that a hierarchical distinction existed between the white artist and the black printer, but that was not the case.

fig. 7
Jos Léonard
Compositie (Composition), 1921–24

fig. 5
Jos Léonard
Logo Studio Novio, 1926

fig. 6
Jos Léonard
Compositie nr. 25 (Composition no.25), 1925

The collaboration meant progress for both. For Godenne, it was a way of shepherding his craft into the twentieth century and linking up with the modern movement. For Léonard, it was an important step in the professionalisation of his new career. His transition from fine art to a full-time job as a graphic designer is often described as a move away from his original objectives. But I do not believe it was such a big change for him, either artistically or ideologically.

Tools

Léonard's career change was not accompanied by a drastic redesign of his workspace. The tools that he used as a visual artist hardly differed from the materials that he used to make his design sketches, a few years later.

Let us look at some early abstract compositions. Initially, Léonard rarely painted on canvas; instead he mainly used thick paper, as in the case of *Compositie nr. 25* from 1925 (*Composition no.25*, fig. 6). Just like the pencil, the paper was a constant in his career, as were the drawing pen, the ruler, and the set square. His gouache painting technique is often very thin and semi-transparent. The elongated *Compositie* (*Composition*, 1921–24, fig. 7) shows how much he diluted the paint until it almost became ink. In some paintings, he used India ink instead of black paint.

Especially at the start of Léonard's career as a graphic designer, there is a strong resemblance to his autonomous work. Sometimes it seems as if, as an artist, he had unconsciously prepared himself for the job that he would go on to do for the rest of his life. For example, he preferred a reduced colour palette, comprising what are sometimes referred to as non-colours: black, white, and grey. He often added red, which printers also traditionally chose as a spot colour.

One might assume that Léonard's work was done as soon as he handed over the sketches to the printer, but this is not what happened. He also got involved in the technical process that preceded the actual printing. To give an idea of what the craft of graphic design meant in practice one hundred years ago, I must first provide a brief technical explanation about preparing for print. Of course, it was impossible for a printer to print with a gouache sketch. This had to be converted into a line cliché. As a first step, Léonard made a copy in India ink. A negative photographic image was made from this black-and-white drawing, which was then exposed and etched onto a photosensitive plate. Finally, the etching was fixed onto a metal block. This is called a line block, but, essentially, it is an advanced potato stamp.

I discovered a few line clichés and a number of preparatory drawings in India ink in the Godenne Foundation (fig. 8). I assume that Léonard is the maker and that they have been preserved thanks to Godenne. It is quite possible that Léonard himself was responsible for the clichés – a technology with which he had become familiar during World War I, when he did odd jobs for the Flemish newspaper *De Standaard*. In short, Léonard not only handed over his sketches to the printer, but also the line clichés.

fig. 8
Jos Léonard
Abstract drawings, no date

fig. 9
Jos Léonard
Abstract geometrisch (Abstract geometrical), 1921–24

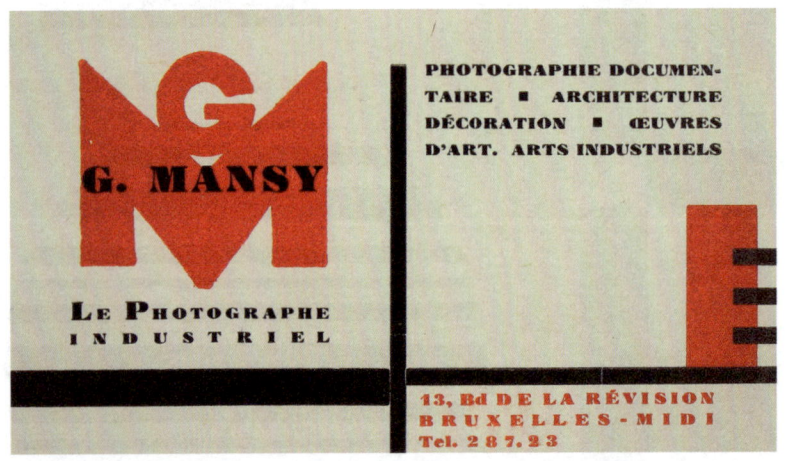

fig. 10
Jos Léonard
Business card for G. Mansy, no date

A stylistic constant

There are also striking similarities between the paintings and Léonard's graphic design in terms of composition. I would like to draw attention to some characteristic compositional elements. First, there is what, for convenience, I call the 'zebra crossing pattern', a motif made up of spaced colour stripes. In ochre brown, in the case of the aforementioned elongated composition, or in red, in the work *Abstract geometrisch* (*Abstract geometrical*, figs. 7 and 9). The same pattern also crops up regularly in early advertising printing, such as the business card for the industrial photographer G. Mansy (fig. 10).

Let us look more closely at this design, and in particular the abstract motif on the right. One would expect from a Constructivist that all graphic elements in the design would have a function. The black bars reveal the construction of the design and the bold capitals in red serve as an eye-catcher. But what is the function of the abstract motif on the right? Purely compositionally, it serves as a counterweight to the heavy red logo on the left-hand side. But otherwise, you can consider it as an autonomous abstract composition within the design. I have come across many of these small artistic additions in Léonard's printed work. They remind us that the creator was an artist.

Another recurring motif is the sequence of rectangular stripes in a colour gradient from light to dark. It appears in *Compositie nr. 25* and in *Abstract geometrisch*, and again in some graphic designs, such as the advertising brochure for the Brussels furniture company Vanderborght Frères (1928, fig. 11). We can speculate about why Godenne kept a sketch like this long after the printing was done and, moreover, long after the death of his companion, Léonard, but I believe it is because he valued it and maybe even considered it a painting.

fig. 11
Jos Léonard
Sketch for brochure of Vanderborght Frères, 1928

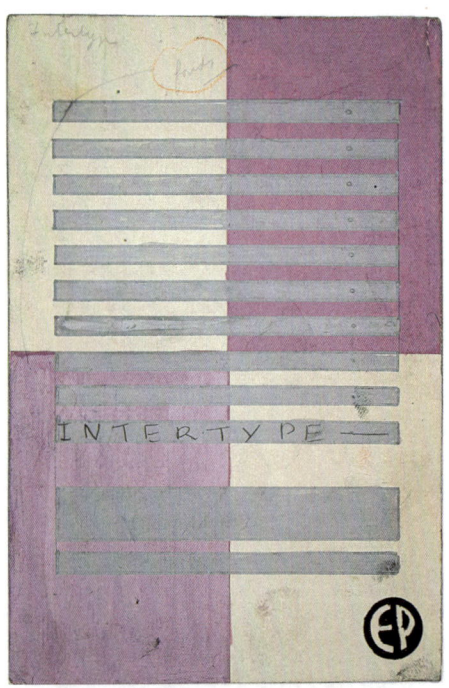

figs. 12
Jos Léonard
Design sketches, no date

Materialising the modernist utopia

I have already pointed out the similarity between Léonard's paintings and his graphic designs, both materially and stylistically. You could take it a step further and argue that they were not so dissimilar in terms of function either.

Léonard did not paint his abstract compositions 'for art's sake'. As a Constructivist, he believed that art was the visual expression of a new, utopian world. His abstract paintings were therefore functional, because they served a higher purpose. When he began working as a graphic designer, he did not turn his back on his earlier ideals. On the contrary, he was convinced that his work for trade and industry could just as well be the materialisation of that modernist utopia. In fact, he reached a much wider audience, since many of his designs were printed and distributed in large numbers.

That must have been a great boost, because abstract art in Belgium elicited few reactions at the time, let alone positive ones. Graphic design was an efficient way for Léonard to find and convince a broader public of the importance of a new visual language. The fact that he could also earn more money with it was an advantage, and not only on a personal level. The modernists viewed the applied arts as a way to breathe life into the economy, which had been hit hard during World War I.

And yet, Léonard's career change is often dismissed as an act of apostasy, motivated purely by personal gain. This point of view neglects the impact of modernist discourse on the fledgling discipline of graphic design. In an early interview in *Meer en Beter*, a Belgian graphic design journal, author Eugeen Allard calls Léonard more modern than visual artists, because he contributes to economic progress: 'He makes art for practical life and thus fulfils an economic role. He is more modern than those who limit themselves to the liberal arts.'[4]

And what about typography?

Léonard's sketches provide insight into the methods of a modernist graphic designer (figs. 12). What is striking is the absence of typography. We see no letters or words, but, instead, grey stripes in varying sizes. Léonard looked at typography as abstract shapes with which to create a composition. Sometimes, he added a few words or letters, but soon they became scribbles as a reminder for himself and the printer.

With regard to the typography, he was particularly interested in the rectangular area that the letters would occupy in the composition. Hence, his preference for re-sizing the lines, so that each line has exactly the same length and the typography fits perfectly in a block. A synonym for this is 'block rule' – a term that Léonard himself used, as can be seen in the sketch for the advertising brochure for Thybaert & De Graaf (1926, figs. 13). It is always interesting when both the sketch and the printed design have been preserved, as in this case.

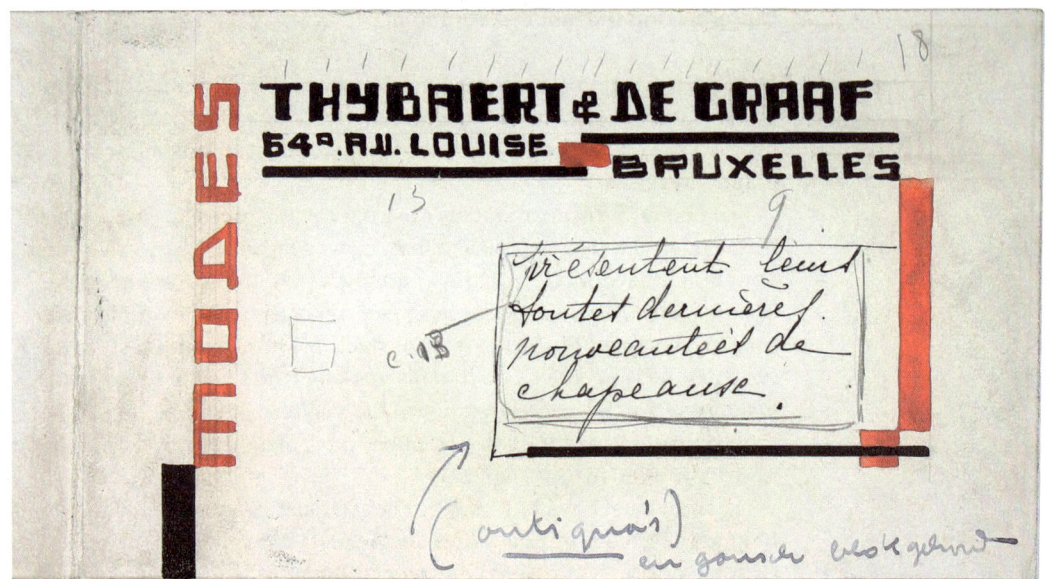

fig. 13
Jos Léonard
Leaflet for Thybaert & De Graaf, 1926
Sketch (top) / Printed copy (bottom)

Godenne did as Léonard told him, albeit probably through gritted teeth. As a proud master printer, he must have had trouble with the much too wide letter spacing of the word 'chapeaux' on the last line. The block rule is a constant in the oeuvre of Léonard and modernist graphic designers. Even for short text fragments, they resized the text, which often resulted in typesetting with letter or word spacing that was far too loose. Occasionally, Léonard came up with a solution for these ugly 'gaps'. He filled them in with thick lines that were the same height as the font size (fig. 14). An elegant solution, and typical of the international Constructivist movement.

However interested the young Léonard was in typography, it is only later in his career that it becomes important and that he acts as a typographer. By constructing a powerful image with simple geometric shapes, Léonard looks and thinks like a painter.

fig. 14
Jos Léonard
Leaflet for Etablissements Vve Hennebert & fils, no date

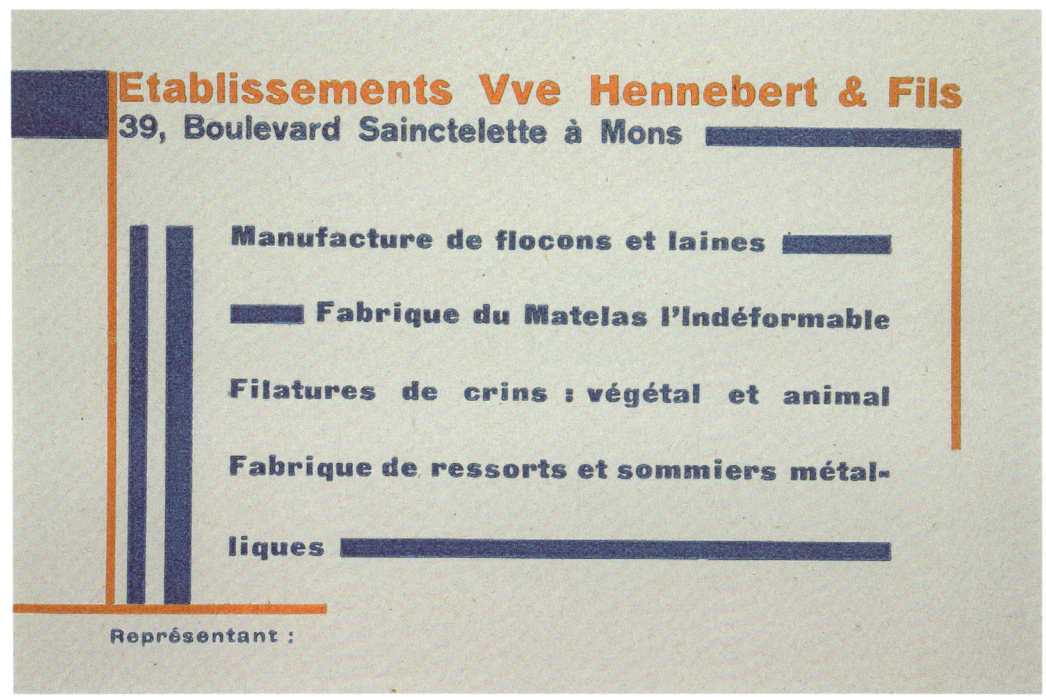

1 Van Haute, Katrien, *Jos Léonard en de ontstaansgeschiedenis van het grafisch ontwerp in België (1918-1936)* (PhD dissertation, KU Leuven, 2009).
2 This subject is elaborated in: Van Haute, Katrien, 'Jos Léonard. Een pragmatische idealist' in *Flouquet / Kassák / Léonard: De architectuur van het beeld tijdens het interbellum*, Van den Bossche, Phillip; Gonnissen, Adriaan; Mafundikwa, Saki; et al. (ed.) (Ostend: Mu.ZEE, 2018).
3 De Bondt, Sara, interview with Herman Lampaert, *Off the Grid: Belgian Graphic Design from the 1960s and 1970s as Seen by Sara De Bondt*, Design Museum Gent, 25 October 2019 – 16 February 2020.
(See excerpt on pp.109–12).
4 *Meer en Beter* was the journal of the 'Vereeniging voor Reklamestudie' (the Association for Advertising Studies), the first professional association of graphic designers in Belgium.

Jo De Baerdemaeker

TYPO BELGIËQUE

Jo De Baerdemaeker (1974) is an independent typeface designer and scholar, currently researching the history of Belgian type design in his project *Typo Belgiëque*. He holds a Master in Typeface Design and a PhD from the University of Reading. He designs and writes about world script typefaces (in particular, Tibetan, Lantsa, Mongolian, and Javanese fonts) and multilingual typography. He regularly speaks at international conferences. See studiotype.be

The title of this paper may suggest that this will be a historical overview of the highlights of Belgian typography. However, I am not going to talk about the master calligrapher and printer from Bruges, Colard Mansion, or the typeface that was specially developed for the book *Utopia* by Thomas More, which was published in Leuven in 1516. Much has also been written about Joost Lambrechts, and the punchcutters who worked for Christophe Plantin and his *Officina Plantiniana*. The origin and importance of the first, Brussels-based type foundries of Jacques-François Rosart and his son Matthias Rosart have already been explained in detail in the facsimiles of their type specimens.[1] Henry van de Velde's oeuvre has been discussed several times, such as his decorative lithographs for *Tropon* (1898), or Antiqua – the printing type he asked painter Georges Lemmen to design for Friedrich Nietzsche's publication *Thus Spoke Zarathustra* (1908). Pioneering works such as Paul van Ostaijen's kinetic typography, the expressive modernist alphabets of Jozef Peeters (see p.150), and the experimental but timeless lettering by Lucien De Roeck (see p.239) can be found in numerous reference works.

Of course, all these examples of letterform expressions from Belgium are undoubtedly very important. Nevertheless, I would rather use the following paragraphs to elaborate on *Typo Belgiëque*, my research project that examines an unknown episode of Belgian typography, from the period around the establishment of the Kingdom of Belgium in 1830 to the mid-twentieth century.

Unopened boxes

The literature about the history of typography in the Low Countries during the nineteenth century focuses mainly on developments in the Netherlands. Relatively little is known about the type foundries and printing houses that were active on Belgian soil in that period.

Recently, some unopened boxes of printing material were dusted off in the archives of Imprimarium, the Printing Museum at the Royal Library of Belgium in Brussels. Closer inspection revealed that they included original punches and matrices, with occasional references to traditional punchcutters and type foundries from Brussels. Based on a thorough analysis of this material, I want to sketch an overview of the visual design of textual information in Belgium in the nineteenth century, and make visible this missing link in the typographic history and identity of Belgium, the Low Countries, and Europe – while simultaneously giving it renewed impetus by digitising the typefaces. The focus will primarily be on typefounding activity in Brussels and Antwerp. Examples include the type collections of Carabin-Schildknecht (Brussels), A. Vanderborght & Dumont (Brussels), Van Loey-Nouri (Brussels), Charles-Jacques Hartung (Antwerp), and Établissements Plantin S.A. (Brussels).

Prior to the creation of Belgium in 1830 – when the current state seceded from the Kingdom of the Netherlands following the Belgian revolution – Dutch King Willem I had already made ambitious investments to establish his own type foundry and printing house in

Brussels. Willem I and his government had bought the type and casting material for this Fonderie et Imprimerie Normale in 1828, from the type foundry and typographic workshop of Jules Didot and his father Pierre Didot, both in Paris, for the sum of 400,000 Francs. Under the leadership of Mr Weemaels, however, the type foundry and associated printing house had little success. Although the Fonderie et Imprimerie Normale had 68 employees in 1829, and already 85 employees in 1830, the foundry, complete with all its contents, would move to The Hague in 1837. Thirteen years later, the Haarlem type foundry Johannes Enschedé en Zonen (Johannes Enschedé and Sons) bought up all its type material. In doing so, it enriched its own, already extensive collection with another 4,320 stamps and 6,858 dies from the Didot family.

Special awards

In the 1820s, other type foundries were active in Brussels, including Delemer, Gando, Foudriat, Theodore Lejeune, Dumont, Pennequin, Vaultier-Bonnard, Conrad & Joniau, and Clément. This was mainly because, in the mid-nineteenth century, Belgium, and especially Brussels, excelled in producing copies. That was the case until 1852: that year, Belgium signed a copyright treaty with France, which abruptly banned all pirate reprints. Each of these typographic workshops used type material from France, as a result of which the neoclassical Didot style – fonts with a strong contrast between thick and thin letter strokes – dominated typography in Belgium.

The house of Vanderborght was founded in 1834 by Michel-Joseph Vanderborght (fig. 1). As the son of a printer, a practising typographer himself, he knew only too well how difficult it was to obtain metal printing types. Since they had to be purchased from abroad on every occasion, he decided to develop and manufacture his own printing types in Belgium. While the type foundries in France and Germany used the Didot point to calculate the height of the lead letter body (also called *French* or *Paris height*), Vanderborght decided to also cast the type on the Fournier point system, because he believed it to be the closest to the metric system, which was common in Belgium at that time.

Vanderborght not only cast type for various Belgian printers, but he also manufactured and sold printing presses and other equipment. His success did not go unnoticed, and the house of Vanderborght was awarded the highest honour during the *Exposition des produits de l'Industrie nationale* in Brussels, in 1841. From October 1858, the newspaper *L'Echo de Bruxelles* was printed with printing types cast according to the new Vanderborght process. In 1870, Vanderborght senior left his company to his sons, Alexandre and François Vanderborght. When François stepped back in 1901 for health reasons, Jean Dumont was recruited as a new business partner. Under the professional and perfectionist leadership of Dumont and Alexandre Vanderborght, the house enjoyed many successful years. It is likely that they also produced printing types using stereotyping and electroplating methods, but the house distinguished itself from the other type foundries

fig. 1
A. Vanderborght & Dumont
Embellished display type,
ca. 1895

fig. 2
Carabin-Schildknecht
Wood block letters, ca. 1903

Le Mont-Blanc en Suisse	DORURE ET RELIURE
17 **BRUXELLES** 65	9 Atelier de Machines 5
7803 — Corps 12 — Env. 3 kil. — Prix : 15 fr.	7801 — Corps 8 — Env. 2 kil. Prix : 14 fr.

8169 — Corps 60 — Env. 10 kil. — Prix : fr. 36.50

Euphrate, 2

Paraphe 8170 — Fr. 4.50

Dans les gouvernements DE CHARLEROI & MONS
7154 — Corps 18 — Env. 5 kil. — Prix : 27 fr.

La Société pour l'amélioration des routes
JOURS PRIS POUR LES JEUX DE SPA
7155 — Corps 6 — Env. 2 1/2 kil. — Prix : 18 fr.

Grande course aux ânes à Ostende
FÊTES AU BOIS DE LA CAMBRE
7156 — Corps 8 — Env. 4 kil. — Prix : 22 fr.

Les nouveaux Journaux en
AUTRICHE-HONGRIE
7157 — Corps 9 — Env. 5 kil. — Prix : 25 fr.

Grande et Jolie Collection
UNE FONDERIE ANCIENNE
7158 — Corps 10 — Env. 6 kil. — Prix : 22 fr.

Une exposition DE CHIENS
7163 — Corps 18 — Env. 6 kil. — Prix : 25 fr.

Continuer MOINES
7164 — Corps 24 — Env. 7 kil. — Prix : 27 fr.

Concert de Bienfaisance au bénéfice
DE LA SOCIÉTÉ DES SECOURS
7165 — Corps 8 — Env. 3 kil. — Prix : 18 fr.

Les bons moments du
JEUNE CAUSEUR AU BOIS
7166 — Corps 16 — Env. 5 kil. — Prix : 25 fr.

Mon Beau Sourire 8
7908 — Corps 48 — Env. 8 kil. — Prix : 32 fr.

Dimanche 23 Octobre GRANDS CONCOURS
7906 — Corps 24 — Env. 4 kil. — Prix : 22 fr.

La Fonderie de Caractères
Grandes Nouveautés
TRAVAUX AU BALANCIER
7904 — Corps 12 — Env. 2 kil. Prix : 14 fr.

Carabin-Schildknecht

with its impressively detailed wooden display type with its large character heights, which were specifically designed for the typesetting of titles, advertisements, posters, and pamphlets.

In the second half of the nineteenth century, the type foundry of Gustave Schildknecht established itself in Brussels. The company also offered other printing equipment, and it housed a large bookbindery. To date, little is known about the operations of this enterprise, other than that Schildknecht started working with Carabin around the turn of the century and that, together, they formed the Fonderie Typographique Carabin-Schildknecht (figs. 2, 3 and 4). It had its own typeface collection and also offered both electroplated as well as lead clichés. Carabin-Schildknecht was a representative of Schelter & Giesecke, a renowned type foundry from Leipzig, Germany. Consequently, it was the only one able to provide Belgian printers with fonts with original German style characteristics.

The Fonderie Typographique Maison Van Loey-Nouri (figs. 5 and 6) was another key player. It primarily offered French typefaces, which could be cast and delivered at both Didot and Fournier heights. In addition, the company, led by Henri Van Loey, had a wide range of typographic devices and graphic products for printing houses. Van Loey-Nouri also placed a strong focus on the creative sector of advertising and magazines, with a wide range of decorative display fonts, embellishments, borders, and vignettes – each one a captivating artistic creation.

Apart from Brussels, Antwerp also had various type foundries, such as those of Jan Baptiste van Wolsschaten, Johannes De Groot, Charles-Jacques Hartung, and Joseph-Ernest Buschmann.

New life for old fonts

Little is written, let alone known, about all these type foundries from Brussels and Antwerp. *Typo Belgiëque* hopes to shed more light on the fonts and the activities of these extraordinary companies. By way of preparation, the material from the archives of Imprimarium is photographed and archived by means of a digital database. By systematically collating the punches and matrices with the original type specimens from the respective Belgian type foundries, I can supplement the visual material with statistical data about the dimensions, background, underlying data, and form analyses of the typefaces.

When I mapped the frontispieces of the above Belgian type specimens in various libraries and archives onto the current street plan of Brussels, I discovered that the buildings of two original Belgian type foundries are still standing. The main entrance to the office of Établissements Plantin S.A. was at Rue Dansaert 70; the entrance to the factory workshop was to the rear of the adjacent building at Rue de la Braie 11–19. Établissements Plantin opened in Brussels in 1911, as a daughter company of the Amsterdam Type Foundry, formerly Tetterode (figs. 7 and 8). The second surviving building is that of the Fonderie et Gravure Typographiques A & F Vanderborght, close to Brussels-North station.

fig. 3
Carabin-Schildknecht
Typeface catalogue, 1903

fig. 4
Carabin-Schildknecht
Geometric sans-serif font, ca. 1903

In a second phase of the project, I subject a selection of the fonts to a stylistic analysis: an evaluation of the letterforms should map the trends and tendencies within the printing activities of this period in Belgium. At the same time, I investigate and describe the social and historic context of literary and printing technology developments.

In a final phase, I select six to eight typefaces that I want to revive as digital fonts for contemporary use in the Belgian publishing and media sectors.

While newspapers such as *The Guardian*, *NRC Handelsblad*, *Le Monde*, *The New York Times*, and *La Gazzetta dello Sport* use exclusively designed font families to underscore their visual identity, the Belgian press currently uses typefaces designed by, among others, Dutch, American, French, German, and British design studios. The licences are not exclusive and therefore are also used by other national and international publishers, advertising agencies, and design studios, so recognisability is not guaranteed. Moreover, some of these fonts do not always work optimally for online and screen use, which is problematic for digital readability. Consequently, Belgian media usually fall back on standard system fonts for their websites, social media, or applications on smartphones and tablets.

Typo Belgiëque seeks to fill this gap. The project will study historical Belgian type families from these until present unknown type foundries, and explore the possibilities for redeveloping a Belgian visual identity. As a result, publishers will be able to choose from an original collection of font families. These will be developed following the latest variable font technology: this guarantees a maximum readability and makes them suited for responsive web and screen typography. In this way, these historical and unique typefaces will get a new life.

fig. 5
Van Loey-Nouri
Sans-serif font Antiques grasses, ca. 1913

fig. 6
Van Loey-Nouri
Order form for various sizes of Elzévir block letters, 1909

1   Rosart, Jacques-Francois. With an introduction and notes by Baudin, Fernand and Hoeflake, Netty, *The Type Specimen of Jacques-Francois Rosart, Brussels, 1768: A Facsimile* (Amsterdam: Van Gendt, 1973).

fig. 7
Établissements Plantin
Wood block border decorations, 1920

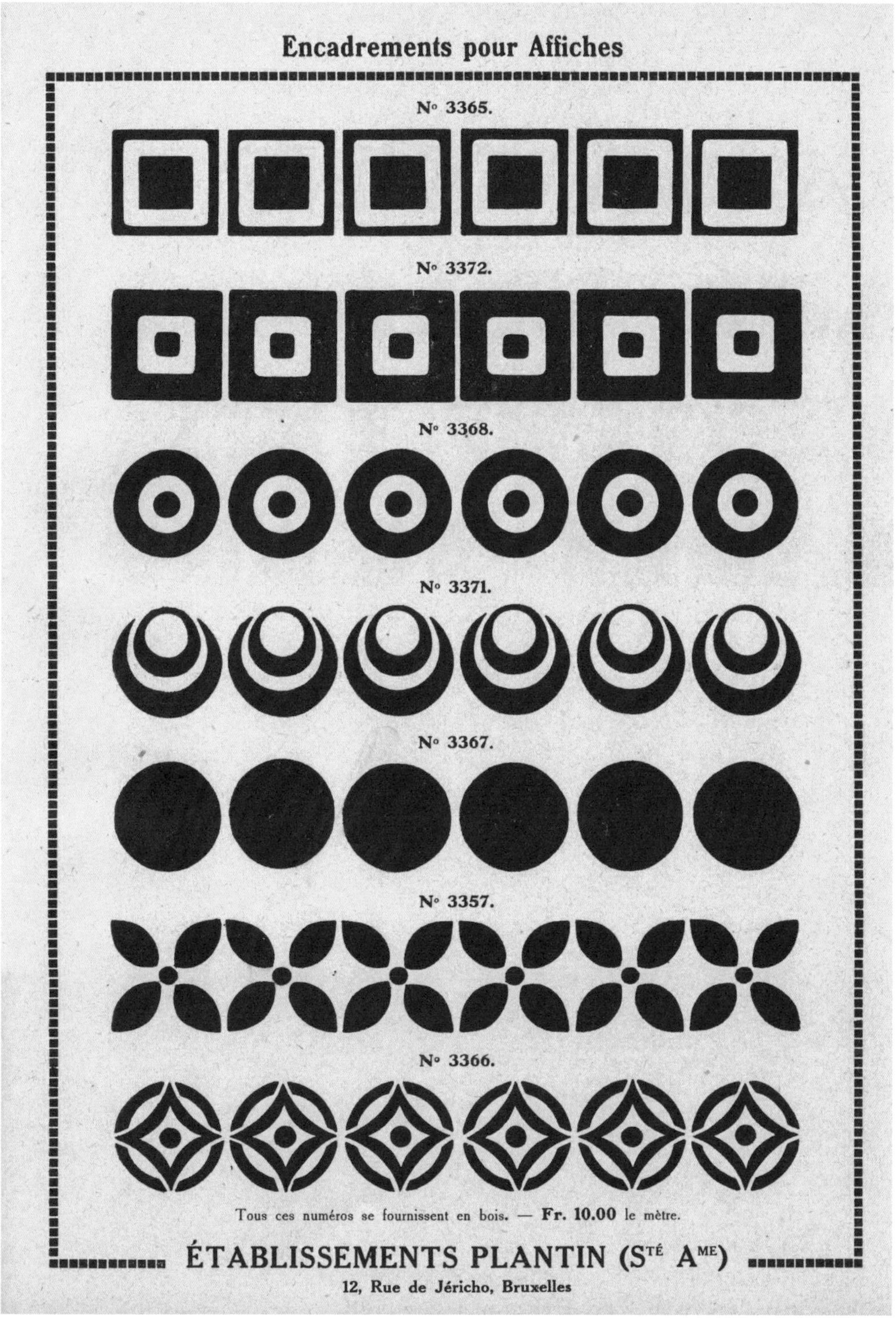

fig. 8
Établissements Plantin
Wood block border decorations, 1920

Richard Hollis

LA CAMBRE AND GRAPHIC DESIGN: THE EARLY YEARS

Richard Hollis is a British graphic designer, teacher and writer. He is the author of such notable books on graphic design history as *Graphic Design: A Concise History* (2001), *Swiss Graphic Design: The Origins and Growth of an International Style, 1920–1965* (2006) and *About Graphic Design* (2012). His most recent book is *Henry van de Velde: The Artist as Designer* (2019). See richardhollis.com

The Institut Supérieur des Arts Décoratifs (ISAD) at La Cambre was the realisation of Belgian architect Henry van de Velde's dream. At the opening in 1926, he told the press that since leaving behind his school in Weimar fourteen years earlier, and throughout years in exile, his ambition had been to set up a new institute in Belgium. He aimed to establish something more than a trade school and 'raise the social level of workers in the visual arts to that of doctor or magistrate'. Its foundation was brought about by Camille Huysmans, Minister of Arts and Education, who lobbied King Albert I for approval to set up a 'school of decorative arts'.

From its first days, the Institut Supérieur des Arts Décoratifs included two courses in graphic design. They were taught as *Le cours de publicité* (The advertising course) and *Le cours du livre* (The book course). The multifaceted artist and illustrator Joris Minne led the two-year advertising course. Students were expected to have studied drawing and basic geometry beforehand. The original syllabus of 1927 set out the following programme:

The first year comprised:
1. Simplified forms of the human figure and objects (diagrammatic symbols)
2. Design and drawing of letterforms, decorative elements suited to publicity
3. Design for announcement cards, advertisements, cartons, trademarks, packaging, labels
4. Making images for lithographic reproduction
5. Signboards, banners
6. Slides – film titling
7. Illuminated signs
8. Headlines and copywriting

The second year:
1. The poster: lithographic and letterpress (in collaboration with Joseph Buschmann)
2. Decorative design for banknotes, titles, postage stamps, etc.
3. Window display

Photographs show Joris Minne and students working on designs for posters in 1930. The sketches are on a small scale, on paper not much larger than A4. Students are grouped around a table with no drawing boards, which may not have been the usual arrangement of the studio. A later photograph shows a more spacious typography class studio setting.

The typography class was under the direction of Lucien De Roeck (fig. 1). In 1932, he had enrolled at La Cambre, aged 17. De Roeck had a long and successful career as a designer – among other things, he designed the identity of the 1958 Brussels World Fair, Expo 58 (see p.233). He may have been an exceptional student. When looking at the photographic documentation in the La Cambre archive, student work in the publicity course seems unadventurous, indistinguishable in style from commercial posters of the time (fig. 2).

The book design course, which took place on Tuesdays, Thursdays and Saturdays, was headed by the craftsman printer-bookbinder Joseph Buschmann. No syllabus seems to have been recorded. Photographs suggest that the class was run as a workshop. It is most remarkable for its choice of typefaces. In the typecases were several weights and sizes of the first version of Paul Renner's Futura font, which had become available only two years before the school opened (fig. 3). In addition to Futura there were Garamond, an extra-bold Bodoni-style font, a hefty art-deco type known as Indépendant, and the text size of Antiqua, designed by van de Velde's friend Georges Lemmen. Van de Velde presented the department with the printing press that had been given to him by his poet friend Max Elskamp and was reputed to have belonged to William Morris. The intention was to publish limited editions of work produced in the school with money raised by an Association of Friends of La Cambre. The project was not a success, although in 1930, one 48-page book, van de Velde's extended essay *Le Nouveau*, was printed in an edition of 300 and typeset in Futura.

The book design class begun by Buschmann was later taught by the journalist Fernand Geersens. He appears in a photograph of the print workshop in 1935, standing at a bench with a student discussing a page. His role is unclear, but van de Velde may have chosen him for his understanding and experience of printed media, thinking of the school's public relations and the role of the press. World War II gave Geersens a public face and a new name. As Jan Moedwil, he was the Dutch-language voice on Radio Belgique, the Belgian National Radio broadcast from London.

Unlike the pioneering graphic design and typography at the Bauhaus – which moved out of its van de Velde-designed Weimar building the same year ISAD opened – La Cambre did not leave an international legacy in graphic design. Yet some of the best-known Belgian designers, such as Michel Olyff, passed their student years at La Cambre. Many new generations continued the country's strong graphic traditions in the twentieth century.

fig. 1
Atelier de typographie (Typography Class), La Cambre, 1959 (from left to right: Marina Wery; Claude Laporte; Boudewijn Delaere; Paul Ghesqiere; unknown; and Lucien De Roeck)

fig. 2
Atelier de typographie (Typography Class), La Cambre, ca. 1957

fig. 3
Typeface collection specimen
(Brussels: École nationale Supérieure des Arts Visuels, La Cambre, 2021), pp.31-32

Ornements Futura

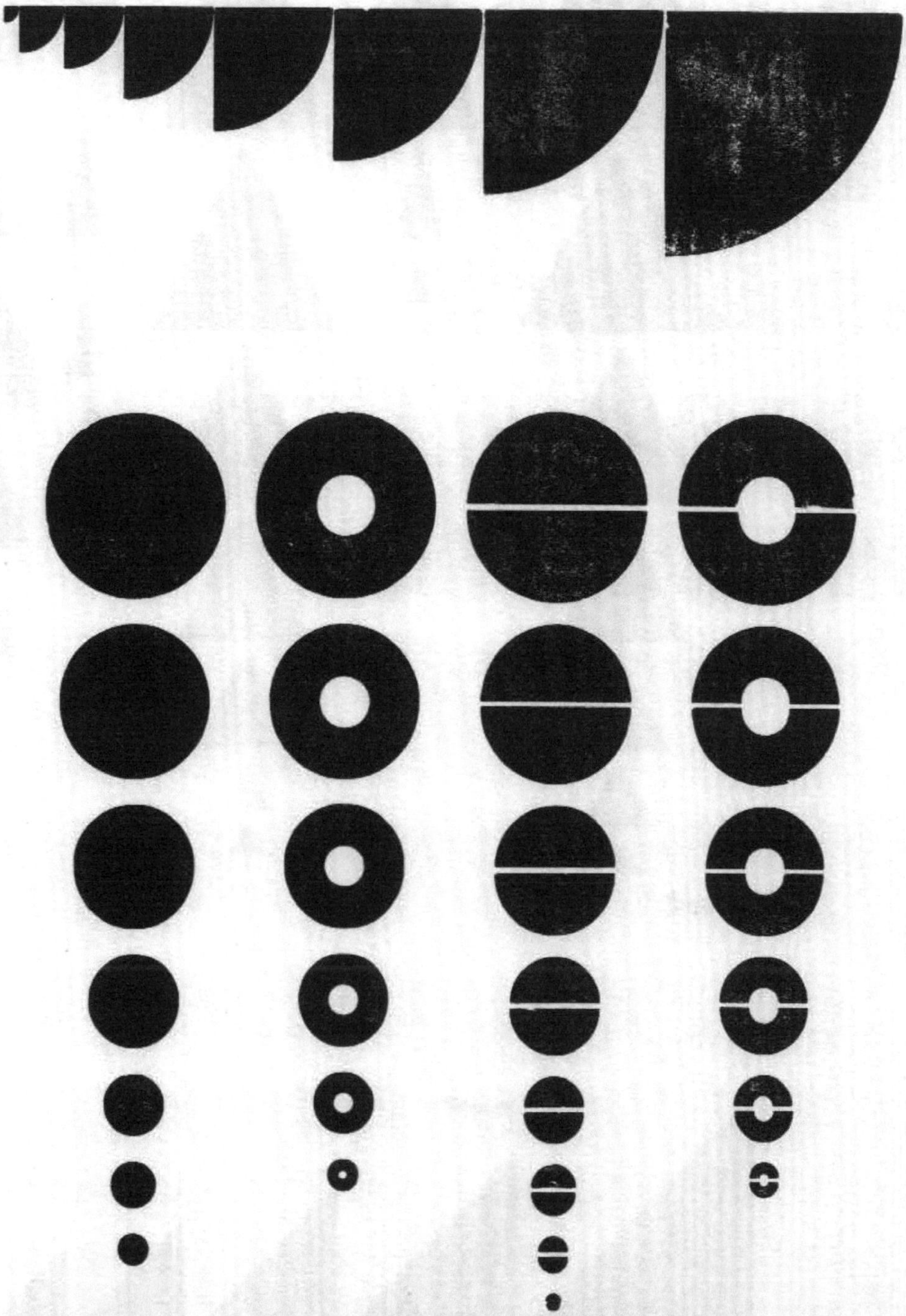

Sara De Bondt

GRAPHIC DESIGN AND THE COLONISATION OF CONGO

Sara De Bondt (1977) is a graphic designer, teacher, publisher, and researcher. She teaches at KASK School of Arts in Ghent. See saradebondt.com

On 30 June 2020, the statue of King Leopold II was removed from the Zuidpark in Ghent. A few weeks before, other statues were vandalised or removed in Brussels and Antwerp. In recent years, the Belgian colonisation of Congo has once again come under the spotlight, in television programmes, exhibitions, and publications. Today, this decolonising movement is accelerating, part of a global reassessment of the continuing impact of colonialism on institutions, curricula and political and civic discourses.

Decolonisation is also increasingly being discussed in graphic design. As early as 1998, the African-American designer Silvia Harris wrote of the need to dismantle the white canon: 'Black designers are working at a disadvantage when they do not feel a kinship with existing design traditions and also have no evidence of an alternative African or African-American design tradition upon which to base their work.'[1] More recent initiatives point to the considerable work that still needs to be done – think of Silas Munro's digital lesson series *BIPOC Design History*; the platform *Decolonising Design* by Danah Abdulla, Ahmed Ansari, et al.; the online *Decolonising Design Reader* by Ramon Tejada; or the exhibition *As, Not For: Dethroning Our Absolutes* by Jerome Harris. These examples come mainly from the United States and are not universal. Yet they have made it clear that the subject should not be absent from this overview of Belgian graphic design history.

What was the role of Belgian graphic designers in the colonisation of Congo between 1885 and 1960? Lucien De Roeck's poster *ANTWERPEN* (1935, fig. 2) is one of the best-known icons: the design is mentioned in the text of Jean-Michel Meyers in this volume (see p.231). But if you view the poster in the tradition of the maritime colonisation propaganda of the port of Antwerp, you see that the design did not come out of nowhere. It fits in a series of posters of the same size and with a comparable composition. This text deals only with a handful of examples, yet they demonstrate how graphic design, implicitly or explicitly, supported Belgium's colonising enterprise, giving it the visual and typographic tools it needed to carry out its task.

fig. 1
Louis Royon
Poster for Anvers-Congo /
Compagnie Belge Maritime
du Congo, 1925

fig. 2
Lucien De Roeck
Poster for City of Antwerp,
1935

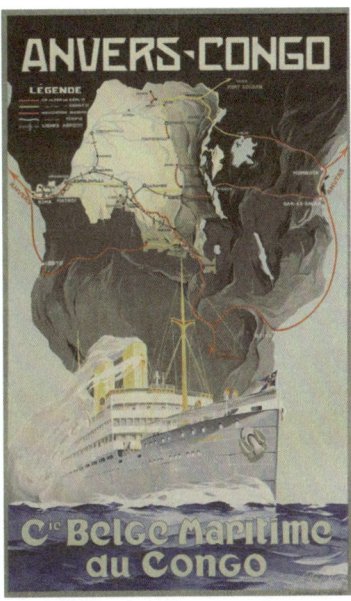

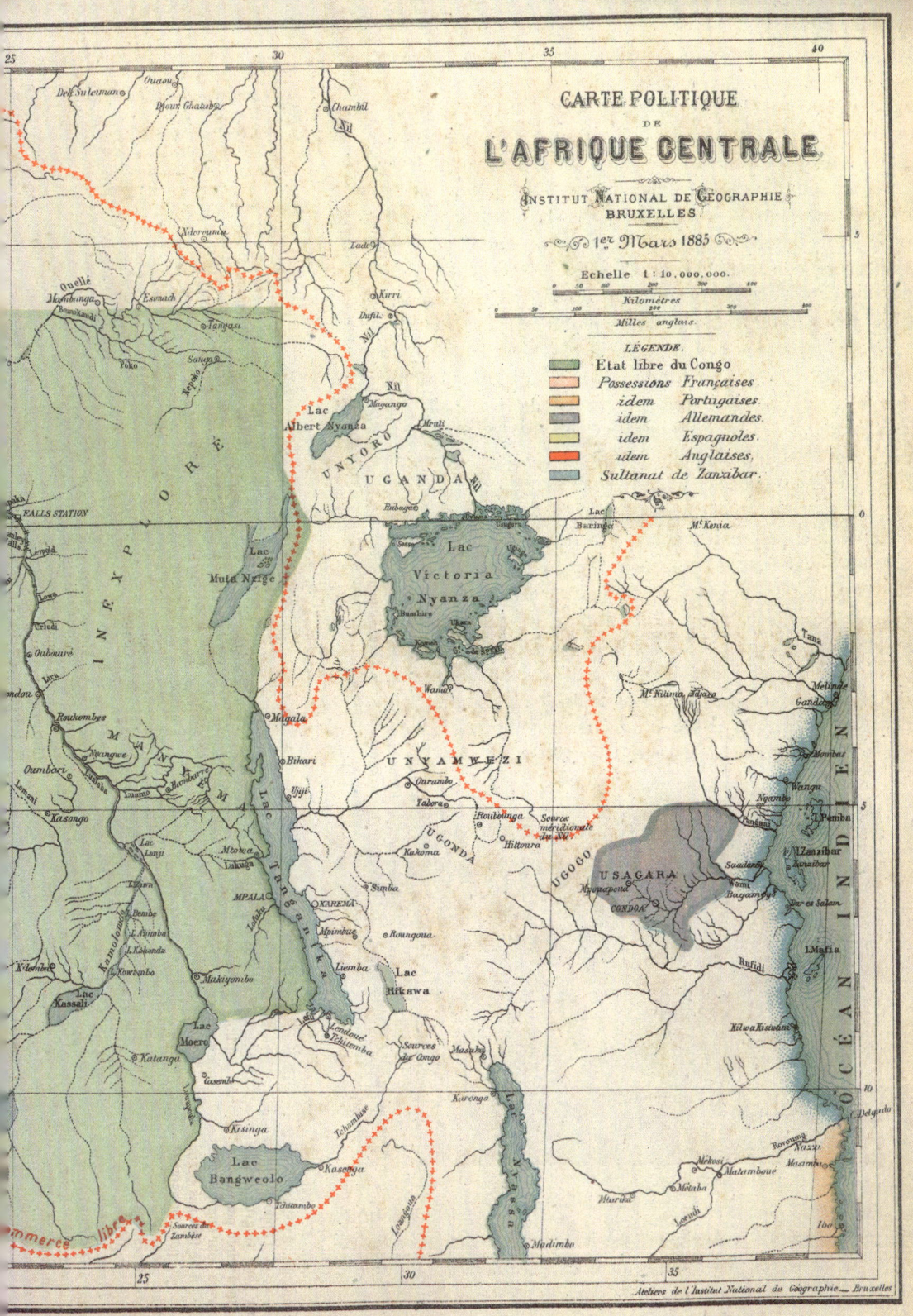

The symbols of Leopold II's power

Alphonse-Jules Wauters was a graphic designer *avant la lettre*. He was a publisher, journalist, geographer, painter, and art teacher. His weekly magazine *Mouvement Géographique* (1884–1922) was an influential promotional tool for the colonisation of Congo.[2] The magazine, printed on newsprint, appeared every Sunday. For several years, it was accompanied by the supplement *Le Congo Illustré* (1891–95). Nowhere in Europe were maps of colonised areas so regularly distributed. His map of 8 March 1885 (fig. 3) visualises how Leopold II took over a large part of the African continent at the Berlin Conference (1884–85). The word 'Possessions' appears next to a brightly coloured legend: pink for France; orange for Portugal; red for Great Britain etc. The largest part of the map, however, is a calming, positive green colour, captioned 'État libre du Congo' (Congo Free State). Its boundaries are drawn crudely with a ruler, as if they were vague and not definitive. In this way, the map created the false impression that Congo belonged to everyone, while in fact it became Leopold's own colony.

The king transformed his private property into a genocidal marauding machine. Yet he never set foot in the country himself. Graphic design was a useful communication tool for showing off his conquests. Motherland and colony are sometimes depicted side by side on the relentless stream of maps.[3] This gives tiny Belgium a powerful status, comparable with its gigantic area of exploitation, which was 77 times the country's size.[4] While the maps were deliberately vague, the flag was a clear symbol (fig. 4). Leopold II recycled the banner of the Association Internationale Africaine as an emblem for his Congo Free State.[5] The flag, with its yellow star on a bright blue background, was planted all over the newly conquered territories.

fig. 3
Previous spread:
Alphonse-Jules Wauters (attributed to)
Political map of Middle Africa. Institut national de géographie. Supplement to *Mouvement géographique*, 1885

fig. 4
Flag of Congo Free State (1885–1908) and Belgian Congo (1908–60)

Successful designers such as Victor Horta, Paul Hankar, and Henry van de Velde also worked at the service of the colonisation agenda. In order to arouse interest in his colony among the initially unenthusiastic Belgian population, Leopold II started a propaganda campaign, with magazines books, posters, monuments, and exhibitions.

Van de Velde – whose brother Willy had travelled through Congo with Henry Morton Stanley – designed furniture for the colonial exhibition in Tervuren (1897).[6] The extravagant Hotel van Eetvelde by Horta, today a UNESCO World Heritage site, was paid for by Edmond van Eetvelde, the head of the Congo Free State and a personal friend of Leopold II. Articles have been published about the links between Art Nouveau and Congo (to the point that Art Nouveau was even called 'Congo style' and its characteristic graphic line the 'whip line').[7] For example, Debora L. Silverman describes in great detail how violent suppression mechanisms – such as the *chicotte* (the whip used to administer corporal punishment on the Congolese), scarification, and vines from rubber plantations – had a direct influence on van de Velde's designs for book covers.[8]

figs. 5 (from left to right)
Henri Privat-Livemont
Poster for *International exhibition Brussels. Park of the Golden Year and Park of Tervuren*, 1897
J. Gilbert and P. Van Brempt
Poster for *General World Exhibition of Brussels*, 1910
Robert Hens
Poster for *3rd Official Colonial Fair, Antwerp*, 1926

Architects were not alone in profiting from colonisation. Designers and printers did as well. An important element of Leopold's colonialist propaganda were the many World's Fairs in Belgium (Brussels, 1897, 1910, 1935, 1958; Liège, 1905; Ghent, 1913). 'Between 1810 and 1940 [...] nearly 1.5 billion visitors were reached.'[9] An arsenal of posters, floor plans, newspaper supplements, and souvenir booklets was designed for these events. Minor printers and graphic arts schools advertised in the commemorative publications. As the AfricaMuseum has argued: 'This mass culture has undoubtedly contributed to the racism that is still present in Western societies today.'[10] Posters for colonial exhibitions, designed by Henri Privat-Livemont (Brussels, 1987), J. Gilbert & P. Van Brempt (Brussels, 1910), and Robert Hens (Antwerp, 1926), promote stereotypes: the represented figures have exaggerated features, are scantily clothed and submissive, and look away from the viewer (figs. 5).

The presence of typography can be an instrument of power. By installing signage in public space, things are named and given a certain status. During these colonial exhibitions in Belgium, Congolese men, women and children were staged in fake villages, as also happened abroad. By certain accounts, Belgium was 'champion in exhibiting people'.[11] Housed in appalling conditions, many became sick or died. In Antwerp, in 1894, seven 'exhibited' people were buried in an anonymous grave without any indication of their presence there.[12] In Tervuren, in 1897, seven Congolese who died there were buried 'in unconsecrated ground, reserved for adulterers and suicides'; it was not until 1953 that they were transferred to the Church of St John the Evangelist in the town centre. The lettering on their gravestones today has almost disappeared (figs. 6).[13]

Belgian graphic design in the service of institutionalised racism

In 1908, the Belgian state took over the colony from Leopold II. A look at the graphic design from this period suggests that the takeover was, in many ways, an extension of Leopold's reign. The same blue flag with

figs. 6
Thombstone lettering, Church of St John the Evangelist, Tervuren, 2021

a yellow star hung in the Belgian Congo until independence in 1960. The Ministry of the Colonies was given a Colonial Office to shape the propaganda in Belgium. The figure of Leopold in particular was often portrayed as a 'visionary colonial genius'.[14] The death of the king in 1909 and the end of World War I heralded a rehabilitation of the Congo Free State and a renewed nationalism: 'Every summer, "colonial days" were held, during which the Belgian population took to the streets to celebrate its African colony.'[15] Joseph van den Bergh's duotone poster *Journées Coloniales* (1924, fig. 7) illustrates the attempt to elevate the monarch, with his recognisable square beard, to the status of an icon. At that time, Albert I had already been king for 15 years, but the portrait of Leopold II had become a logo for colonisation.

fig. 7
Joseph van den Berg
Poster for *Colonial Days – Under the high patronage of His Majesty the King, 6 Juy 1924*, 1923

Belgians tried to justify their presence in the colony by presenting it as a civilising mission. They invested in transport, healthcare, religion, and education. Healthcare was partly financed by income from the Loterie Coloniale (Colonial Lottery), founded in 1934.[16] The lottery advertisements were often derogatory. In Jean Dratz's design, *On saisit la fortune par les cheveux...* (1935), a blindfolded black woman is assaulted by six white men who try to grab her money (fig. 8). The images were present in Belgian streets, such as on the corner of the Place Saint-Josse in Brussels in 1936, where 'Mangbetu women and words like win and millions took up no less than four floors.'[17] (fig. 9) The link between images of black people and slogans about money reveals what colonisation actually entailed: economic exploitation. After independence, the name was changed, first to African Lottery and in 1962 to National Lottery, but it too continued to portray 'exotic' figures to sell lottery tickets.

Other Belgian companies employed similar racist visual tropes. Alimenta, producer of Côte d'Or chocolate, was very prominent at the Brussels World Fair of 1935, where the 50th anniversary of the colonisation was celebrated. There, the company introduced the Mignonnette packaging, which is still used today.[18] When World War II hindered the procurement of cocoa beans, the manufacturer launched a surrogate chocolate bar, and changed its name to 'Congobar' (1940, figs. 11). The advertisements featured a winking Congolese with an enlarged chocolate bar. He wears the uniform of the Force Publique, set up under Leopold II, a force of white officers and black soldiers that exercised a reign of terror in Congo.

fig. 8 (left)
Jean Dratz
Poster for Loterie Coloniale which reads: 'Fortune is grabbed by the hair… by buying a colonial lottery ticket', 1935

fig. 9 (right)
Colonial Lottery advertising, Brussels, ca. 1936

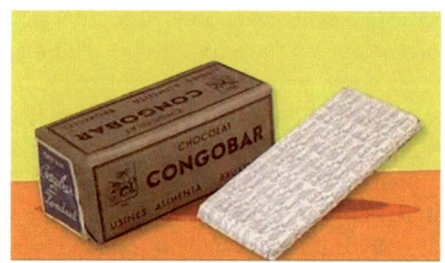

figs. 11 (bottom left)
Alimenta / Côte d'Or, Congo Bar packaging and advert, 1940

From Indépendant to independence

Congo was central to the commemorations of Belgium's centenary in 1930. To celebrate the anniversary, Joan Collette and Jos Dufour designed the Indépendant typeface for the Établissements Plantin type foundry. Henry van de Velde was effusive in his praise: 'I warmly congratulate you on this achievement. It is complete. It is striking, legible, and all the letters are perfectly in balance with each other.'[19] As Katrien Van Haute has argued: 'By referring to national independence, the Indépendant set itself up as a concept specific to Belgium.'[20] The architect Joseph van Neck used Indépendant on the buildings of the Centenary Palace, the centrepiece of the Brussels World Fair of 1935 (fig. 12).

fig. 12
Indépendant lettering on Brussels World Fair building, 1935

Meanwhile, 'the exploitation of Congo continued.'[21] During World War II, Congolese industry became a key source of income for the allies. Posters and other printed matter emphasised this productive use to which the colony was put. A series of placards testifies that: 'In the past years, Congo has supplied approximately 6% of the world's copper production, the figure for 1942 was thus 165,000 tons, enough to equip 180 large warships.' Many Congolese were forced to leave their families and go to work in urban centres.

Even after the war, the propaganda machine in Congo continued to run at full speed. All media were deployed: film, radio, newspapers, magazines, and posters. In Kalina, an administrative district of Kinshasa, at the time Léopoldville, the bi-monthly photographic magazine *Nos Images* was published, aimed at Congolese readers. The loose photo album layout was combined with graphic display letters. Paternalistic reportages alternated with regular features such as photos of subscribers, or manuals for making a Belgian chair, table, or brick house. On the *La vie au Congo / La vie en Belgique* pages, life in both countries was compared. The Belgian nationalist typeface Indépendant was chosen for the Congolese pages, but for

figs. 13
Nos images, 9th year, no.132, 1 April 1956

the Belgian pages, the Transito typeface by the famous German designer Jan Tschichold was used (figs. 13). As Van Haute asks: 'Was perhaps Transito, as a heavier display face, simply more appealing and did Indépendant maybe seem just a little too Latin?'[22] Although Indépendant symbolised the Belgian identity, Transito had more prestige internationally.

Work is a recurring topic in *Nos Images*. Congolese are pictured in the army, on rubber plantations, and in silk farming, but also in the graphic industry. In a photo reportage from March 1956, a white father teaches graphic design to three black students, with the caption: 'The Sint-Lucas School in Léopoldville has been training Congolese sculptors and painters for many years.'[23] (fig. 14) In the Christmas issue of that same year, we see four black printers of *Nos Images* working with a composing stick at a Belgian typesetting block in the printing house of the *Courrier d'Afrique* newspaper.

fig. 14 (top)
Poster design class,
Sint-Lucas Academy,
Kinshasa (then Léopoldville),
1956

fig. 15 (bottom)
Typesetter at work for
Le Courrier d'Afrique, 1956

The printing house employed 40 white and 350 black workers with separate unions.²⁴ Belgian printer Pierre Ryckaert remembers the financial benefits for the white printers: 'At that time, there were machine setters who went home with 18,000 Francs. I am talking about 1950, imagine that! That was extremely well paid.'²⁵ The dependence on Belgium led to financial and logistical problems: 'We did have problems with the typesetting machines in Congo. The maintenance and especially the repairs were not what they should have been. If a technician had to be involved, if there was a major breakdown, then he had to come from Brussels. That cost a bomb.'²⁶

The photographer Albert Bayidikila documented an awareness campaign about safety at work for the Information and Documentation Centre of Belgian Congo and Rwanda-Urundi (figs. 16). The warnings leave little to the imagination. Where *Nos Images* was bilingual Kiswahili and French, here they only use the latter. As Saki Mafundikwa observes: 'Language was one of the most powerful weapons against the colonised people of Africa.'²⁷ Some posters aim to increase productivity ('Wear your goggles while welding!' or 'Push your cart into the mine instead of pulling it!') while others focus on social control ('Don't let your children play in the street!'). The lettering has Art Deco style features – just like Indépendant. According to the American designer Rob Giampietro, the stereotypical use of typefaces such as Neuland and Lithos for contemporary Afro-American products went back to Art Deco.²⁸ The repeated used of specific typefaces for certain ethnicities 'prevents the public from seeing representations of minorities being treated with the same respect as those of the dominant cultures', adds Dutch design researcher Ruben Pater.²⁹

figs. 16
Victor Wallenda (Brother Marc-Stanislas)
Government announcements, 1951

Congolese who refused to perform forced labour were emprisoned.³⁰ It was Indépendant which was used to apply the word 'Prison' to the façade of the penal institution in in Kalemie, then Albertville (fig. 17). It shows how scrupulously and with what level of detail the Belgian state orchestrated colonisation: a typeface designed to celebrate Belgium's independence was used to oppress Congolese people. The prison is still in use today. The blue flag with star has been painted over, but the rusted letters have not been removed.

fig. 17
Albertville prison with Indépendant lettering, 1955

On a campaign for the Radio Congo Belge programme *Mme Sabine* (1958, fig. 18), black actors in smart suits and dresses feature in Western interiors. They work, laugh, and eat, but the slogans leave nothing to the imagination: women must be proud of their husband, support their family, and shop frugally. In the Belgian era, Congolese society was based on a system of apartheid.³¹ 'After 1945, an educated elite, often described as 'modern', emerged in Belgian Congo: the so-called *évolués*. They were Congolese who had trained as office workers, teachers, or priests.'³²
The accompanying posters were colourful but paternalistic. They are still sold as souvenirs in museum shops today, such as during the exhibition *100 × Congo* in the MAS in Antwerp in 2021.³³

There is a striking difference between the way in which the Congolese were portrayed on the posters for the Belgian and Congolese markets. On advertising posters in Belgium, such as those for the World's Fairs or the Colonial Lottery, Congolese are represented semi-naked, vulnerable, and submissive. In the colonisation propaganda in Congo, such as that for the Information and Documentation Centre or Radio Congo Belge, they look dressed, enterprising, and productive. Yet it concerns the same people, the same government, the same period.

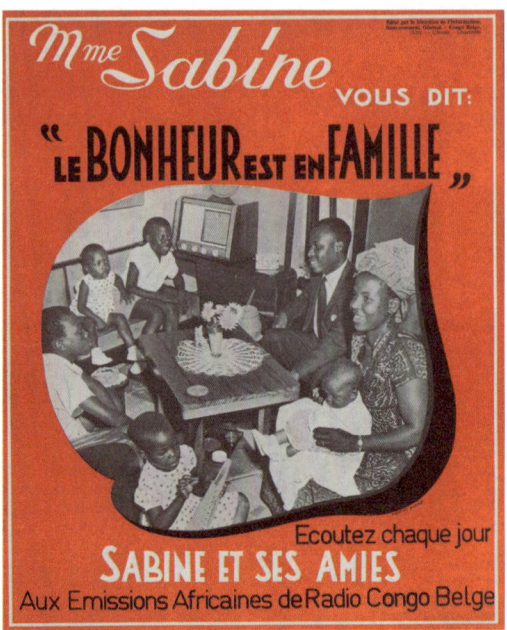

fig. 18
A. Noiret
Posters for *Mme Sabine* radio programme, Radio Congo Belge, 1958

Graphic design, a daily manifesto

As late as the 1958 World's Fair, which had a colonial section, Belgium was still trying to justify its presence in Congo.[34] Many modernist designers contributed to Expo 58: De Roeck drew its star-shaped logo; Jacques Richez designed the poster; Jacqueline Ost designed the interior of the Ministry of Health Pavilion; and Paul Ibou made an advertisement for Pan American Airways. The designs for the US and UK pavilions by Robert Brownjohn, Peggy Angus, and others are widely admired.

Together with the architect Constantin Brodzki, Belgian graphic designer Corneille Hannoset designed the building, scenography, and graphics for the Congo Fauna Pavilion. The sunken, spherical building was one of seven pavilions on Belgian Congo and Ruanda-Urundi at Expo 58.[35] A stylised floor plan guided visitors through various themes and past stuffed animals. At the end of the route stood an imposing elephant, around which the building was designed. Hannoset had travelled to Congo and London to kill and stuff the animal, boasting: 'I was made an Honorary Lieutenant of the Hunt in Léopoldville, for services rendered.'[36] The arched walls of the pavilion were lined with photographs of nature, animals, and Congolese people. In combination with contrasting lighting and minimal typography, these extreme enlargements (sometimes up to eight metres tall) created a dramatic effect. Animal skulls and human masks hung together in display cases. As Brodzki explained: 'There are no straight lines in nature. So, why would I draw a straight exhibition pavilion?'[37] The scenography reinforced racist stereotypes 'at the moment when the call for independence was already ringing.'[38]

fig. 19
Constantin Brodzki and Corneille Hannoset
Congo Fauna Pavilion, 1958

Right next to this Fauna Pavilion was – again – a human zoo. Behind a fence, Congolese adults and children performed in fake villages. After several weeks, these actors walked out in protest against the humiliating conditions. Congolese intellectuals visited Brussels during the Expo.[39] Among them was Patrice Lumumba, who would be elected chairman of one of Congo's first political parties, the Mouvement National Congolais (MNC), nine days before the end of the exhibition.

Graphic design was one of the tools that the MNC used in its non-violent struggle for independence. The party published papers such as *L'Indépendance* (*Independence*, fig. 20 and 21) and *Uhuru* (*Freedom*, fig. 22). The headline of *L'Indépendance* is set in a bold, condensed typeface and contains a red key with contours of Congo: the country is opening up. Underneath it read: 'Manifesto of the Congolese National Movement for the Liberation of Congo.'[40] The layout is bursting at the seams; not a millimetre has been spared, texts have even been turned 90 degrees to make them fit. Every inch of available white space is filled with anti-Belgian slogans, such as 'The Belgians will vote in Congo. That is absurd!'[41] It seems as if all small business owners wanted to place an advertisement. A dozen different typefaces were used interchangeably, but the decorative Art Deco fonts of the coloniser are rarely employed. While the Belgians governed with a divide-and-rule strategy, Lumumba tried to promote unity in Congo. The page layout and typeface choice of *L'Indépendance* and *Uhuru* reflect this polyphony.

Congo became independent in 1960. The Democratic Republic of Congo has been liberated from Belgium for more than 60 years now, but the colonisation is not over. 'A survey in 2020 by the University of Antwerp and the Royal Museum for Central Africa shows that Belgians have little factual knowledge about the colonial past of their country.'[42] The sources that I have consulted for this chapter come exclusively from Belgian archives, and many voices are missing from this text. This is only a first step in the extensive research that still has to be done on the history of Belgian graphic design in relation to colonialism, both then and now.

fig. 20 (bottom left)
L'Indépendance, Issue 7,
6 November 1959

fig. 21 (opposite)
L'Indépendance, Issue n. 6,
30 October 1959

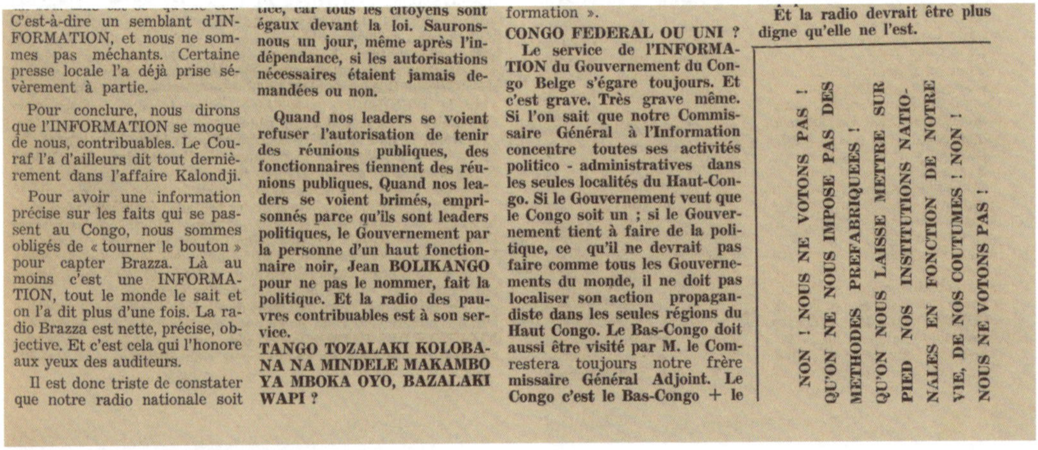

1re Année. — N° 6. — Vendredi 30 octobre 1959.   PRIX : Léo : 3 fr. — Intérieur : 4 fr.

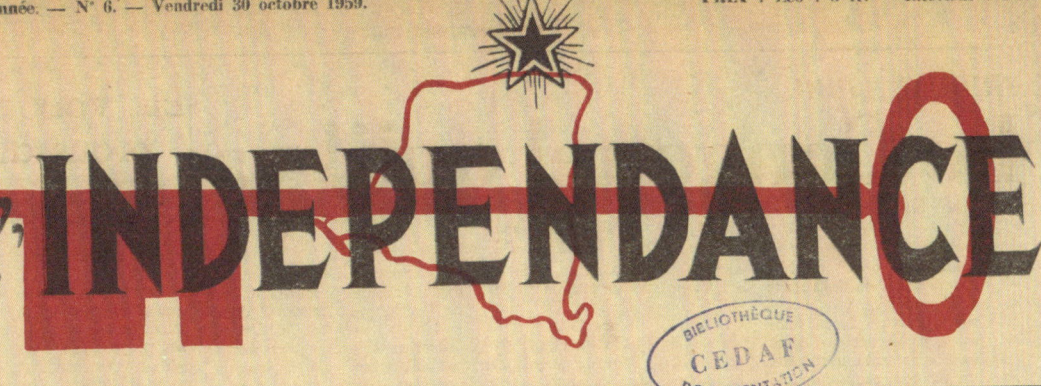

l'INDEPENDANCE

...gane de combat du Mouvement National Congolais pour la libération du Congo
HEBDOMADAIRE D'OPINION NOIRE

| BUREAUX : | Administration
Rédaction
Publicité
Abonnements | : | **112, RUE DE KALEMBELEMBE**
B. P. 8201. — Téléphone : 8385
LEOPOLDVILLE | Directeur : Patrice LUMUMBA
Rédacteur en chef : EKATOU M.C. |

EDITORIAL

Le Divorce ! NOUS DEMANDONS LE DIVORCE

La Belgique, depuis qu'elle nous a eus, s'est mise délibérément à exploiter notre pays et a acquis ainsi l'habitude d'amasser tant et plus pour son propre profit qu'elle nous a relégués au dernier rang de ses soucis, nous jugeant une quantité négligeable.

Pour une brasse d'indigo drill et une cuillerée de sel, ses enfants se sont accaparés des plus belles de nos terres dont ils tirent de fabuleux bénéfices.

Ils nous usent jusqu'à l'os et, le moment venu, nous laissent tomber, tel ce citron dont on a extrait jusqu'à la dernière goutte. C'est assez dire qu'ils nous font travailler — ils le disent eux-mêmes — comme des nègres jusqu'au moment où nous serons tout juste bons pour la « mitraille ».

Nos chefs coutumiers, propriétaires fonciers, ne peuvent pas disposer de leurs terres. Chaque fois qu'ils veulent le faire, il y a l'urbanisme ou quelqu'autre invention en « isme » qui les en empêche. Et qu'on ne parle pas d'indemnité d'expropriation ; un nègre n'a pas le droit d'en parler, sans quoi, c'est l'ombre et tout ce qui s'ensuit.

Depuis la fin de la dernière guerre mondiale, les Belges n'ont pas seulement réalisé que nous valions les autres hommes de la création, mais ils se sont rendu compte, par eux-mêmes, qu'ils dépassaient très largement la mesure de l'exploitation. Pour un Belge qui se respecte, le Congolais est moins qu'un outil. C'est assez dire que la valeur intrinsèque de l'outil est de loin supérieure à celle de l'homme noir.

Depuis la fin de la dernière guerre mondiale, les Belges ont commencé timidement à faire quelques petits gestes. Quelques petits gestes qui ne représentent en somme rien, mais que, pour les besoins de la cause, ils grossissent démesurément aux yeux du monde.

Ils sont les premiers à clamer sur tous les tons que nous ne sommes pas encore mûrs pour ceci ou cela, ô contrate, ils clament, également sur tous les tons, qu'ils nous ont formés, éduqués, civilisés ; qu'ils ont beaucoup fait. Et nous reconnaîtrons volontiers

(Suite en page 14)

UNE ERREUR GRAVE !

La première édition de « NOTRE KONGO », organe d'expression française de l'ABAKO a été saisie. Nous ne savons pas pour quel article cette mesure a été prise. On conviendra avec nous que la LIBERTE DE PRESSE n'est pas garantie. On convien-

(Suite en page 14)

...es Belges voteront au Congo. C'est une ineptie !

6 SEPTEMBRE 1960   Mercredi 28 Septembre 1960   Stan 4 frs. — Intérieur : 5 fs.   1ère ANNÉE N° 36

UHURU

BUREAUX : Administration
Rédaction
Publicité
Abonnements

AVENUE DES COCOTIERS
(Ex - Stanleyvillois) Bloc Wogenia
B. P. 355 - Tél. 2600
STANLEYVILLE

QUOTIDIEN ORGANE DE COMBAT DU MOUVEMENT NATIONAL CONGOLAIS
Directeur et Editeur responsable : Patrice LUMUMBA

ABONNEMENTS

VILLE :	TRIMESTRIEL	Frs. 200
	ANNUEL	Frs. 700
	SEMESTRIEL	Frs. 375
INTERIEUR :	TRIMESTRIEL	Frs. 200
VOIE ORDINAIRE)	SEMESTRIEL	Frs. 375
	ANNUEL	Frs. 700
EXTERIEUR)	ANNUEL Dol.	50
PAR AVION)		

UNE DELEGATION MILITAIRE EXPRIME A Mr. P. LUMUMBA SON DESIR DE VOIR FONCTIONNER UN GOUVERNEMENT

Le Premier Ministre, M. Patrice LUMUMBA a déclaré lundi soir à Léopoldville qu'une délégation de 26 militaires représentant les différentes ethnies de l'Armée Congolaise, s'était rendue à sa résidence pour lui exprimer leur désir de voir fonctionner sans retard un gouvernement.

Selon M. Patrice LUMUMBA, cette délégation aurait obtenu l'accord de M. KASA-VUBU et TSHOMBE lui-même.

aurait déclaré qu'il serait intégré dans le gouvernement des représentants de l'opposition.

Et c'est en cet effet, continue M. Lumumba, que des militaires auraient insisté sur la nécessité d'une grande réunion nationale qui se tiendrait au Parlement de Léopold.

M. Lumumba a ajouté que la délégation de 26 militaires aurait insisté sur la nécessité d'une grande réunion nationale qui se tiendrait au Parlement de Léopold.

ville et que la présence de M. Tshombe serait nécessaire pour arriver enfin à trouver une solution à la crise Congolaise.

(suite page 4)

Mr Khroutchev nettement contre le Colonialisme

NEW-YORK

Mr. Nikita "K", Président du Conseil soviétique, a joint une note explicative à sa demande soumise vendredi à l'Assemblée Générale de l'O.N.U. où il demande qu'il soit procédé à un débat d'ensemble sur la question de l'Indépendance des divers colonies et territoires encore sous mandat. Cette note dont le texte a été publié samedi, déclare notamment que le dirigeant soviétique est guidé par les hauts principes et buts de l'O.N.U. ainsi que par l'idéal noble et humain de l'égalité et de l'autodétermination des peuples et des Nations. Au cours des 15 dernières années quelques 1.500 millions de gens, plus de la moitié de la population du monde se sont libérés des chaînes de l'oppression coloniale. Des dizaines de nouveaux Etats sont sortis des ruines des anciens empires coloniaux. Dans sa note, Mr. "K" ajoute que les membres des Nations-Unies ne peuvent pas rester indifférents au fait que plus de 100 millions d'êtres humains vivent encore dans des conditions d'oppression et d'exploitation. La note attaque également la guerre coloniale française en Algérie, le régime portugais dans les territoires africains et les activités belges au Congo. La note du dirigeant soviétique s'attaque encore aux bases militaires en Territoire étranger.

L'ONU continue à envoyer au Congo des troupes de renfort

Le transport de troupe américain BEXAR à bord duquel se trouve 1.200 soldats indonésiens se rendant au Congo a fait hier escale à SINONSTORM, la base navale sud-africaine.

Le lieutenant Colonel SO- LICHIM qui commande les troupes a déclaré qu'un groupe de garnisons a été envoyé le vendredi dernier au Congo. Ces soldats seront envoyés dans la Province de l'Equateur et ont tous été entraînés pour la plupart à la Guerre de jungle.

Sékou-Touré s'entretient avec des Ministres Marocains sur le Congo

RABAT :

Un communiqué du ministère marocain de l'Information fait savoir que les entretiens qu'a eu dimanche soir Mr SEKOU TOURE, Président de la République de Guinée, avec de nombreux ministres marocains, ont porté sur les problèmes congolais, algériens et mauritaniens. Ces entretiens, selon le communiqué, se sont déroulés dans une atmosphère pleine de compréhension amicale et ont été marqués par une volonté de collaboration et d'entente. Ils se sont poursuivis hier matin avec le départ du chef de l'Etat guinéen, avec pour ordre du jour "l'Unité africaine et le rôle qu'elle doit jouer sur la question d'un tel facteur de la libération des peuples d'Afrique. Le ministère de l'Information marocain annonce également que Mr SEKOU TOURE a fait exprimer au roi la ferme volonté de la Guinée d'établir des relations solides et étroites dans les domaines culturel, politique et économique avec le Maroc.

Pas d'union entre les républiques du Congo ex - Français et du Congo (Léopoldville)

LAGOS

Dans une déclaration qu'il a faite dimanche soir à l'Agence France Presse, Mr. Ngouala, qui présente le Congo ex-français aux fêtes de l'Indépendance de la Nigéria, a notamment révélé qu'il n'est pas question actuellement d'une union ou d'un rapprochement constitutionnel entre Congo ex-français et la République Congolaise.

Le ministre des travaux publics du gouvernement Youlou a ajouté que les deux pays sont encore trop différents. En ce qui concerne les rapports entre leur gouvernement et celui de la Nigéria, Mr. Paul Ngouala a dit qu'il apportait un message d'amitié pour le gouvernement nigérien et formait les vœux pour une entente solide entre Brazzaville et Lagos.

Les Russes sont prêts à établir le siège de l'ONU en U.R.S.S.

Un Architecte Russe en chef de l'Institut National Soviétique du Progrès vient de déclarer à la Pravda : « Nous sommes prêts à établir le siège des bâtiments de l'O.N.U.
Et les techniciens ont-il précisé,

avaient été très intéressés par la suggestion de M. KHROUCHTCHEV, selon laquelle on peut transporter le siège de l'O.N.U. dans un autre pays de l'Union Soviétique.

Des troubles se produisent au Nigeria

LAGOS

Au moment où arrive la princesse Alexandra qui représentera sa cousine la reine Elisabeth aux fêtes de l'Indépendance Nigérienne et signale de nouveaux désordres dans le secteur de Nukuri,

Nigérie du Nord. Un communiqué officiel publié à Kadum Capitale signale que des bandes de Tive (indigènes paiens) se sont livrés à des pillages et incendiés à Wuhari. Des renforts de Police ont été envoyés et plusieurs arrestations ont été opérées.

Les troupes Israéliennes à la frontière de la R.A.U.

DAMAS :
Les observateurs Militaires affirment que les troupes israéliennes se concentrent depuis vendredi à la frontière de la Province

Syrienne depuis deux semaines.

membre de la R.A.U. Un journal arabe rappelle que des troupes jordaniennes se concentrent également à la frontière de la Province

WASHINGTON

L'Association internationale du développement entre en vigueur

L'Association internationale de développement entre en vigueur à la séance inaugurale de l'Assemblée annuelle des gouverneurs du fonds monétaire et de la banque Mondiale. Mr. Haroldhold (Australie) a annoncé l'entrée en vigueur de l'Association internationale de développement. Cette nouvelle organisation dont la création avait été décidée l'année dernière doit permettre aux pays sous- développés d'obtenir des prêts plus avantageux que ceux qui pouvaient leur être consentis d'ordinaire par les organismes internationaux. Quinze pays se sont déjà engagés à apporter leur contribution qui totalise 690 millions de dollars.

Un mémoire sur l'Union Sud-Africaine est soumis à l'ONU

JOHANNESBOURG :

Le Sunday Times annonce qu'un africain, ENOCH MBHELE, a quitté secrètement il y a quelques semaines le PONDOLAND en Afrique du Sud, porteur d'un mémoire à l'ONU. Ce document signale une agitation dans le Territoire, un vif mécontentement à l'égard des autorités bantoues et du nouveau système d'éducation séparée et réclame l'égalité des droits civils et politiques pour les africains.

LEOPOLDVILLE :

Un film documentaire pour les Congolais se rendant en Amérique.

Un film sur l'Amérique a été montré à Léopoldville au Congolais qui en moins de deux siècles ont bâti un pays admirable en vue de leurs plans. Il a en outre permis aux spectateurs d'avoir déjà une idée du pays où ils se rendent. A la clôture Monsieur Pierre ILEKA, Directeur de l'Assistance technique au Ministère des Affaires Etrangères a remercié les fonctionnaires américains au Congo et tous à la Mission spéciale des Etats-Unis au Congo et leur a demandé de transmettre, par leur ambassadeur à Léopoldville, les sentiments de vive

évolution des Etats-Unis d'Amérique qui en moins de deux siècles ont bâti un pays admirable en vue de leurs plans. Il a en outre permis aux spectateurs d'avoir déjà une idée du pays où ils se rendent. A la clôture Monsieur Pierre ILEKA, Directeur de l'Assistance technique au Ministère des Affaires Etrangères a remercié

gratitude du Gouvernement Congolais des Etats-Unis qui ont accès sion du Congo à notre République ce a accordé à notre République des bourses d'études et de stage dans des conditions un peu plus généreuses. Mr ILEKA a formulé le vœu que les Congolais qui bénéficient de cette aide mettent à profit leur savoir au service de leur pays. Les premiers départs sont fixés au 30 septembre et 15 octobre prochains.

Mr Khroutchev nettement contre le Colonialisme (PARIS)

Le premier colloque international sur la physique à Grenoble

Plus de cent physiciens et ingénieurs, la plupart venus des Etats-Unis, de la Grande-Bretagne et de l'UNION SOVIETIQUE, vont tenir à Grenoble, sur l'initiative du C.N.R.S. Centre National de la Recherche Scientifique le premier Colloque international sur la physique des forces électro-statiques, et ses applications. Grenoble a été choisi pour cette réunion, car depuis 15 ans, le laboratoire électrostatique du C.N.R.S. y est installé et fait œuvre de pionnier dans le domaine des générateurs électro-statiques, ce qui amené à la fabrication de toute une gamme de nouvelles machines de tous pays à l'étranger et a été récemment couronné au grand Oscar de l'exportation.

ces applications des forces électro-statiques prennent, semble-t-il une importance de plus en plus grande dans des domaines très variés.

En Amérique et en France, on étudie actuellement la possibilité d'emploi des machines électro-statiques spéciales fonctionnant dans le vide sidéral pour alimenter les fusées ioniques qui augmenteraient prodigieusement le rayon d'action des véhicules spaticaux.

DAKAR :

Mr Sékou-Touré fait escale à Dakar

Venant de Rabat par avion, M. SEKOU-TOURE qui retourne à Konakry, a fait hier au milieu de la journée une escale technique à Dakar. A sa descente d'avion il a été salué notamment par MM. Léopold SENGHOR, Président du Sénégal et MAMADOU DIA, Président du Conseil sénégalais. Le premier Guinéen a eu un long entretien avec ces deux personnalités.

VOTRE ASSUREUR

1. Harris, Silvia, 'Searching for a Black Aesthetic in American Graphic Design', in Heller, Steven, *The Education of a Graphic Designer* (New York, Allworth Press, 1998), p.125.
2. Henry, Elise, 'Le *Mouvement Géographique*, entre géographie et propagande coloniale', *Belgeo, Belgisch Tijdschrift voor Geografie*, 2021, 1, pp.27–46. Available at: https://doi.org/10.4000/belgeo.10172; last accessed on 10 August 2021.
3. Silverman, Debora L., 'Art Nouveau, Art of Darkness: African Lineages of Belgian Modernism, Part I', *West 86th: A Journal of Decorative Arts, Design History and Material Culture*, 18: 2 (Fall-Winter 2011), pp.139–181.
4. Bodenstein, Wulf, *Kaarten van Afrika* (Tervuren: Koninklijk Museum Voor Midden-Afrika, 2017).
5. Adriaenssens, Werner, 'De Congostijl: Belgische art nouveau als koloniale propaganda', in Huygens, Frank and Simon Thomas, Mienke, *Design Derby: Nederland België 1815–2015* (Rotterdam: Museum Boijmans Van Beuningen, 2015), p.76.
6. Hollis, Richard, *Henry van de Velde: The Artist as Designer* (London: Occasional Papers, 2019), p.86.
7. Silverman, Debora L., 'Art Nouveau, Art of Darkness: African Lineages of Belgian Modernism, Part I', pp.139–181; Idem, 'Art Nouveau, Art of Darkness: African Lineages of Belgian Modernism, Part II', *West 86th: A Journal of Decorative Arts, Design History, and Material Culture*, 19: 2 (Spring–Summer 2012), pp.175–195; Idem, 'Art Nouveau, Art of Darkness: African Lineages of Belgian Modernism, Part III', *West 86th: A Journal of Decorative Arts, Design History, and Material Culture*, 20: 1 (Spring–Summer 2013), pp.3–61; Sacks, Ruth, 'Style Congo in the Congo: Tracing Art Nouveau in Mbanza-Ngungu', paper for Art Nouveau International Congress (Barcelona, 27–30 June 2018); Hollis, Richard, *Henry van de Velde: The Artist as Designer* (London: Occasional Papers, 2019), p.86; Jarrassé, Dominique, 'Art Nouveau or Congolese Art? The Colonial Museum in Tervuren: A Synthesis of the Arts', *Gradhiva, Revue d'anthropologie et d'histoire des arts*, 23 (2016), pp.122–145. Available at: https://journals.openedition.org/gradhiva/3159; last accessed on 19 July 2021.
8. Silverman, Debora L., 'Art Nouveau, Art of Darkness: African Lineages of Belgian Modernism, Part II', p.182.
9. 'De menselijke zoo van Tervuren (1897)', AfricaMuseum. Available at: https://www.africamuseum.be/nl/discover/history_articles/the_human_zoo_of_tervuren_1897; last accessed on 23 May 2021.
10. *Ibid.*
11. Vandenbussche, Liselotte; Brouckaert, Tine; Andriessen, Laura, 'The "Other", Power Relations, and the Zoo Humain: An Interview with Theatre Artist Chokri Ben Chikha', DiGeSt. Journal of Diversity and Gender Studies, 3: 2 (2016), pp.75–90. Available at: https://www.jstor.org/stable/10.11116/jdivegendstud.3.2.0075; last accessed 25 August 2021.
12. Visitor's Guide, *100 x Congo: Een eeuw Congolese kunst in Antwerpen* (Antwerp: MAS, 2020), p.25.
13. 'De menselijke zoo van Tervuren (1897)', AfricaMuseum.
14. Stanard, Matthew G., 'De koloniale propaganda: het ontwaken van een Belgisch koloniaal bewustzijn?', in Lauro, Amandine; Goddeeris, Idesbald; Vanthemsche, Guy (eds.), *Notities uit Koloniaal Congo. Een geschiedenis in vragen* (Kalmthout: Polis, 2020), ch. 24.
15. *Ibid.*
16. Scheerlinck, Karl, 'Dromen van papier. Affiches uit de collectie van de Nationale Loterij', *Openbaar Kunstbezit Vlaanderen*, 1 (2015), p.32.
17. De Geest, Joost, 'Kunstenaars en Loterijbiljetten', *Openbaar Kunstbezit Vlaanderen*, 1 (2015), p.29.
18. Van den Berghe, Gie, *WILD: Exotische dieren en mensen op Belgische wereldtentoonstellingen*. Available at: http://www.serendib.be/boeken/WILD.htm; last accessed on 3 August 2021.
19. Van Haute, Katrien, 'The Indépendant: A Typeface as Period Document', *Quaerendo*, 38 : 1 (2008), p.61.
20. *Ibid.*
21. Lauro, Amandine; Goddeeris, Idesbald; Vanthemsche, Guy (eds.), *Notities uit Koloniaal Congo*, ch. 24, p.5.
22. Van Haute, Katrien, 'The Indépendant: A Typeface as Period Document', p.61.
23. 'Une École d'art Congolaise', *Nos Images*, (Léopoldville: Kalina, 15 March 1956), n. 132, p.6. Original text: 'L'école Saint-Luc de Léopoldville s'occupe depuis de nombreuses années de former des sculpteurs et des peintres congolais.'
24. Dujardin, Carin, '"Out of Africa": Le Courrier d'Afrique (1947–1970)' in *KADOC nieuwsbrief*, 2012 / 2 (Leuven: Interfacultair centrum KU Leuven), p.12.
25. 'De Zetter: Pierre Ryckaert', *VIAT - Tijdschrift voor geschiedenis van techniek en industriële cultuur*, 7: 2 (1989), p.30.
26. *Ibid.*
27. Mafundikwa, Saki, *Afrikan Alphabets: The Story of Writing in Africa* (New York: Mark Batty Publisher, 2007), p.2.
28. Giampietro, Rob, 'New Black Face: Neuland and Lithos as Stereotypography', *Lined and Underlined* (blog), 2004. Available at: https://linedandunlined.com/archive/new-black-face/; last accessed on 26 May 2021.
29. Pater, Ruben, *The Politics of Design: A (Not So) Global Manual to Visual Communication* (Amsterdam: BIS Publishers, 2016) p.45.
30. 'Between 1945 and 1960, a period for which we have quite reliable figures, 3 to 7 per cent of the male population, depending on the region, would have been in prison, a much higher percentage than in Belgium itself.' Dewulf, Valentine, *Réprimer, enfermer, éloigner en situation coloniale. Pratiques de confinement et logiques au Congo belge, 1908–1960*, PhD dissertation ULB, forthcoming (2016–2020)', quoted in: Lauro, Amandine; Henriet, Benoît, 'Repressie. Was Congo na Leopold II een minder gewelddadige kolonie?', in Amandine Lauro, Idesbald Goddeeris, and Guy Vanthemsche (eds.), *Notities uit Koloniaal Congo*, ch. 15.
31. Buelens, Frans, 'De grote conglomeraten. Hoe werd de kapitalistische economie in Congo ingeplant?', in Lauro, Amandine; Goddeeris, Idesbald; Vanthemsche, Guy (eds.), *Notities uit Koloniaal Congo*, ch. 8.
32. Tödt, Daniel, 'De koloniale staat en de Afriaanse elites: een geschiedenis van onderwerping?', in Lauro, Amandine; Goddeeris, Idesbald; Vanthemsche, Guy (eds.), *Notities uit Koloniaal Congo*, ch. 18.
33. Visit by the author on 20 July 2021.
34. 'De menselijke zoo van Tervuren (1897)', AfricaMuseum.
35. Hannoset, Corneille, portfolio (Brussels: Catherine Hannoset archive).
36. Hannoset, Corneille, *Voyages Chroniques* (Alentours: Éditions Tandem, 1997), p.51. Original text: 'Je fus nommé à Léopoldville, pour service rendu, Lieutenant Honoraire de Chasse.'
37. Demeulemeester, Thijs, 'Iconisch Brussels kantoorgebouw krijgt make-over', *De Tijd*, 9 May 2018. Available at: https://www.tijd.be/sabato/design/iconisch-brussels-kantoorgebouw-krijgt-make-over/10010377.html; last accessed on 19 July 2021.
38. 'De menselijke zoo van Tervuren (1897)', AfricaMuseum.
39. Van Reybrouck, David, *Congo* (Amsterdam: De Bezige Bij, 2019), ch. 16.
40. Original text: 'Quotidien organe de combat du mouvement national congolais'.
41. *L'Indépendance*, Léopoldville, 1er année, no.6, 30 October 1959, p.1. Original text: 'Les Belges voteront au Congo. C'est une ineptie!'
42. Avoy, Bénédicte, 'Vooraleer we de pagina kunnen omslaan, moeten we ze lezen', AfricaMuseum. Available at: https://www.africamuseum.be/nl/learn/history_articles; last accessed 23 May 2021.

Sara De Bondt

THE BELGIAN CHAMBER OF GRAPHIC DESIGNERS

Sara De Bondt (1977) is a graphic designer, teacher, publisher, and researcher. She teaches at KASK School of Arts in Ghent. See saradebondt.com

'Een Kamer waar niet geslapen wordt!
(*A chamber where nobody sleeps!*)'[1]

The question of why so little is known about the history of Belgian graphic design is met with all kinds of responses: the lack of dedicated archive institutions; the absence of exhibition policy; the structure of artistic education; the complex Belgian federal structures; underinvestment by public and private clients; a *laisser-faire* approach; the hierarchy between liberal and applied arts; the lack of a specialised press, and so on.[2] These are all plausible reasons. But one could also wonder where the responsibility of the designers themselves lies.

In the 1950s, Masaru Katsumie, the Japanese designer and editor of the journal *Graphic Design*, boldly got to the heart of the matter. He claimed that the substandard quality of the work was the problem: 'Between 1951 and 1960, as the curator of the World Commercial Design exhibition [in Tokyo], I had the opportunity to take a closer look at the graphic production of all the countries in the world: almost everything I saw from Belgium was of a very mediocre level.'[3] It is likely that very few Belgians were selected for this exhibition, but ten years later his claim was subverted. Suddenly, international cover stories about the work of the talented Belgians appeared (figs. 1), not only in Katsumie's own journal, but also in other international publications, such as the Japanese *IDEA*, the German *Gebrauchsgraphik*, the Polish *Projekt*, the British *Vista*, and Switzerland's *Graphis*. Expo 58 undoubtedly had an impact, but there was more to it.

figs. 1 (from left to right)
Josse Goffin
Cover of *Graphis*, no.144, 1969
Boudewijn Delaere
Cover of *Gebrauchsgraphik: International Advertising Art*, 4/1970
Jacques Richez
Cover of *Gebrauchsgraphik: International Advertising Art*, 9/1971

The government played an important role in the turnaround of the promotion of Belgian design abroad. In 1962, it had established the Brussels Design Centre, an institution that promoted 'good' industrial design. This had a significant effect. Under the direction of the driven Josine des Cressonnières, the centre organised exhibitions, awards ceremonies and events, and published *Infordesign*, a magazine about design.[4] Its well-known, restrained house style was created by Michel Olyff (see p.146).

The Design Centre regularly staged graphic design exhibitions. There were group exhibitions on a specific theme, such as *Hoe maakt men het gezicht van een onderneming? (How to create the face of a company?*, 1966), featuring the house styles of 17 Belgian companies, or *Pakkende verpakkingen (Captivating Packagin*, 1969) with some 70 examples of 'good packaging'. Other group exhibitions had a wider angle, such as *Graphic Design 67* (1967) and *Leven van Grafisme (Living off Graphic Design*, 1968). And occasionally, graphic designers were given solo exhibitions, for example the Antwerp Design-Team (1971).[5]

The famous G logo made by graphic designer Jacques Richez for Belgium's Generale Bank (fig. 2) was central to the *Het imago van een belangrijke bank (The Image of an Important Bank*, 1970) exhibition. Richez emphasised how great the effect of the Design Centre was:

fig. 2
Jacques Richez
Logo for Generale Bank, 1966

> 'The turning point was spectacularly taken with the exhibition held in the Design Centre in 1969 on the occasion of a conference of the International Council of Graphic Design Associations. *Graphis* underlined in its report that, "the clouds that hung over the Belgian graphic landscape suddenly disappeared." Hope [...] finally took shape: we existed on an international level.'[6]

Despite the positive results, there was also criticism of the Centre. Design critic Karel Elno thought it was too hierarchical and called the Design Centre a 'status centre'.[7] Several of the graphic design exhibitions in the Design Centre were organised by an external group, an alliance of practitioners that was perhaps more accessible and had a broader mandate. Their organisation was founded and run by designers themselves, without government support. Its approach was less nationalistic than the Centre. It was created in 1948 as the Chambre Belge des Artistes et Artisans Publicitaires (Belgian Chamber of Advertising Artists and Artisans) by Richez, a Frenchman based in Brussels, and London-based Belgian illustrator Mark Severin. After 14 years, the then chairman Charles Rohonyi, a poster artist from Hungary, gave the organisation a new, bilingual name: Belgische Kamer van Grafici / Chambre Belge des Graphistes (Belgian Chamber of Graphic Designers, CBG).[8]

While the Design Centre was a government organisation, the Chambre Belge des Graphistes was run by volunteer designers, with few resources. According to Richez, it was a courageous gang that deserved greater recognition: 'A brave (many think: rash) enterprise run by a handful of stubborn volunteers and which, incidentally, should get a little more attention from the government.'[9] On paper, the CBG was a professional association, but in practice it was much more than that. It was a space where designers could meet each other, exchange experiences and contacts, and discuss each other's work. It also defended the interests of designers at economic, social, and educational levels.

Exchanges and exhibitions

One of the CBG's main objectives was the national and international promotion of its members. Sometimes, it set up exhibitions through institutional partnerships, such as in Warsaw and Łódź in 1970.[10] There were also more improvised exchanges. For example, as one of its many reports states: 'Guy Schockaert and Hilde Van der Velden, together with our corresponding [...] member in Paris, Servaes Goddyn, installed the Belgian contribution at the *Première Expo des Techniques et des Arts de la Communication*, which featured the work of 12 members.'[11] Several designers were affiliated to comparable organisations abroad, which facilitated this kind of contact. Writer and typographer Fernand Baudin was an active member of the Association Typographique Internationale, which, to this day, promotes research and organises an annual conference on type design and typography. During the summer holidays, the sociable Olyff invariably travelled to Lurs in the south of France, where designers still meet during the *Rencontres internationales de Lure (International meetings of Lure)* for lectures, workshops, and social gatherings (figs. 3 and 4). Under Olyff's chairmanship, the CBG would enjoy its most productive years. Gilles Fiszman and Richez were members of the prestigious graphic design association, Alliance Graphique Internationale. And, as a group, the CBG was proud to be part of the umbrella organisation, the International Council of Graphic Design Associations. Thanks to such informal international contacts and displays, the CBG's network grew.

fig. 3 (left)
Fernand Baudin (far right)
Rencontres internationales de Lure, 1964

fig. 4 (right)
Lucien De Roeck (far right)
Rencontres internationales de Lure, 1979

Alternative exhibition sites were also sought within Belgium. In the centre of Brussels, nine designers hung preliminary studies and propositions to a transparent zigzag frame structure, which was designed by CBG member Corneille Hannoset and placed in the public space of the Hubertus Gallery. *Manifest van de 9 (Manifesto of the 9)* (1961, fig. 5) presented designs without commissions: 'Not commissions, but proposals originating from one's own vision, questioning whether graphic designers should become their own clients rather than wait for commissions.'[12] Today, the term *speculative design* would be used to describe this approach.

fig. 5
Corneille Hannoset
Exhibition design for *Manifest van de 9*, Brussels, 1961

Over time, larger institutions followed. With the help of the CBG, the then assistant curator Pierre Baudson put together the exhibition *Van beeld tot grafiek (From Image to Graphics,* 1975) at the Royal Museum of Fine Arts of Belgium.[13] It remains one of the few exhibitions about graphic design in a Belgian museum to this date. The catalogue was designed by CBG chairman Fiszman and the cover by Olyff, who had just drawn the logo for the Museum. In the catalogue Baudson writes about the power of graphic design and the impact that it can have on others: 'graphic designs, at the highest level, [can] be an extraordinary method of achieving self-realisation [...] and that of others.'[14] The CBG recognised the importance of collective action.

The House of Graphic Designers

By 1972, the 'handful of stubborn volunteers' had grown into a group of 92 members and the Brussels room above the Au Vieux Saint Martin restaurant was becoming too small for the monthly meetings. They decided to set up La maison des graphistes (The House of Graphic Designers), with a documentation room, an info wall, a library with reading room, studio spaces with photomechanical equipment, a lab, and a cafeteria. The socio-cultural dimension was paramount: 'A house of graphic designers? Not a building, not a villa, not a tent, but a House. The House's aims are socially and culturally motivated. There are no commercial objectives.'[15]

Two years later, the House opened in Schaarbeek with a rich exhibition programme, featuring work by its own designers and by non-members.[16] The designers did everything themselves: scenography, construction, and deconstruction. In one of the newsletters, members were asked to bring their 'blue jeans' and DIY materials. Despite the short running time, the exhibitions were open outside office hours and free of charge, so that they could reach a wide audience.

A bar was also set up in the House, the Rekto-Verso Club. Every Friday evening from nine o'clock, designers could find each other there to 'drink, eat, talk, watch, listen, etc.'[17] Michel Waxmann, designer of the Letraset disco typefaces (see p.159), organised a party with 'slide projection, fanfare, discussion evening, competition, puppet theatre', and refreshments. On another occasion, the *Night of the Graphic Designers* treated the attendees to 'five orchestras with light show, and hot-dog and snails sale'.[18]

But no matter how much work and leisure got mixed up, partying was not the only objective. The House had five committees: professional practice, competitions, exhibitions, public relations, and education.[19] Workshops on transfer letters and seminars on book design took place in the reading room. To fund the library, members donated work for the *Poster Show*: 'It is a "graphic designer's supermarket" where House members can obtain fly posters, posters, etc.'[20] Designer Francine De Boeck was responsible for the archive and encouraged members to provide printed matter, dated and with a brief description of the nature of the project.[21] The work was photographed, and those slides were used for both archiving and promotion. Among other projects, De Boeck organised slide projections in the city, including in the Théâtre du Parvis, for which she had designed the logo and house style.

The education committee was aimed at both professional players and the general public. They tried to improve the low quality of vocational training and, to this end, spoke to the Minister of Education. A discussion evening followed: *'Would you recommend your children to go to a Belgian school for graphic designers?'* After several independent magazines and newspapers folded, the CBG organised a debate about the freedom of information 'in the presence of the main managers and principal motivators.'[22][23] The annual *International Day of Graphic Design* tried to 'inform the general public and especially students, about the development of visual communication.'[24] The *Atelier d'Expression Libre*, educational workshops for children and 'old children aged 60+', were announced with a fold-out flyer (fig. 6).

Political awareness

Social engagement was important in the CBG. For example, the former Brussels Atelier Populaire members Colette Denaeyer-Van Poelvoorde, Roland Denaeyer, and Olyff, together with artists Jo Dustin and Bernard Villers, staged the *42/60* poster campaign in 1974 (fig. 7). It was an invitation to design posters for a good cause. The title referred to the economical print format, 42 × 60 cm:

'Graphic designers, poets, journalists, painters, etchers, photographers, cartoonists and everyone else... What do we do, what can we do, we who live in a 'rich' country, we who make a living from it and especially those of us without surplus financial resources? What should we do and what can we do other than give our time to try to improve the lot of those who do not have access to a level of freedom, a level of dignity, a minimum in life, a privilege that is all too often reserved for a few of their fellow citizens?'[25]

The back of the invitation contained suggestions on topics such as the torture of prisoners in South Vietnam, immigration, educational reform, consumer society, feminism, the workers' struggle, the environment, etc. Denaeyer-Van Poelvoorde coordinated the action.[26] From the first set of 68 entries, 11 designs were chosen and 300 copies were printed. The posters were sold in all sorts of places, from flea markets to bookshops, and the sale was a success: the campaign raised 59,907 Belgian Francs for good causes.[27] Ten years earlier, in the renowned *First Things First* manifesto (1964), British designer Ken Garland and his colleagues had called on designers to use their talents for purposes other than advertising: 'We think that there are other things more worth using our skill and experience on.' But CBG members went further than just putting their names to a message. They used their talent in a way that had a direct financial impact on the causes they believed in.

fig. 6 (below)
Poster for *Atelier d'expression libre* workshop at La maison des graphistes, 1973

fig. 7 (opposite)
Roland Denaeyer and Michel Olyff
42/60 – C'est pas trop cher à imprimer et c'est suffisant pour s'exprimer (42/60, It's not too expensive to print and it's enough to express yourself), 1974

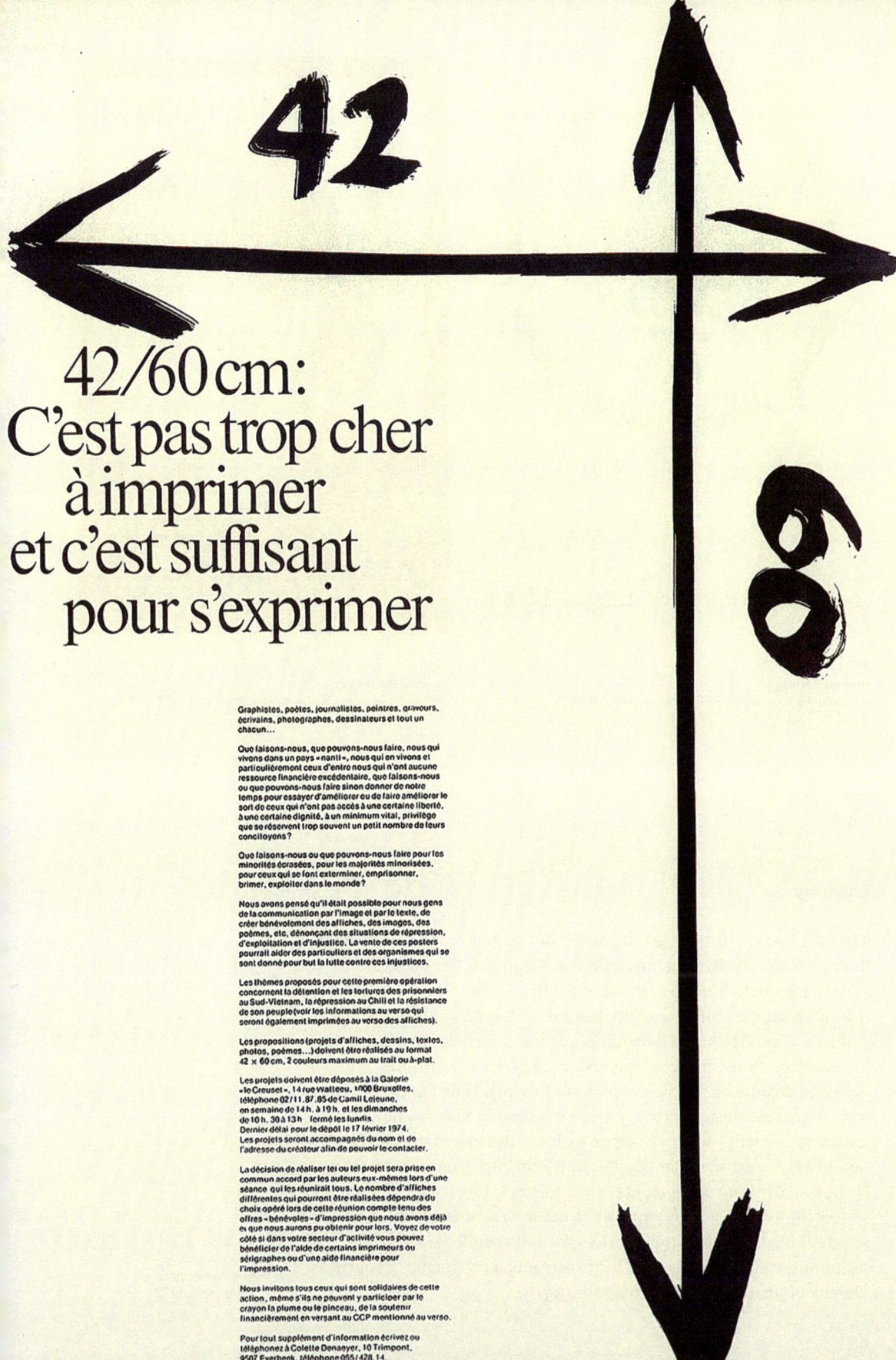

fig. 8
Roland Denaeyer
Poster for Fête de la paix 73 (Peace Festival 73), 1973

fig. 9
Roland Denaeyer
Poster for Meeting Vietnam. Mrs. Nguyen Thi Binh, 1971

Economy

The CBG had no 'profitable purpose,'[28] but that did not mean that the financial aspect of design practice was forgotten. For example, in 1972, several members tried to convince the Minister of Finance to lower the VAT status of self-employed designers. After a conference of the Alliance Typographique Internationale, an optimistic Baudin contacted the Ministry about the protection of the copyright of graphic and typeface designers.[29] A sleek brochure for potential clients explained what a graphic designer is: 'a person who combines the knowledge of a technician and the creativity of an artist.'[30] But one of the most radical initiatives occurred under Olyff's chairmanship, from 1972 to 1974. Designers drew up agreements about tariffs in a price list document, so that they would not undercut each other's remuneration. The folded sheets of paper contain guide prices for both small assignments, such as the lettering on a slide, and large projects, such as the corporate identity of an international company (fig. 10).

fig. 10
Chambre Belge des graphistes, pricing agreement, 1972

			A	B	C
formulieren		6.	Lay-out te berekenen op uurloonbasis met een minimum zoals voorzien bij 4 (binnenpaginas). Basislay-out ereloonraming rekening houdend met de moeilijkheidsgraad.		
advertentie		7	Een ganse pagina in de dagbladpers of reklame in huis aan huisbestelling.		
			• Lay-out	10.000-15.000	15.000-20.000	20.000-30.000
			• Grafische konseptie	15.000-20.000	20.000-30.000	30.000-50.000
			• Totale konseptie	20.000-30.000	30.000-50.000	40.000-60.000
			- Prijs voor tijdschriften · — 30 %. - Prijs voor gespecialiseerde tijdschriften — 50 %. - Prijs voor 1/2 pagina — 30 %. - Prijs voor 1/4 pagina en minder — 50 %. - Resizing prijs voor aanpassingen, in het raam van het zelfde medium, die geen totale herwerking van het lay-out vragen — 90 % met een minimum van 3.000 F of berekend op uurloonbasis. - Prijs voor totale herwerking zie 4 (lay-out binnenbladzijde).		
omslag		8.1	(prospekt, plooifolder)		
			lay-out	2.000	3.000	5.000
			konseptie	5.000-7.500	7.500-12.500	10.000-15.000
		8.2	(kataloog, broschure, magazine, enz.)		
			lay-out	4.000	6.000	10.000
			konseptie	10.000-15.000	15.000-25.000	20.000-30.000
gelegenheidsdrukwerk		9.	(wenskaart, verhuisaankondiging, vakantiemededeling, uitnodiging, telegram, enz.)	5.000-10.000	7.500-15.000	vanaf 20.000
kalender		10.	Grafische konseptie illustraties, zie 20.	10.000-25.000	20.000-30.000	25.000-40.000
verpakking		11	• Etiket	8.000-10.000	20.000-30.000	vanaf 30.000
			• Buitenverpakking voor gegeven en bestaande binnenverpakking	10.000-20.000	20.000-30.000	vanaf 40.000
			• Design voor totale verpakking	20.000-40.000	40.000-60.000	vanaf 80.000
			- Aanpassingen van verpakkingen voor andere produkten met het doel een reeks of een gamma te vormen ereloonraming. - Aanpassingen van verpakkingen en andere inhoudsmaten of aan andere verpakkings- mogelijkheden prijs te berekenen op uurloonbasis. - Het op punt stellen van een koherent verpakkingssysteem **kontrakt** dient opgesteld. - Verzamelverpakking of groepsverpakking (showbox, floorstand, display) ereloonraming.		
draagzak of inpakpapier		12.	Draagzak of inpakpapier	8.000-10.000	20.000-30.000	vanaf 50.000

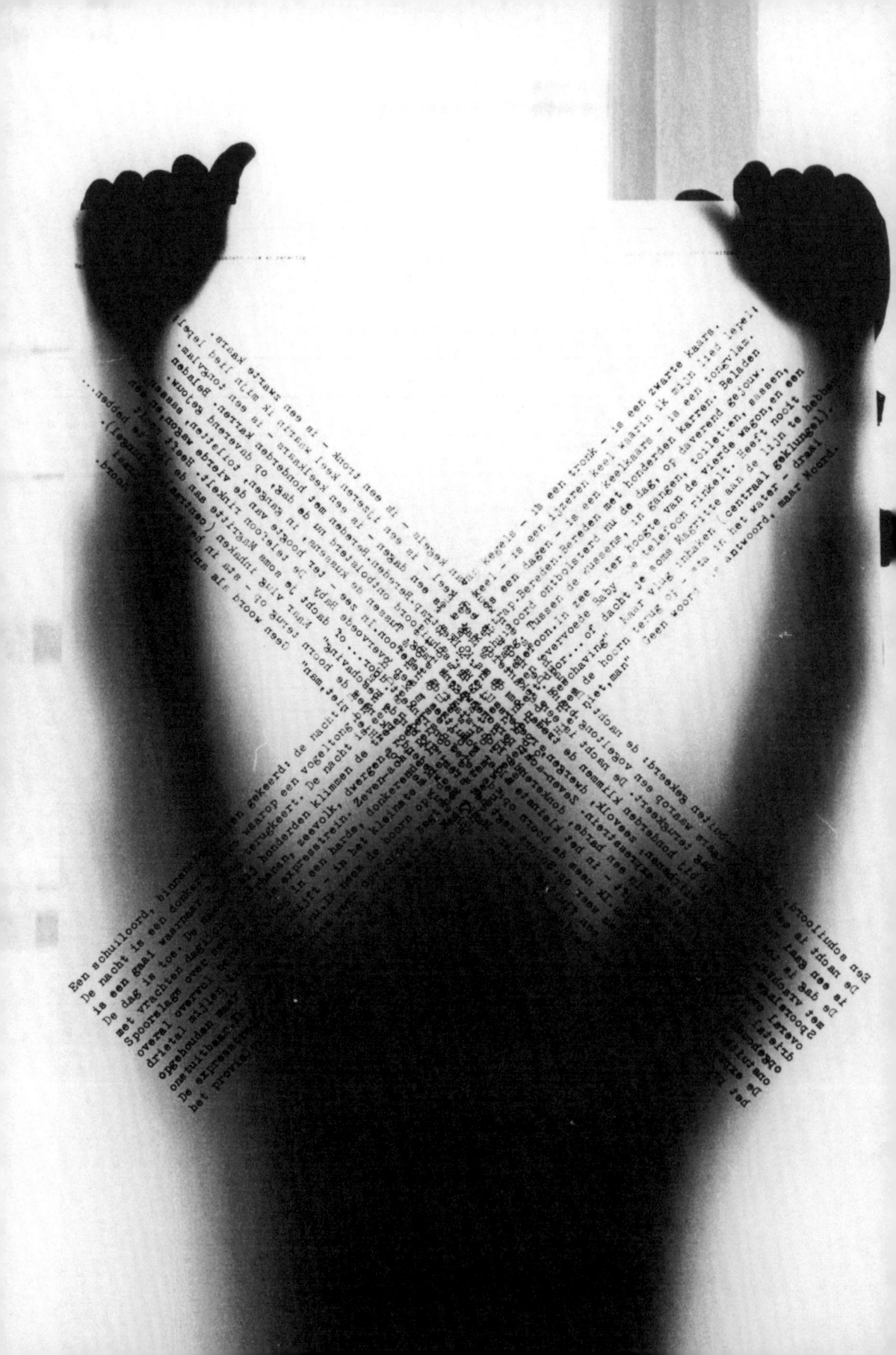

Running the House cost money, and members were creative with fundraising. They sold prints, such as Herman Lampaert's transparent *Dag & Nacht* (*Day & Night*, 1973, fig. 11). Signed self-portraits were sold in the *Ontwerper te koop* (*Designer for Sale*, 1973) auction. Members whose membership fees were overdue were named and asked to pay up in the *CBG News* newsletter. Unfortunately, it was not enough. On 30 October 1978, the balance was reviewed and it turned out that the arrears amounted to 437,851 Belgian Francs. The lease on the House was terminated, debts were settled and the CBG went into liquidation. According to Lampaert, it was immediately missed.[31]

The closing had a dramatic effect on the representation of Belgian graphic designers, and, arguably, this has never recovered. The CBG was a long-running and innovative member association, although it was not the only one, and contact with designers outside Brussels was sometimes tricky. There were other short-lived initiatives on the Flemish side, but members argued about who was allowed to design the logo, or how much the membership fee should be.[32] In 1981, some former CBG members joined the Union des Designers en Belgique (Federation of Designers in Belgium).[33] Things seem better abroad: the British Design and Art Direction (D&AD), the Dutch Beroepsorganisatie Nederlandse Ontwerpers (Association of Dutch Designers) and the American Institute of Graphic Arts (AIGA) are examples of flourishing professional associations by and for graphic designers today.

The Design Centre also no longer exists: following the death of des Cressonnières in 1983, the government shut down its agency. Belgium's state reforms in the 1980s meant that culture and economy, two pillars of the design sector, were no longer managed by the same federal authority. The fragmentation signified the end of a central body for the promotion of Belgian design.[34] In Flanders, the successors were VIZO, Design Vlaanderen, and the Flanders Fashion Institute. Today these are merged into the non-profit Flanders DC, but its focus is an economic one. In Brussels, there is MAD, a 'home of creators' with a focus on local fashion and design. And then there is Wallonie Design, which aims to 'increase the use of design and its methods within Walloon companies'.[35]

Nowadays, designers are increasingly subjected to malpractice: unpaid pitches, unpaid internships, zero-hour contracts, pressure to perform on social media, increasing demands with respect to knowledge of technology, loss of copyright. Nevertheless, there is an active design scene in Belgium, which is once again finding international resonance. During *Off the Grid*, many of them participated in a discussion during the one-day radio programme *Talking Letterheads* (2020). Although few radio guests bought into the idea of pricing scales, the event marked the official start of the new Belgisch Instituut Grafisch Ontwerp (Belgian Institute Graphic Design). It aims to become a knowledge centre and presentation platform for graphic design in and beyond Belgium.[36] Hopefully, this will usher in a new phase of mutual respect and support for Belgian graphic designers.

fig. 11
Herman Lampaert
Poster for CBG portfolio, 1973

1. Brochure for Belgian Chamber for Graphic Designers (no date), Boudewijn Delaere Archive.
2. See Crombez, Thomas and 3BA Grafisch Ontwerp, *Made in Belgium: Een debat over de (ontbrekende?) geschiedenis van grafisch ontwerp in België*. Available at: https://www.letterwerk.be/madeinbelgium/20181130.html; last accessed on 20 May 2021.
3. Richez, Jacques, 'Au nom des graphistes les plus mal employés du monde' in *Clés pour les arts* (Brussels: Association pour l'information culturelle, February 1975), p.36.
4. Designed by Corneille Hannoset with a logo by Michel Olyff.
5. Serulus, Katarina, *Design & Politics: The Public Promotion of Industrial Design in Postwar Belgium (1950–1986)* (Leuven: KU Leuven Press, 2018), p.185.
6. Richez, Jacques, 'Au nom des graphistes les plus mal employés du monde', p.36.
7. Elno, Karel, *De Nieuwe*, 24 June 1966.
8. Lampaert, Herman, 'De naoorlogse periode. Een schets', in Johan Valcke, *In koeien van letters: 50 jaar grafische vormgeving in Vlaanderen* (Brussels: VIZO, 1997), p.58.
9. Richez, Jacques, 'Au nom des graphistes les plus mal employés du monde', p.36.
10. Brochure for Belgian Chamber for Graphic Designers (no date), Boudewijn Delaere Archive.
11. Meeting report (29 September 1971), Boudewijn Delaere Archive.
12. Lampaert, Herman, 'De naoorlogse periode: Een schets', p.82.
13. *Van beeld tot grafiek. Aspecten van de affiche en de grafiek in België van de jaren twintig tot heden*, Royal Museums for Fine Arts of Belgium, 21 February–13 April 1975.
14. Baudson, Pierre, 'Introduction', in *De l'image au graphisme: aspects de l'affiche et du graphisme en Belgique des années vingt à nos jours* (Brussels: Musée provisoire d'art moderne, 1975), p.11.
15. Brochure for Belgian Chamber for Graphic Designers (no date), Boudewijn Delaere Archive.
16. Some examples: *18 screen-prints by BKG members* (1973); *Heinz Edelmann, The face of a radio* (1973); *Olaf Leu: International Design* (1973); *Young Polish Film Posters* (1973); *American Depression Posters 1929* (1974); *Original posters for Chile* (1974); *Dick Bruna draws for children* (1974).
17. *De Recto-Verso vrijdagen* (*The Recto-Verso Fridays*) (no date), p.1, Letterenhuis, Luk Mestdagh Archive.
18. CBG Newsletter (no date), p.1, Letterenhuis, Luk Mestdagh Archive.
19. Brochure for Belgian Chamber for Graphic Designers (no date), Boudewijn Delaere Archive.
20. CBG Newsletter (no date), p.1, Letterenhuis, Luk Mestdagh Archive.
21. Letter from Francine De Boeck (15 November 1972), Letterenhuis, Luk Mestdagh Archive.
22. *Perscommuniqué, Maison des Graphistes* (no date), Letterenhuis, Luk Mestdagh Archive.
23. Some of the magazines and newspapers that disappeared included *Les Cahiers du Grif*, *Clés pour les Arts*, *La Metropole*, *La Flandre Liberale*, *Le Matin*, *Theatre-Poème*, *Journal d'Europe*, *Spot*, *Le Peuple*, *Europe 74*, and *Infor-Jeunes*.
24. Brochure for the Belgian Chamber for Graphic Designers (no date), Boudewijn Delaere Archive.
25. Original text: 'Graphistes, poètes, journalistes, peintres, graveurs, écrivains, photographes, dessinateurs et tout un chacun… Que faisons-nous, que pouvons-nous faire, nous qui vivons dans un pays 'nanti', nous qui en vivons et particulièrement ceux d'entre nous qui n'ont aucune ressource financière excédentaire, que faisons-nous et que pouvons-nous faire sinon donner de notre temps pour essayer d'améliorer le sort de ceux qui n'ont pas accès à une certaine liberté, à une certaine dignité, à un minimum vital, privilège que s réservent trop souvent un petit nombre de leurs concitoyens?' Denaeyer, Roland; Olyff, Michel, *42/60 – C'est pas trop cher à imprimer et c'est suffisant pour s'exprimer*, poster, 1974.
26. Hemmerijckx, Rik, 'De politieke affiches van Roland Denaeyer', *Brood en Rozen. Tijdschrift voor de geschiedenis van sociale bewegingen*, 5: 1 (2000), pp.89–95.
27. Denayer, Colette, letter (November 1974), Letterenhuis, Luk Mestdagh Archive and *Mai 68: L'imagination au pouvoir* (Brussels: Éditions Luc Pire, 2008), p.65.
28. Brochure for Belgian Chamber for Graphic Designers (no date), Boudewijn Delaere Archive.
29. *CBG/BKG Typo* (no date), Letterenhuis, Luk Mestdagh Archive.
30. Brochure for Belgian Chamber for Graphic Designers (no date), Boudewijn Delaere Archive.
31. Lampaert, Herman, 'De naoorlogse periode. Een schets', p.116.
32. These were: the Vlaams Verbond van Grafici (VVG); the Grafische Vormgevers Vlaanderen (GVV); Beroepsvereniging Grafische Vormgevers (BGV); and the Vereniging van Vlaamse Ontwerpers (VVVO). Already in 1836, only six years after the creation of Belgium, printer Adolphe Wahlen founded the Société Typographique Belge for printers. (Baudin, Fernand, *Belgian Books, 1830*–1980, lecture in the Library of Congress, 29 May 1980 (typescript), from Sunier, Coline and Mazé, Charles (eds.), *Dossier Fernand Baudin* (Dijon: Les presses du réel, 2013), p.116). On 13 April 1967, the establishment of the Vlaams Verbond van Grafici (VVG) was published in the Belgian Official Gazette and signed by Gerard Alsteens, Jeanine Behaeghel, Hugo Dekempeneer, Boudewijn Delaere, Paul Ibou, Luk Mestdagh, Robert Neirynck, Albert Setola, Geert Setola, and Ernest Verkest. (*Belgisch Staatsblad*, 13 April 1967, p.785). Boudewijn Delaere designed the logo. (Verkest, Ernest, letter to Boudewijn Delaere, 6 April 1967 (Boudewijn Delaere Archive)). The organisation ceased to exist in 1974. (Ibou, Paul, 'Ontstaan en groei van beroepsverenigigingen voor grafische vormgevers in België en Nederland', June 1987 (Boudewijn Delaere Archive), p.5). The Vereniging van Vlaamse Ontwerpers vzw (VVVO) was founded in Ghent in 1983. The Grafische Vormgevers Vlaanderen (GVV) was founded in Zandhoven, in 1986, under the chairmanship of Paul Ibou. (Ibou, Paul, *Ontstaan en groei van beroepsverenigigingen voor grafische vormgevers in België en Nederland*, June 1987 (Boudewijn Delaere Archive), p.5). In 1990, the Beroepsvereniging Grafische Vormgevers (BGV) published a charter written by chairman Misjel Vossen. Febelgra, the Federation of the Belgian Graphic Industry, still exists today. Available at: https://www.febelgra.be/nl; last accessed on 7 July 2021. This organisation is the amalgamation of Unigra, the union of graphic and book industries nfp, Brussels and the Chambre Syndicale des Maîtres Imprimeurs de Bruxelles. Available at: https://etwie.be/nl/kennisbank/nieuws/historische-drukkerij-turnhout-ontrafelt-geschiedenis-houten-drukpers; last accessed on 7 July 2021.
33. Letter (24 February 1978), Letterenhuis, Luk Mestdagh Archive.
34. Valcke, Johan, 'Design en de publieke sector in België sinds 1975', in Huygens, Frank and Mienke, Simon Thomas (eds.), *Design Derby: Nederland België 1815–2015* (Rotterdam: Museum Boijmans Van Beuningen, 2015), p.188.
35. http://www2.walloniedesign.be/a-propos/; last accessed on 7 July 2021.
36. https://belgischinstituutgrafischontwerp.be/2/; last accessed on 7 July 2021.

EEN HUIS VAN GRAFISCHE ONTWERPERS?

Geen building, geen villa, geen tent maar een Huis.

Een ontmoetingsplaats, een werklokaal, een Huis van de grafische ontwerpers. Waarom ?

Door groeiend ledenaantal en door de verscheidene aktiviteiten werd de noodzaak aangevoeld een eigen vaste plaats te hebben om er een aktief sekretariaat in onder te kunnen brengen, en er de leden en hun genodigden de mogelijkheid te bieden konferenties, seminaries en werkvergaderingen te houden.

Met een grote meerderheid werd daarom door een algemene ledenvergadering, op 15 november 1972, besloten het projekt, Huis van de grafische ontwerpers, te realiseren. Dit, door de BKG beheerd Huis, bevindt zich op de Eugène Demolderlaan 24, te 1030 Brussel (Schaarbeek), tel. 41.05.64.

Door de animatoren wordt, met toestemming van de beheerraad, het auto-beheer van het Huis verzekerd.

Sociale en kulturele motieven vormen het doel van het Huis.
Er zijn geen kommersiële doelstellingen.

fig. 12
Brochure about the House of Graphic Designers, no date

Katarina Serulus

Practices in the Margins of Design History: Club Culture and Graphic Design in Belgium

Katarina Serulus (1988) studied Art Studies and Design Cultures at KU Leuven and the Vrije Universiteit Amsterdam. In 2016, she defended her PhD, *Design & Politics. The Public Promotion of Industrial Design in Postwar Belgium (1950–1986)* at the Faculty of Design Studies at the University of Antwerp. It was published in book form in 2018 by Leuven University Press. An earlier version of this text first appeared in *Designing The Night: Graphic Design of Belgian Club Culture 1970–2000* (Brussels: ADAM and CFC-Éditions, 2019).

Graphic design in Belgium has been little studied from a historical perspective. My first encounter with this unknown aspect of design history was in the context of my PhD research: *Design & Politics: The Public Promotion of Industrial Design in Postwar Belgium (1950–1986)*.[1] This study outlines the political history of design in post-war Belgium. During my research, I discovered the work of Corneille Hannoset, Michel Olyff, Jacques Richez, Boudewijn Delaere, Sophie and Sami Alouf, Anne-Judith Van Loock, Jean-Jacques Stiefenhofer, Julian Key, and Gilles Fiszman – just a few of the many designers active in Belgium in the post-war period. Limited by the scope of my research, I only covered a small part of their practice, namely, the graphic design that was promoted as – or served to promote – Belgian design, in accordance with the international modernistic canon. At the time, it was held in high esteem by institutes financed by the Belgian government, such as the Design Centre in Brussels (1964–85).

A few years later, I discovered a very different dimension to the history of graphic design in Belgium – a dimension that is even less known and documented than the modernist designs explored in my doctoral thesis. This happened during research for two exhibition projects on club culture. For these projects, I exchanged the institutional context for the underground and discovered the design cultures of the night. Together with Cat Rossi and Jochen Eisenbrand, in 2018 I curated the exhibition *Night Fever: Designing Club Culture 1960–Today*, a coproduction of the Vitra Design Museum in Weil am Rhein and the Design Museum Brussels. It was the first international retrospective about the relationship between design and club culture, from 1960 to date. The wealth of graphic material about the Belgian scene that I discovered during that project resulted in the smaller exhibition *Designing the Night. Graphic Design of Belgian Club Culture 1970–2000*, at the Design Museum Brussels, in 2019.[2] That exhibition explored graphic design as an essential part of Belgian club culture in the 1970s. Graphic design, together with music, dance, architecture, and lighting effects, shaped a temporary universe in which clubbers could immerse themselves to escape from everyday life.

It required a different view and approach to study design that was created outside of the institutional frameworks and at the margins of disciplinary practices. In contrast to the cultures of the day, night culture – and certainly club culture, with its subversive and temporary nature – is hardly documented in public archives and collections. In documenting the fleeting, almost elusive club nights, graphic design occupies a special position. Flyers and posters are often the only physical mementos left after a club night. However, they are not made for longevity. They are often hastily produced objects that, unlike books or other more durable graphic artefacts, are quickly consumed and then disappear just as rapidly. For this reason, design historian Alice Twemlow describes nightlife graphics as 'the most ephemeral part of graphic design, a discipline that is intrinsically highly transient.'[3] Yet, it is often these rare specimens that give us an idea today of the subcultures, music genres, graphic strategies, identities, and the huge creativity in night and club life.

Club graphics not only tell us something about the club culture of the time, but also shed light on alternative practices of graphic design that are frequently absent from general overviews, both Belgian and international. Authorship is often still the peg on which design history is hung, and the frequently anonymous club logos, flyers, and posters remain in the margins. The focus was not so much on the designer, but rather on the different communities in which these graphic ephemera functioned as a means of communication and helped to shape identities with which the youth and clubbers could identify. In most cases, the makers had not received any training in graphic design. However, they were often part of the group of habitués who claimed their place in the club almost every week. Consequently, they spontaneously mastered the visual codes to appeal to visitors with a similar taste in music and lifestyle. Their idiosyncratic position, outside the institutional and professional design world, allowed them to experiment with the limits of the medium. For example, some flyers were little more than a photocopied sheet of paper, stripped of all graphic elements, with only an indication of the date and location of the club night. But, equally, new technological gadgets were used or senses were stimulated with the integration of smell, sound, or movement. The carrier of the flyer was also played with: paper was sometimes replaced by CDs, cassettes, energy drinks, or even shower gel samples (fig. 1).

This short essay takes a look at the design of these fleetingly produced and quickly consumed objects and reveals the wide range of lifestyles, graphic strategies, subcultures, music genres, identities, and creativity that Belgian club life fostered. Since nightlife is hardly documented in public collections, I have mainly relied on documents from private archives and interviews with key figures. This text therefore does not provide a complete overview, but rather highlights a number of prevailing strategies, trends, and themes that coloured Belgian club culture from its pioneering work in the 1970s to the emergence of electronic music festivals at the turn of this century.

fig. 1
Shower gel flyer for 'It's Clean, it's Fuse', Brussels, 1997

Cut and paste

Punk and post-punk were important youth cultures in the mid-1970s, with a profound influence on the world of music, art, and design.[4] The challenging visual language and attitude had a lasting influence on the graphic design of nightlife. The aesthetic is characterised by the unabashed recycling and appropriation of existing images, a straightforward DIY approach, and the use of handwriting, transfers and adhesive letters. Designers found the source material for their cut-and-paste work in daily mass media, such as newspapers, magazines, and books. The visual strategies that emerged within the punk movement turned out to be very effective and would quickly find their way beyond that movement itself.

The most iconic Belgian post-punk graphics are, without a doubt, the posters for Joy Division's performances at the Brussels avant-garde centre Plan K.[5] This multidisciplinary venue was founded in

fig. 2
Marc Borgers
Poster for the opening night of Plan K, Brussels, 1979

fig. 3
Jocelyne Coster
Poster for Joy Division and Digital Dance in Plan K, Brussels, 1980

1979 by the eponymous dance and theatre company in a former sugar refinery in Molenbeek.[6] Journalists Annik Honoré and Michel Duval were responsible for the musical programming and booked legendary performances by, among others, A Certain Ratio, Section 25, Echo & The Bunnymen, and Front 242. For the club's opening night in 1979, the duo arranged the first foreign show by Joy Division, the post-punk cult band led by Ian Curtis. The headliners were performances by the avant-garde author William S. Burroughs and artist Brion Gysin; these were supplemented with film screenings, lectures, and concerts by, in addition to Joy Division, Cabaret Voltaire. Graphic artist Marc Borgers created the poster, which clearly shows the visual language of the punk movement at that time (fig. 2). The aesthetics were characterised by the appropriation of pre-existing images, a straightforward DIY spirit, handwriting, and dry-transfer lettering.

Three months later, Ian Curtis and his entourage were invited to Plan K again, this time as headliner. The poster for this was created by artist Jocelyne Coster, then a student at La Cambre (fig. 3). She set to work with one of the most common tropes within the punk movement: the recycling and appropriation of existing images. She cut out a black-and-white image of three boys in tuxedos and glued it to a grid, then added the band names and location to the artwork with black and red transfer letters. The poster was printed on cheap newsprint by POUR, a left-wing Brussels organisation and monthly magazine, and has become one of the most sought-after artefacts of punk memorabilia. It has even secured a place in the collection of the Museum of Modern Art in New York.

fig. 4
Bruno Bulté
Poster for Cabaret Voltaire at Klacik, Brussels, 1980

fig. 5
Bruno Bulté
Poster for 'Nuit 1960' in Le Pluriel, Brussels, 1980

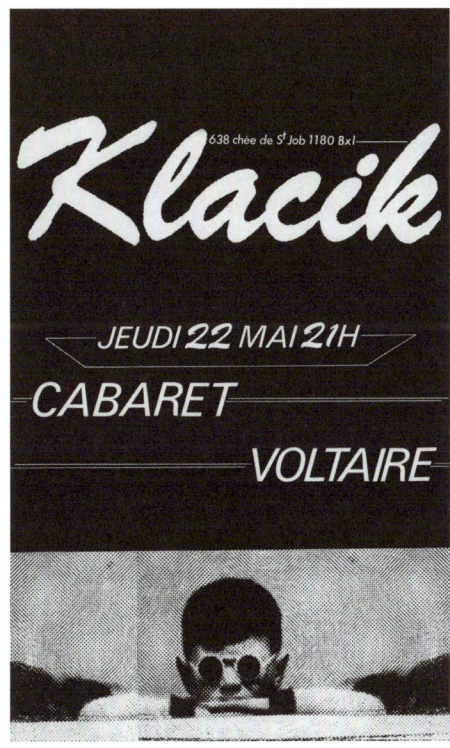

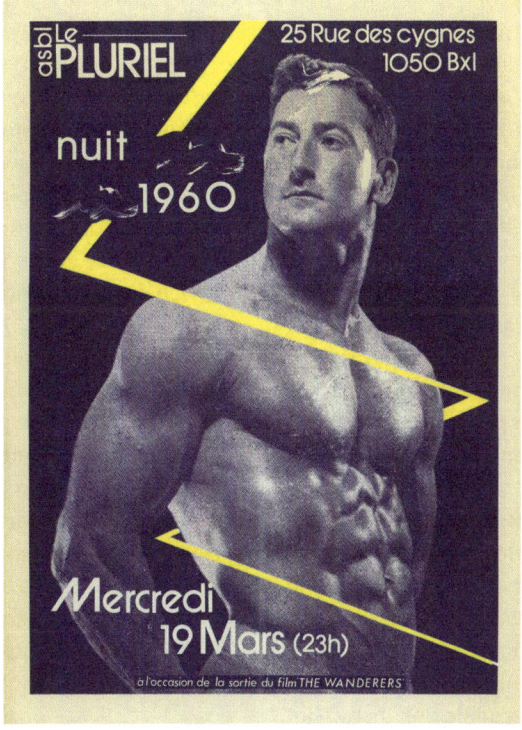

The punk idiom is also prominent in the artwork of the small avant-garde venue Klacik, founded in 1978 by three young rebellious minds: Bernard Cauchie, Thierry Balasse, and Thierry Melatre.[7] The club quickly became a hotspot for experimental and alternative music. Together with journalist Gilles Verlant, they programmed, among others, Simple Minds, Cabaret Voltaire, and The Cure, long before these bands would fill the largest concert halls in the country. The artist Bruno Bulté started working as Klacik's artistic director after training as an architect at the Brussels Académie Royale des Beaux-Arts (Royal Academy of Fine Arts). Bulté drew his greatest inspiration from the mass media. He collected images from magazines, periodicals, and books. For example, he was able to produce a new poster for an evening concert or a club night in just a few hours, by adding drawings and lettering to one or more images from his collection (figs. 4 and 5).

The rich punk aesthetic was also used for announcements from Alkaselser, the brainchild of the Brussels DJ and artist Philippe Itterbeek.[8] These club nights were organised at various locations in the city, with the recurring punk style, with drawn- and typed-on photo montages forming the common thread. The name Alkaselser was inspired by the popular painkiller from the 1980s, a well-known hangover cure after a heavy night out. The parties were attended by a colourful mix of guests from various Brussels artistic circles and the film industry.

New wave meets disco

At about the same time as post-punk and new wave, disco made its appearance: a style of music that would strongly determine future club scenes. In the early 1970s, a mainly gay, Afro-American, and Latino public were dancing to disco at underground club nights in New York, but the genre finally reached a wider Western audience when the blockbuster *Saturday Night Fever* (1977) appeared in cinemas. Discotheques became places where young people experimented with alternative lifestyles and questioned established social norms. The cross-pollination of the glitter of the disco scene with the nostalgic style of new wave resulted in a rich graphic design production within club culture.

An important exponent of this mash-up between the new wave and disco aesthetics was the talented artist Aldo Gigli. He played a prominent role in Brussels nightlife as a graphic designer and set builder for the Brussels disco temple Mirano Continental[9] and its predecessor, the Canotier.[10] Located in an old 1930s cinema, the Mirano Continental was conceived by its founders – Paul Sterck, Gigli, Marco Rolland, and Jacques Goossens-Bara – as a cross between the legendary Studio 54 in New York and Le Palace in Paris. Inspired by those two references, the club adopted a very exclusive door policy, based on looks and style, and organised spectacular themed events and experimental performances with sensational décor and impressive graphic design by Gigli.

fig. 6
Aldo Gigli
Flyer for 'Disko Futura' at Canotier, Brussels, 1979

fig. 7
Aldo Gigli
Poster for 'Les Bacchanales Romaines' at Mirano Continental, Brussels, 1984

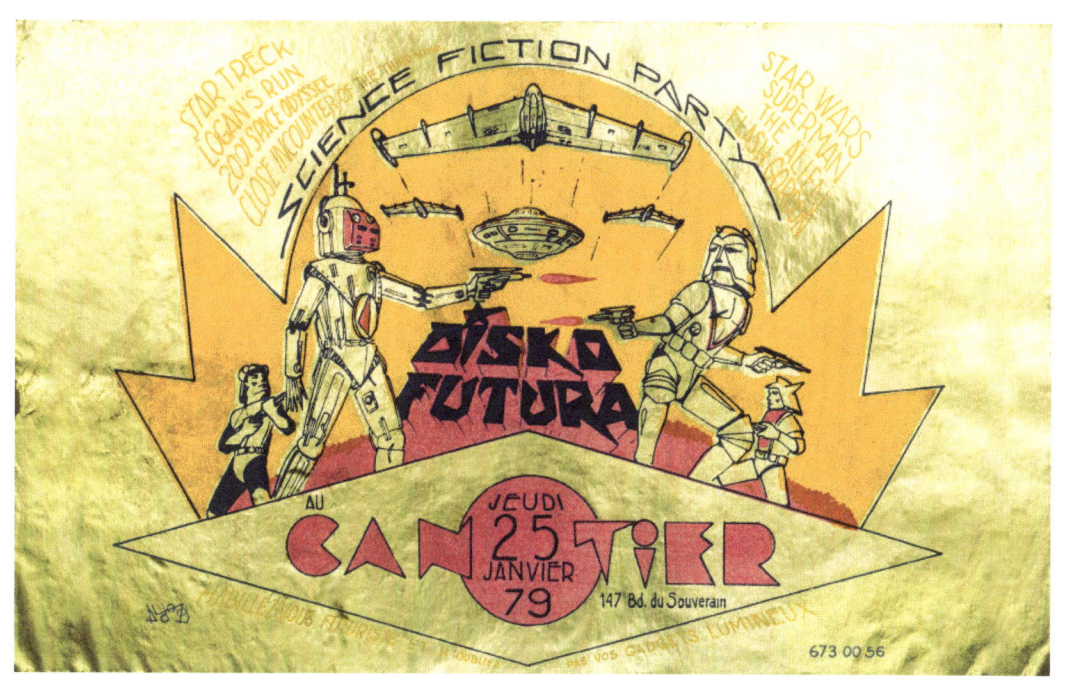

Gigli used a wide range of visual references in his artwork: from disco glitter and new wave colours to cartoon characters and futuristic beings. The flyer for the *Disko Futura* club night in the Canotier, in 1979 (fig. 6) is a good example, with laser-gun-shooting robots and spaceships whizzing around overhead. Against a gold background with fluorescent pink details, he wrote: 'Dress futuristically and don't forget your luminous gadgets'. He found inspiration for this futuristic setting in the Canotier's recently renovated interior. In 1979, it was the first club in Brussels to install a laser light, a technology previously only used for scientific purposes.

The Canotier got the ideas from discotheque Le Palace (1978), which architect Patrick Berger furnished with innovations such as neon and lasers. Gigli translated that element into his artwork, creating his own unique, artificial world.

Fashioning the body

The body was (and is) central to the club experience. It was immersed in a parallel reality with flickering lights, thumping beats, atmospheric decor, drugs, and alcohol. It should come as no surprise, therefore, that the human body is one of the most common tropes in the graphic design of club culture: from references to body piercing and the physical pleasure of drug use to iconic images from the mass media or high art, cartoonish depictions and cyborgs. However, the one-sided and stereotypical use of naked or eroticised male or female bodies also raises questions about gender (in)equality within a club scene that was particularly male oriented.[11]

Fashion was an important element of the hedonistic and physical culture of the club scene, a form of expression that made it possible to experiment with different identities during a night out.[12] Clubs and record labels brought out their own clothing lines featuring their logos and visual identity. In 1988, Antler-Subway Records, known for the first new-beat releases, launched a complete clothing collection inspired by that brand-new Belgian music genre. They simply called the collection New Beat Fashion and enlisted the help of two fashion students from Antwerp, Idriz Jossa and Bart Declercq, for the design (fig. 9). The clothing was dark, with a strong nod to new wave and religious-inspired prints and accessories. Characteristic was the oval badge with a photographic portrait of an older woman. This recurring graphic motif was inspired by the ceramic photographs found on gravestones. It was the darker alternative to the acid-house generation's smiley face (fig. 8). In the mid-1990s, the logo of the legendary Bonzai dance label graced bomber jackets and long-sleeved T-shirts en masse. The logo was designed by the then 17-year-old Alec Van and features an abstract bonsai tree with Asian typography, allegedly inspired by the menu from an Asian restaurant (fig. 10). It remains one of the most iconic logos in Belgian club culture.

fig. 8
Flyers for 'Acid Love Forever' and 'Acid Test Evolution' organised by Philippe Motteux (Fifi) at Café d'Anvers, Antwerp, 1993

fig. 9
Brochure for the 'New Beat Fashion' collection, 1988

fig. 10
Bart Gijsens
Flyer for 'The First Rebirth Party', Bonzai Records, 1994

Glitches and fractals

The new beat was a new sound that broke through in the Belgian underground club scene in the late 1980s, with slow and deep beats flooding the dancefloor.[13] Young people from all over Western Europe would converge in Belgian discotheques to dance the night away. The success of this new music laid the foundations for the further development of an authentic Belgian house and techno culture in the 1990s. Technology played a central role. Computers, sequencers, and synthesisers provided the new digital sound, with the Roland TB-303 and TR-808 drum machines becoming welcome guests in the producer's studio.

These new technologies not only heavily influenced the new sounds in the nightclubs, but also the graphic design. Clubbers, promotors, and DJs experimented with the new digital applications to design the most striking, stylish, or attractive flyers, posters, or record covers. The new technologies also spurred the development of 3D animations and futuristic landscapes brimming with fractals, glitches, cyborgs, and planets (fig. 11). But due to the limited speed of computers at the time, it took 10 to 12 hours to save a file, and making a poster took several days.

fig. 11
Bart Gijsens
Flyer for 'Extreme on Monday's', Affligem, 1990s

Brands and branding

To promote club nights, the club scene also drew inspiration from consumer culture and its visual style. A common strategy was the ironic recycling of advertising campaigns by hyper-capitalist companies (figs. 12). The many parodies of fashion brands, washing powder or toothpaste advertisements, and cigarette brands may have poked fun at the advertising industry, but at the same time they also exploited this strong visual language for their own promotion.[14] This, in turn, introduced an alternative form of collectivity to the market, which was experienced through music, drugs, and dance.

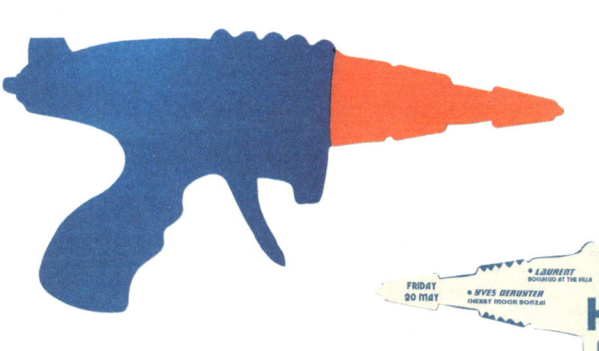

figs. 12
Clockwise from top right:
Flyer for 'Hardfloor' at Cherry Moon, Lokeren, 1994
Flyer for 'The Magic Mushroom Party' at Cherry Moon, Lokeren, 1994
Flyer for 'Save the Robots' organised by Philippe Motteux (Fifi)
at Café d'Anvers, Antwerp, 1995
Flyer for 'Ça Mousse' at Fuse, Brussels, 1996

presents

I ♥ TECHNO

featuring

RICHIE HAWTIN
JEFF MILLS
PIERRE TRISH

live

DAFT PUNK

FRIDAY 10th NOVEMBER
21.00 - 05.00

VOORUIT - GENT

Sint-Pietersnieuwstraat 23
info : 09/243.77.77 • 02/567.16.97
vvk : Fnac, Music Mania, Music Man (Gent), Usa Import (Antwerpen)
The Fuse CD-release weekender part 1

  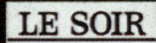 

The flyers and posters for La Demence,[15] the legendary monthly gay parties organised by Thierry Coppens in Brussels' Fuse since 1992,[16] invariably went to town with the visual codes of consumer society. For example, the layout of the well-known Belgian cigarette brand Tigra was adopted for a flyer for a Tarzan party in 2001. The head of the famous model Angelina Saey, depicted in the iconic tiger costume on a green background, was replaced with a man's head (fig. 14). This subversive twist references the entrenched gender roles and hetero-normative standards that dominated advertising and product branding.

In the mid-1990s, club culture became commercialised. Discotheques evolved into global brands, DJs became superstars earning staggering wages. The once sullen underground electronic music scene became part of the mainstream and conformed to commercial interests. This was reflected in the design of posters and flyers, which now dedicated increasing space to the names of famous DJs and logos. At the same time, the first indoor dance events were launched. These events pulled in thousands of clubbers and set the tone for the many electronic music festivals that continue to define Belgium's thriving club scene to this day.

fig. 13
Marc Meulemans
Flyer for the first edition of 'I Love Techno', 1995

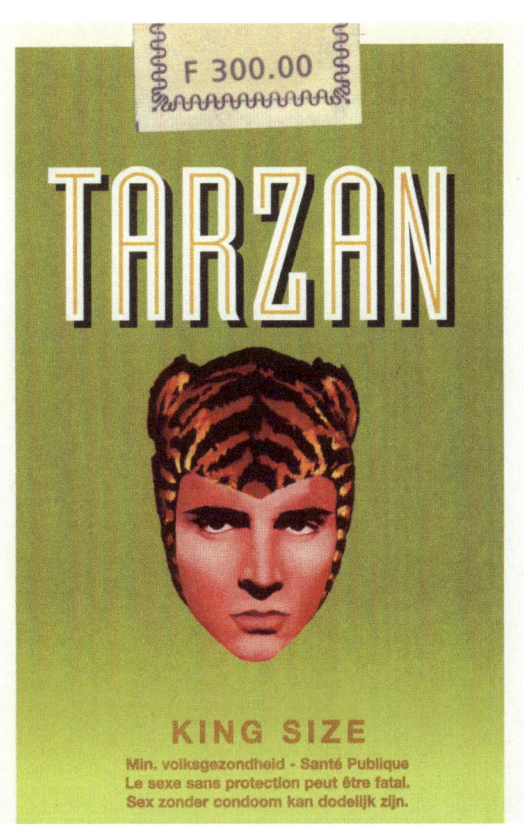

fig. 14
Flyer for 'Tarzan' at La Démence, Brussels, 1996

1. Serulus, Katarina, *Design & Politics. The Public Promotion of Industrial Design in Postwar Belgium (1950–1986)*. (Leuven: Leuven University Press, 2018).
2. Eisenbrand, Jochen and Rossi, Cat, 'Night Fever: Designing Club Culture 1960-Today', in Mateo Kries; Eisenbrand, Jochen; Rossi, Cat (eds.), *Night Fever. Design Club Culture 1960-Today* (Weil am Rhein: Vitra Design Museum, 2018); Serulus, Katarina, *Designing the Night. Graphic Design of Belgian Club Culture 1970-2000* (Brussels: CFC Editions, 2019).
3. Twemlow, Alice, 'Smiley Faces: The Graphic Language of Electronic Dance Music Promotion', in Kries, Mateo; Eisenbrand, Jochen; Rossi, Cat, *Night Fever. Design Club Culture 1960-Today*, p.218.
4. Blauvelt, Andrew, *Too Fast to Live, Too Young to Die: Punk Graphics, 1976-1986* (Bloomfield Hills: Cranbrook Art Museum, 2018); De Chassey, Eric (ed.), *Europunk: The Visual Culture of Punk in Europe, 1976-1980* (Rome: Drago, 2011).
5. Plan K (1979-1980s), Rue de Manchester 21, 1080 Brussels.
6. Carly, Philippe (ed.), *Au plan K: Joy Division & Postpunk at La Raffinerie du Plan K, Brussels 1979-2009* (Brussels: ARP2 Editions, 2017); Nice, James, *Shadowplayers. The Rise and Fall of Factory Records* (London: Aurum Press, 2010), pp.83-86.
7. Klacik (1978-1981), Chau. de Saint-Job 63, 1180 Brussels.
8. Alkaselser (1980-2005).
9. Mirano Continental (1981-to date), Chau. de Louvain 38, 1210 Brussels.
10. Canotier (1976-1986), Bd du Souverain 147, 1160 Brussels.
11. Twemlow, Alice, 'Smiley Faces', p.223.
12. For more information about the relationship between fashion and Belgian club culture, see: Serulus, Katarina, 'Club Culture, New Beat, and Belgian Fashion', in Kries, Mateo; Eisenbrand, Jochen; Rossi, Cat (eds.), *Night Fever. Design Club Culture 1960-Today*, pp.282-291.
13. Brewster, Bill; Broughton, Frank, *Last Night a DJ Saved My Life: The History of the Disc Jockey* (New York: Grove Press, 2006), pp.384-385; Reynolds, Simon, *Energy Flash: A Journey through Rave Music and Dance Culture* (London: Faber and Faber, 2013), p.134. For more information about new beat, see the 2012 documentary 'The Sound of Belgium', directed by Jozef Devillé (production Visualantics).
14. Twemlow, Alice, *Night Fever. Design Club Culture 1960-Today*, pp.222-223.
15. La Demence (1992-now), Rue Blaes 208, 1000 Brussels, and Paleis 12, Av. de Miramar, 1020 Brussels.
16. Fuse (1994-now), Rue Blaes 208, 1000 Brussels.

IN THEIR OWN WORDS

This chapter includes transcripts of video interviews
from the *Off the Grid* exhibition at Design Museum Gent (2019–20).
They were filmed in the designers' studios and edited
by Sara De Bondt and Simon van der Zande.

SOPHIE ALOUF-BERTOT

I studied at La Cambre. Lou Bertot, my mother, had been one of the first female students at the school and taught there when I began. That made it easier for me to get started. She taught 3D, everything related to the third dimension, shop window design and things like that. Luc Van Malderen was the head of department and Fernand Baudin taught typography. Van Malderen concentrated on image, Baudin on letters, because these were still separate subjects at that time.

After my studies, I was immediately hired by the cosmetics manufacturer Elizabeth Arden to design shop windows for the Benelux. That was a nice job; I sometimes went to Paris for meetings and everything went very smoothly. I was well paid and worked with them for almost a year and a half. After that, my husband, Sami Alouf, and I started our own studio, S+S Alouf. The first year was really difficult. When we became independent, we had to start from scratch and look for clients, which was not always so obvious. We had a tiny house, with a studio where we worked. It was nice to be able to do this from home, according to our own rules and schedule.

Colour is crucial

We were lucky, because early on we met a client who needed a graphic identity for the Woluwe and Westland Shopping Centres. Every two to three months, he organised thematic exhibitions there. Sami and I designed a lot of posters for him (see pp.156–57). Since it wasn't a large print run, we could afford to have the posters screen-printed. This technique resulted in a beautiful colour and print quality. It also fitted in well with my work, which is important.

Gradually, we got other clients. We had a style that was clearly 1970s, on the one hand, but also very personal, on the other. For me, colour is crucial, and clients who wanted colour came to us. Many colleagues were experimenting with black and white, but I used a lot of bright surfaces and geometric shapes in my designs. I'm heavily influenced by the work of Sonia Delaunay, Bauhaus, and De Stijl; I love their sense of contrast and composition.

We had several clients from the cultural sector, such as the Design Centre and the Palais des Beaux-Arts (Centre for Fine Arts). I mostly designed posters, while Sami was busy with lettering and logos. We designed a lot of signage for hotels abroad, including in Lebanon and the United States. As soon as you become part of a network and produce good work, the assignments come by themselves, through word of mouth.

GALERIES ANSPACH · MILTON MARVAN

LA FEMME
ET LES METIERS
DE CREATION
DESIGN CENTRE
7·2/26·4·1975

Cut and paste

In addition to my design practice, I'm a painter. I've always liked having that freedom. My paintings are very graphic; it's a constant cross-pollination with my other work. I proceed in the same way when making a poster as I do when creating a painting. I start with cut pieces of paper, although you wouldn't say that at first glance. I stick the clippings on a transparent film, so that I can make and try out different backgrounds. That gives me the opportunity to be playful, because I don't have to keep starting all over again. I only stop when everything feels right. Many of my posters are almost paintings.

I usually started with the image and added text later on. Then, I added the mocked-up text. I'd calculate the number of letters and come up with a layout in the chosen font. Often, that was Futura, Frutiger, or Helvetica. Since I didn't know much about typography, I used well-known typefaces. For me, the complete image was important – not the text and the image separately, but together, as a whole, with the text as part of the image.

Sami and I worked with a really good printer. He always came to our office with the proofs, which were still done in photogravure at that time. Offset is a completely different process from screen printing, which I was more confident with. I was a bit disappointed with offset, because the colour density wasn't quite as intense. Every now and then, I was really not happy and then the printer would have to start again. We got along very well. I've worked with fantastic people.

Wonderful adventure

I taught for years – first at La Cambre, where I taught colour and image classes in the typography studio. Later, I mainly focused on the École supérieure des arts Saint-Luc in Brussels, where I became head of the graphic design studio. I spent a lot of time with my students. For the end-of-year assessment, I often invited foreign designers to come and judge their work. Sometimes this was reciprocal and they invited me to their own school abroad. I really loved that; it was so enriching. Teaching was a wonderful adventure. I've been very fortunate to get a lot back from my students. I still have excellent contact with many of them. They taught me a lot. Contacts with young people call everything into question; they force you to challenge everything, throw your world in the air. I think that's great.

Not a close group

We set up the Chambre Belge des Graphistes (Belgian Chamber of Graphic Designers), and we met at a place in Schaarbeek. That was very cool. That's how we got to know each other and kept in touch. Unfortunately, it was short-lived. Maybe designers are too individualistic. Nevertheless, it was interesting to meet colleagues, such as Michel Olyff and many others. We discussed our sketches and ideas, showed what we'd achieved; we looked at the latest innovations and techniques; we exchanged addresses of good printers and photographers… From time to time, members also exhibited their work together. We followed each other's path, but then we lost touch. Thanks to the former chairman Charles Rohonyi, an article about us appeared in two issues of *Novum Gebrauchsgraphik*, one about posters and another about signage. We had a subscription to *Graphis*, *Novum*, and *IDEA*, so we kept abreast of the latest international trends.

    Belgian designers don't advertise their nationality. We're not a close group of graphic artists, like, for example, Polish graphic designers, who have unionised. But I don't feel the need to be known outside the context of my work. I'm happy with my clients. That's how I am. I don't have to be part of a group.

Brussels, 21 August 2019

ROB BUYTAERT

My first choice of study was architecture at Sint-Lukas Brussels, now LUCA, but I couldn't get on with the maths. One of the teachers was the design historian Karel Elno, and we both left for the Akademie Industriële Vormgeving (Academy for Industrial Design) in Eindhoven – he as professor and I as student. I owe everything to him. He was an incredibly good teacher. The course in Eindhoven lasted four years, with a fifth internship year, which was really good. You had to do internships in at least four different industries, including film, wood, etc. I really learned a lot.

Negotiating with printers

I come from a family of self-employed people, and after my studies I immediately started as a freelancer as well. I received no financial support from home. I had to do it all by myself. My mother owned a fashion company and my father was a businessman. At the time, I worked for, among others, Photogravure De Schutter, who made stereotypes. That was a very large company, employing 350 people in Antwerp and Brussels.

I was always interested in the cultural sector. I had good links with actors who had already broken through internationally, and so I started doing work for them. I've never worked alone. I learned that from my mother. She always had people in the house. If someone asked her to stitch something, then she would say: 'I can't do that, you'll have to ask Maria.' So, I followed her example. Initially, I worked from home, but that was short-lived.

I'm not a great draughtsman, but I could put something on paper. I could visually convey a thought, an idea. I made little sketches, outlining how we could do something. Often, it was about negotiating with printers. If you asked for Helvetica and they didn't have it, then they would dare to print it in another font. You could see it immediately, but we had to work with what was available.

Design-Team

After a few years, it became so busy that I could no longer handle it on my own. I then started Design-Team with a number of colleagues: Antoon De Vylder, Rudi Verelst, and me. But we still couldn't get through all the work, and one day we decided to look for someone else. We all wrote down who we'd most like to ask on a piece of paper. That turned out to be Luk Mestdagh, whom we knew from the professional association. He was from Bruges, and it was a big success. He wasn't an easy guy, but he was a great designer. I don't think we've ever had anyone like him since.

At the time, I was a member of the Chambre Belge des Graphistes (Belgian Chamber of Graphic Designers) in Brussels. They even had

their own house, and we'd go there every month, for a lecture or an exhibition. Nothing like that exists anymore; VIZO and Design Vlaanderen are no longer active either. In those days, you also had the Design Centre, led by Josine des Cressonnières. She was a fantastic woman, passionate about design, who introduced us to the industry and brought us together.

In 1971, we designed the catalogue, poster, lettering, and scenography for the exhibition *Bouwen in België* (*Building in Belgium*). We behaved like a professional design studio, which was exceptional then, because nobody knew what that was. Nobody understood what I did. My brother said: 'Rob, you need to write down what you do, who you are. Because when I'm on the tram, everyone asks me: "What's Rob doing now?"'

To survive, you had to adapt to the context and sometimes make things that were less creative, like for a taxi business, or an insurance company. I had to wear a white shirt, with a jacket and tie. Otherwise the conservative clients wouldn't have accepted it. That wasn't very pleasant, and sometimes we turned down an assignment. In those days, we could still do that. Design-Team was based on Total Design in the Netherlands, but they had significant financial and administrative support – they weren't just designers. We thought that we could do all that ourselves, but we misjudged it. That's how life goes. I didn't stay very long with Design-Team in the end.

Antwerp, 6 August 2019

BOUDEWIJN DELAERE

When I was 12 years old, my father told me I should go to the Technische School Stad Kortrijk (Technical School City of Kortrijk). Its department of textile drawing was a rather boring affair. Everyone was given a piece of chalk and a green board on which you had to copy an existing drawing, in mirror image; a curl on the left, a curl on the right – for a whole year. In the meantime, I took lessons at the Koninklijke Academie voor Schone Kunsten (Royal Academy of Fine Arts), also in Kortrijk. After three years, I obtained my diploma as a textile draughtsman. After that, I studied at Sint-Lucas Gent for a year, but that was a disappointment.

Fortunately, I then took part in an entrance exam for La Cambre and was accepted. That was quite an adventure – the school was in Brussels and classes were taught in French. The groups were very small, with about five students. The most interesting thing about the department was the letterpress studio. There we had to learn to work independently, under the guidance of a full-time printer: designing and preparing things for press. All the printing for the school was produced there. We were allowed to choose from different typefaces, Garamond, Futura, everything. We had to make compositions with them, so that we could feel the letters. We were allowed to work with all those shapes and letters ourselves. We even printed in colour. That was great, a really fun experience.

Most of the professors at La Cambre worked for Expo 58, the Brussels World's Fair – such as Lucien De Roeck, who designed the famous Expo star (see p.233). We bathed in that atmosphere. A few months before the Fair started, all the students were summoned to work there: helping to stick those cork letters. It was a wonderful time.

Army contest

When I graduated from La Cambre in 1960, the Provinciaal Technisch Instituut Kortrijk (Provincial Technical Institute Kortrijk) was looking for a teacher. I could immediately start teaching evening classes. I also began to work for clients. One of the first was a food distribution company, Centra, with shops throughout Flanders and Wallonia. Their own brand was called Gulden Sporen. I applied using my La Cambre portfolio and was hired immediately, on a freelance basis. We designed packaging for coffee, wine, oil, all sorts of things. I did that for 18 months, until I had to do my military service. I spent a year in the army in Germany, but I was also designing there. And I even won an army poster contest!

My career only really started in September 1963, after my return to Kortrijk. I was able to work as a freelance designer for publishers such as Lannoo, Patmos, De Sikkel, and Heideland. My big stroke of luck was that De Hallen convention centre in Kortrijk had just been built. That's when Interieur was founded, the big biennial for design. I started working for them in 1968, and in the end, I spent 30 years taking care of their corporate identity and signage.

art.3 Everyone has the right to life, liberty and security of person.

Universal declaration of human rights (10 december, 1948)

...and nature?

A pattern for Inno

I worked alone, but I did have someone who provided technical support: André Huyzentruyt. He's done that my whole life. When I made designs for Lannoo or Schuurmans, he'd produce the technical drawings. His work was so precise that I hardly had to worry about it. He still does it now.

I produced a lot of work in series, postcards, and so on. Eventually, I was almost a printing press of designs. It was wonderful to get those kinds of assignments. Everything you drew was printed by Lannoo and went straight to the United States. This included religious graphics, communion cards, birth announcements, etc. The kinds of things I was making caused quite a stir in that world because the existing cards were old-fashioned and outdated. When I came along with my innovative designs, the French loved them. I even exhibited in Paris a few times.

The industry in Kortrijk was flourishing: there was the textile industry, the wood industry, furniture company De Coene – there was an unimaginable amount of work. You submitted your work one day, and the next you were given a commission. Wonderful times.

One of my most important designs was the wrapping paper for the Innovation department store (Inno). After the disastrous fire of 1967 in Brussels, Inno needed a new image. My design was chosen via a competition run by the Chambre Belge des Graphistes (Belgian Chamber of Graphic Designers). Instead of a logo, I drew a pattern that could be used for all kinds of things, such as carrier bags, shop windows, and wrapping paper. My design could be reproduced in grey tones, which was cheaper. Inno used it for three decades.

The first conservationists

At a certain point, the Provincie West-Vlaanderen (Province of West Flanders) launched a poster competition about nature conservation. I created a very understated design, a black poster with only text, and submitted it (see p.99). Then I got a message from a colleague who was on the jury – I think it was Rob Buytaert – that I'd won. Subsequently, however, I was told that the provincial government didn't accept the jury's result, because it was 'too intellectual' and that the public wouldn't understand it. The first prize went to a bird in a snare. The council planned to award me third place, but I declined. The following year, Interieur and I had my poster printed in Dutch, French, and English, and I sent it to all the museums in Europe. In 2015, I discovered one of them purely by chance in the exhibition *Critique / Crisis / Desire* at the Koninklijke Musea voor Schone Kunsten van België (Royal Museums for Fine Arts of Belgium). It was hanging between artworks by famous artists such as Luc Tuymans and Francis Bacon!

Technical problem

One of my first printed jobs – for an exhibition by Constant Permeke (1961) – had a serious technical problem, which I only discovered after it had come off the press. Ever since, I've sworn never to trust a printer, and I've always done press checks.

Back then, you only had rub-on letters for typesetting – I got to know them at La Cambre. Letters were printed on a thin cellophane sheet, coated with some sort of adhesive. You had to cut them out, letter by letter, with a special pen, take them off the sheet, and carefully stick them onto a page. Then came transfer letters, like Letraset and Mecanorma. At school, I had a really good gouache technique, because of my textile pattern training; I had designed oriental carpets, things from Louis XIV and Louis XV, really intricate and detailed.

At that time, letterpress still existed. The development of Helvetica had a big impact. No one had that font; the first blocks came from foundries in Switzerland, metal letters in different point sizes. If you wanted to print a title, you had to send them the text and write down the typeface and the point size. The printer then composed your text, a perfect print made on baryta paper, and you had to get a cliché made of that. That's how it went; it was really primitive. It was only later that machines arrived that could project letters onto films.

I usually only made one proposal for an assignment. I hated having to let the client choose from ten options. I had an idea, executed it, and presented it in the best possible way. If they had comments, I generally responded, but sometimes I didn't. Ultimately, that was the best way of working for me. I didn't have to redo many things. One commission, one proposal. When you go to the doctor, you only get prescribed one cure. The doctor will only give you something else if that medication doesn't work.

Outside impulses

I travelled frequently, and kept up with what was happening in the world. I subscribed to every possible foreign magazine, American, British, German: *Graphis*, *Novum Gebrauchsgraphik*, *Bauhaus*, *Art Director's Annual*, *Push Pin Graphic*. I was anxious to get impulses from outside. But I've also been good at keeping my own work. Most of what I've produced is in my archive here at home.

Kortrijk, 9 August 2019

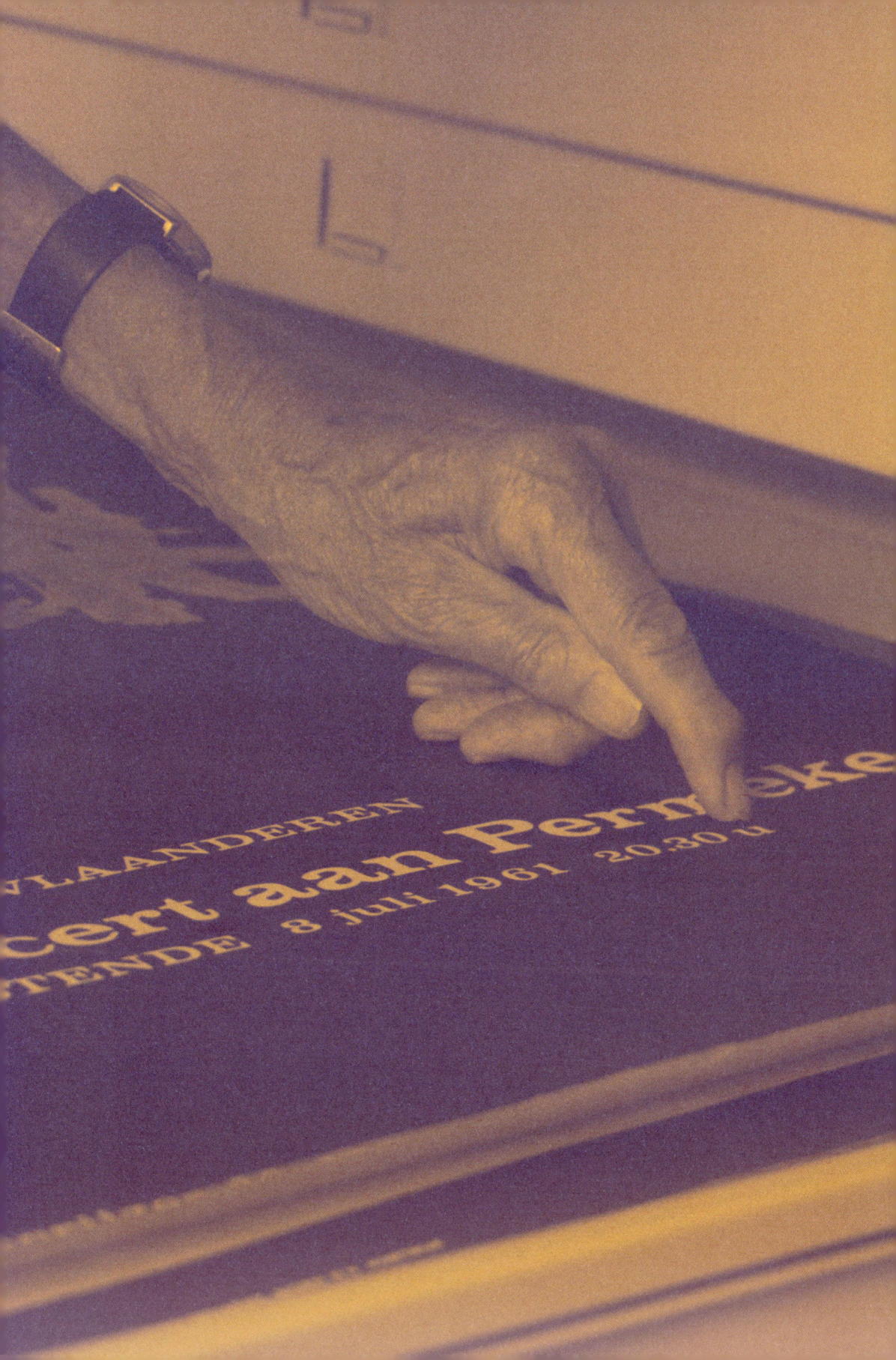

PAUL IBOU

I was born in 1939 as Paul Lodewijk Henri Vermeersch. My father was a professor and successful entrepreneur from Bruges, who had settled in Antwerp in the late 1920s. Shortly after World War II, I often stayed in the hotel-restaurant Huîtrière Devriendt, in Blankenberge – my cousin and godfather owned it. Today it's called De Oesterput, and they still use my logo design. My cousin introduced me to famous artists from that time: Frans Masereel, Constant Permeke, and Willem Van Hecke. Under their influence, I was always drawing. I was obsessed with expressing myself creatively.

On the advice of my family, as a 13-year-old, I went to study Fine Arts at the Koninklijke Academie voor Schone Kunsten (Royal Academy of Fine Arts) in Antwerp. In my free time, I earned money by painting lettering on the windows of cafés and shops, together with artists like Wannes Van de Velde and Raoul Van den Boom. My first real employer was the Van Poppel advertising studio, which provided the marketing for, among others, the Antwerp Zoo.

Due to personal circumstances, I had to switch from day school to night school. I was taught by inspiring teachers, such as Piet Serneels and Hélène van Coppenolle, to whom I owe a lot. I graduated in 1958. After that, I completed my studies at the Plantin Instituut voor Typografie (Plantin Institute of Typography), with people like the Swiss-Belgian poster designer Leo Marfurt and the Dutch typographer Hubert van Krimpen.

During the day, I was employed by Photogravure De Schutter, where I learned everything about printing techniques: helio, offset, typo, and photography. It was a large company with an international market. I became friends with the manager, and he encouraged me to start up on my own, first as a freelance art director for Nutricia in Aartselaar, and from 1 September 1962 with my own agency, under the name Paul Ibou.

Mythical beast

I designed my pseudonym in 1957. The logo is a griffin: a hybrid mythical beast with the body of a lion and the head and wings of an eagle. My first studio was in the centre of Antwerp, in a small house on the main shopping street, the Meir. I immediately received commissions from people who called at the door or by word of mouth.

In 1962, I met my wife, Liliane-Emma Staal. She would play a key role in my design studio. She was multilingual, and had a big cultural network of artists and designers. We were married for 52 years; she was my mainstay. Liliane died in 2015 and I miss her every day.

Our first assignments included title sequences for Belgische Radio- en Televisieomroep (Belgian Radio and Television), hand-painted on rolls. I also created illustrations, for among others, British Petroleum's Belgian magazine. Later on, I worked for Shell

International, with jobs such as magazines, annual reports, and all kinds of prestigious publications. We had clients from all sectors, cultural, financial, and government bodies: Provincie Antwerpen (Province of Antwerp), CERA Bank, Europalia, UNESCO, and many others. In 1967, I travelled to the United States for the first time, because I also had American commissioners, such as Apple, Leaf Brands, and Clarks International.

Working in 3D

I've always designed my logos as sculptures, as tangible objects, three-dimensional symbols. They were made out of different materials and they're now spread all over the world. One of the best known is the oversized B logo for Biënnale Middelheim (Middelheim Biennial) in Antwerp. From 1965, the letter was installed every biennial year, as a 3- to 4-metre-high sculpture, at about 40 locations in the city, the province of Antwerp, and beyond.

Another example is the Koninklijk Ballet Vlaanderen (Royal Ballet of Flanders). They had a large tetrahedron in which dancers performed their movements according to the Laban system. My logo design is based on a stylised photograph of this. These are only two examples of the over 400 logos I designed during my career.

Multi-Art Press

In the early 1970s, Liliane and I developed Paper Art in our gallery, Multi-Art, in Antwerp. These were objects in cardboard and paper by international artists such as Bruno Munari and Günther Kirchberger, but also by Belgians such as Jef Verheyen or Roberte Mestdagh. They were produced in limited editions of 100 or 150 copies and numbered.

I've also made a lot of Paper Art myself, including fold-out calendars, folding cards, and books. My creations *12 Owl Variations* (1970) and *Metamorphosis* (1968) have won awards. They were made in a variety of different types of paper, with fold-out and shifting shapes that form colourful compositions. The paper moves and becomes simultaneously sculptural and cinematic.

From the mid-1970s, I started to focus on Constructivism. I was fascinated by the geometric shapes of Pythagoras – the circle, the square, the triangle, the hexagon. These have had a huge influence on my practice. I used them for applied and free work, without distinguishing between the disciplines, as a *multi-artist*. After Multi-Art gallery closed, I developed *Quadri-Structures*: a geometric system with endless possibilities for making paintings and objects. I was awarded the well-known *Prix de la Jeune Peinture* and the Europa Prize (bronze) for them.

Rehabilitation

In 1984, I had a serious car accident. I had to spend almost a year in rehabilitation. Liliane and I moved to a castle in Zandhoven. There, we received many guests and it allowed me to make work on a much larger scale. Thanks to our many travels, I came in contact with designers and artists in Europe, America, China, and Japan.

Graphic sense

The Dutch have a longstanding professional graphic design association. This never got off the ground in Flanders. In 1966, I took the initiative and founded the professional association Grafische Vormgevers Vlaanderen (Graphic Designers Flanders), but it fizzled out after a few years. In 1962, Charles Rohonyi invited me to become a member of the Chambre Belge des Graphistes (Belgian Chamber of Graphic Designers), but it was primarily French-speaking.

In the 1960s, graphic design in Flanders was an amateurish activity that wasn't as popular as fine art, which had always been seen as at the forefront. Design was an area nobody knew much about. I tried to promote it by publishing books. They were distributed in more than 60 countries by Nippon Shuppan Hanbai from Tokyo: *Banking Symbols*, *Animal Symbols*, *Museum Symbols*, and so on. In 1970, I established the magazine *Vorm in Vlaanderen* (*Form in Flanders*), with several sponsors from the world of graphic design and printing. Our aim was to familiarise government and industry with the heterogeneous community of creative designers in Flanders, in fields such as furniture design, marketing, illustration, cartoons, and graphic design. I'm sure it's had an impact on the graphic sense of our community.

For the last 20 years, I've been involved with Cube Art: monumental geometric art structures. Four of them have been installed in China: in Shenzhen, Chengdu, Beijing, and Shanghai. After this, it was nice to receive the Ultima, a prize for design by the Flemish Community in 2019. And in Zoersel, where I've been living for the past seven years, I'm now an Honorary Citizen.

Zandhoven, 7 August 2019

HERMAN LAMPAERT

We were raised in Dutch, but my father spoke quite good German and my mother perfect French. Their library was filled with books in German, French, and Dutch. I often sat scouring the dictionaries... when I wasn't running around in a cornfield.

My first studies – mainly drawing and painting – were at Sint-Lucas Gent. Teachers such as Gaspard De Vuyst, Gerard Hermans, and Louis Van Mechelen – going to his art history lessons was like walking into a sunrise – had a decisive influence on me. By coincidence, 30 years later, in 1976, I got to design Van Mechelen's text about Robert Venturi for *Aplus* magazine. I used a typewriter font for it.

On a school trip to France, all the attention was focused on the cathedrals in Amiens, Paris, and Chartres; modern architecture was a blind spot. But, together with two classmates, we managed to visit the Fondation Suisse student house, which had been designed by Le Corbusier in 1930. That was the high point of the trip. I was already familiar with modern architecture then, such as the Boekentoren (Book Tower) in Ghent and Villa Colman-Saverys in Knokke, both by Henry van de Velde, and the Hoekhuis (Cornerhouse) in Sint-Amandsberg by Gaston Eysselinck.

After three years at Sint-Lucas, I left with two fellow students for La Cambre in Brussels. A different language, a different audience, a different spirit, interaction with different studios – it was an exciting time. In Henri d'Ursel's film history lesson, we watched the surrealist film *L'Âge d'Or* by Luis Buñuel. Luc Haesaerts spoke just as eloquently about China as he did about the Latem School of Painting. There was French literature and theatre history. Joris Minne and Lucien De Roeck gave us design assignments (but no one told us about Sjoerd de Roos, Eric Gill, or Jan Tschichold). And in the centre of Brussels you had La Proue bookshop, where I held my first exhibition in 1954.

No illusions

During your studies, your fellow students are the most important thing: you fight and you discuss together, with a shared enthusiasm. Michel Olyff and Corneille Hannoset had graduated from La Cambre a few years earlier. Their work was a pinnacle for me: one more exciting than the other, both equally effective.

I also got my first commissions from fellow students, from a teacher, and from friends, such as the photographer Walter De Mulder. This was followed by PetraShoe and the publishers Lannoo and Van Melle. For PetraShoe I started with the redesign of the logo. I placed it horizontally, removed the background, and redesigned the letters in such a way that PetraShoe customers wouldn't expect a new product. Why would you create false illusions?

Manual labour

Working with printers was completely different back then. Now, everything is delivered ready-made, while then you had to specify all the details. Designing was brain- and handwork, cutting and pasting. Anything manual, physical, in varying daylight, is still more stimulating for me. The floor was my biggest work surface. When in doubt about the layout of a book, I spread all the pages on the floor and showed them to my wife, bibi Lonfils. If bibi said: 'On that page, there...' then I had to reconsider. Her input is still important.

Van Melle, Snoeck, and Van Muysewinkel were the best printers at the time. I once designed a model in which texts in five different languages were placed oblique and adjacent to each other. I was worried about the feasibility, but Mr Moerman of Van Melle printers was able to reassure me. It became one of the designs that I still dare to show everywhere today. It's important to stay at the press until the last sheet comes out. Never forget: the last chisel stroke can split a statue.

Don't push

We think that we can change everything at will, but life is full of coincidences. When I'd just graduated from La Cambre, a letter from St Gallen, Switzerland, arrived. Rudolf Hostettler, the editor-in-chief of *Typografische Monatsblätter* (1949), invited me to come and print in his studio: 'I've seen your woodcuts... We have enough room and you could stay with us for a few days.' As we bid each other farewell after my visit, he presented me with a leather-bound copy of his masterfully typeset *The Printer's Terms*.

Here in Belgium, the Design Centre was influential. Fernand Baudin became particularly important to me. His diverse work has no fixed style, no recurring tics. Yet it's still stylish. If a designer's recognisable style imposes itself on you, then something has gone wrong. No reader is asking for that; a reader wants efficacy.

Bringing order to chaos

I also taught. Initially, I loved doing that, until I saw my talents being wasted on words instead of design. My last class – at La Cambre, at the behest of Guy Schockaert – was a comparison of the Paris street guide *L'indispensable* with its Brussels equivalent. The Parisian guide shows the scale and location on each page. The Brussels atlas is less user-friendly and three times thicker and heavier. You sometimes wonder whether designers don't know what's going on in neighbouring countries. Whether you're an author, architect, or graphic designer, your primary task is to try and bring some order to the chaos that constantly surrounds us. Remaining a lifelong student has its benefits.

C'est le chagrin des Belges

During my teaching, my need for historical knowledge grew – I wanted to make my students aware of the wide horizons of our predecessors. I showed them work by colleagues from Ancient Rome, of Carolingian handwriting, but also catalogues by Benno Wissing or a logo by Bram de Does. In 1997, Johan Valcke asked me to write a timeline of the history of Belgian graphic design for the catalogue *In koeien van letters (In Extra-Large Type)*. At the same time, my book, *Kroniek van de vorm (Chronicle of Form)* was published independently.

Belgium versus the Netherlands? Careless Catholics versus pragmatic Protestants? 'Calvinism is in the blood of the Dutch', wrote typographer Jan van Krimpen in 1958. The Dutch design world was better organised and had more influence with the government. The World Wars had less impact there on education and industrial development than they did here. In Belgium, there was an ongoing fragmentation and division.

And that damn bilingualism, wouldn't that be a blessing? At a meeting at the Design Centre we once talked about how we could put ourselves on the national map, whereupon I suggested that we could occasionally show up in Liège or Ostend. Meanwhile, politicians from both linguistic communities turned their backs on each other and everything federal. That took a toll on budgets. Moreover, our designers were seen more as artists (which is fine) than as creators of good solutions for concrete problems.

Brussels, 5 August 2019

PLATES

The following pages feature work made by designers who are mentioned in this book or who were included in the exhibition *Off The Grid* at Design Museum Gent (2019–20).

STEM
SOCIALIST

8

Anonymous designer, 1971

Ausloos & Payot
Poster for Het Nederlands Kamertoneel, 1964

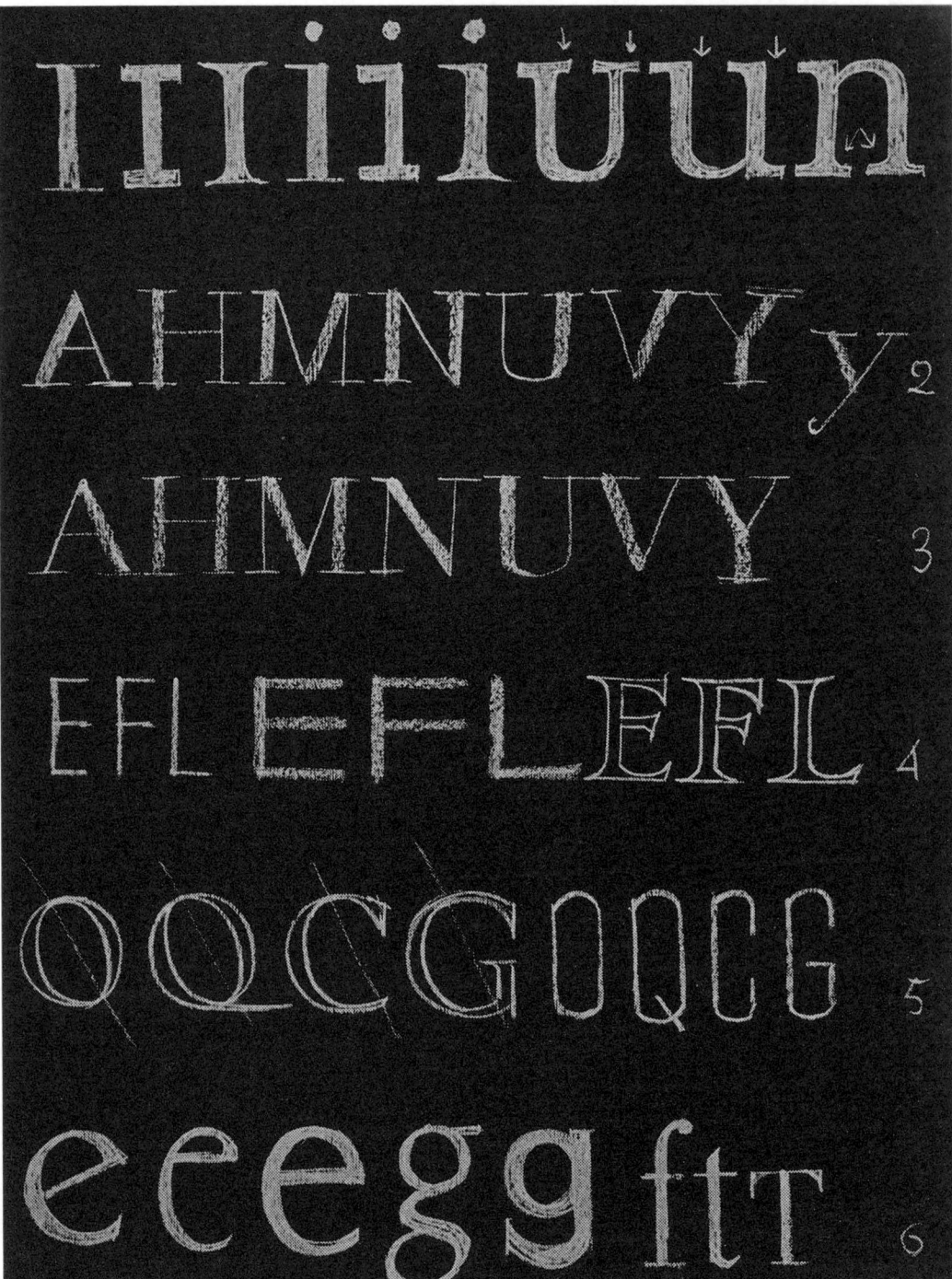

Fernand Baudin
Page from *De Drukletter: Vorm, Vervaardiging, Indeling, Toepassing*, 1965

Fernand Baudin
Spread from *How Typography works (and why it is important)*, 1989

The graphical order is not the alphabetical order. They are altogether different. The former is determined by the similarities between characters made up of mainly straight lines, circles or obliques. The narrowest letter is always the i. The widest ones are always the M & W. When thinness is required it is necessary to accentuate the contrast between narrow & wider letterforms.

WE — Where the E is only one half the width of the W, the proportion, the "rhythm" is good.

WE — Where the E has the same width as the W, the proportion & the optical "rhythm" are bad.

L F E P R B S are approximately one half the width of an N or an H.

I J L F E P B R S

O Q C G D

M W

H U N T

A V X Y Z K

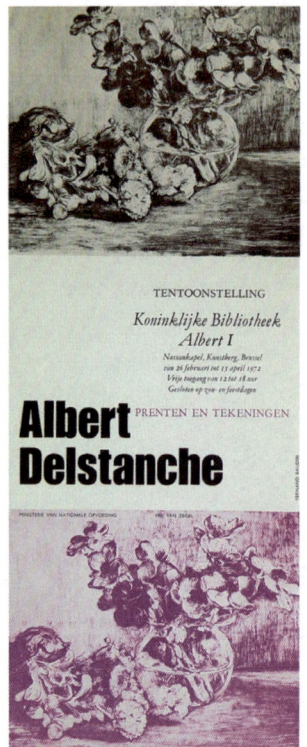

Fernand Baudin
Posters for Koninklijke Bibliotheek Albert I (Royal Library Albert I), 1972–80

Iris Clert

schilderijen objekten

peintures objets

paintings objects

GALERIJ
DE
ZWARTE PANTER

Sint Julianuskapel

Hoogstraat 70-72|69
Antwerpen
België

tel. 03 33 13 45

van 29 september
t.m. 8 oktober 1972
van 13 tot 18 uur

maandag gesloten

Herbert Binneweg
Poster for Galerij De Zwarte Panter, 1972

Frida Craet Burssens
Poster for Museum voor Sierkunst (Museum for Decorative Arts), 1956

Rob Buytaert
Various posters, 1964–74

Rob Buytaert
Poster for Paleis voor Schone Kunsten (Centre for Fine Arts), 1976

Hélène van Coppenolle
Poster for Biënnale Middelheim (Middelheim Biennial), 1959

Martha van Coppenolle
Adverts, 1938–50

Nelly Degouy
Book cover for *De Wonderbare Tocht (The Miraculous Journey)* by Ernest Claes, 1944

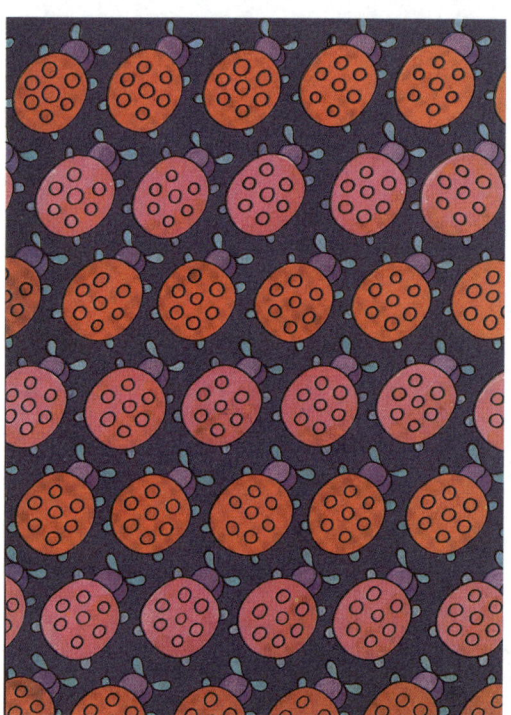

Boudewijn Delaere
Greeting cards, 1960s

Boudewijn Delaere
Poster for painting exhibition, 1964

provincie west-vlaanderen
cultuurdagen 1964

tentoonstelling schilderkunst

brugge provinciaal hof
15 november - 6 december
open 10 -12 en 15 -18 u
vrije toegang

Boudewijn Delaere
New year's greetings, 1970

Jean-Michel Folon
Poster for Europalia, 1975

hugOKÉ
Poster for Koninklijke Nederlandse Schouwburg (Royal Dutch Theatre), 1971

Manfred Hürrig
Poster for Théâtre National, 1978

Paul Ibou
Poster for Biënnale Middelheim (Middelheim Biennial), 1965

8 biennale middelheim antwerpen

20 juni / 30 september '65

Paul Ibou
Logo designs, 1960s–1990s

Frans Dejonck
Poster for Gentse volks-feesten (Ghent folk festivals), 1975

Julian Key
Poster for Salon de la Moto et du Cyclomoteur (Motorbike and Moped Show), 1973

Besloten ekonomie houdt ondermeer in dat te verwerken grondstof zo volledig mogelijk wordt benut en de materiaalafval zo laag mogelijk wordt gehouden. De vormgever zal vooraf dienen na te gaan of het produkt niet heel en al bij éénzelfde producent kan ontstaan uit de voorradige materialen, inkten, formaten, lettertypen, enz. De mogelijkheden van het machinepark zullen overigens de produktiemethode in hoge mate bepalen.

Andersom kan de aard (en oplage) van het te vervaardigen produkt bepalend zijn bij de keuze van de materialen (zie aldaar), producent en drukprocédé.

Copyright is het uitsluitende recht van de vormgever om zijn werk openbaar te maken, te verveelvoudigen of te verspreiden.

Alle werkstukken, ontwerpen, maketten (prototypen enzovoort) blijven het geestelijk eigendom van de vormgever (auteur) en, tenzij uitdrukkelijk anders is overeengekomen, ook diens materieel eigendom.
Bij kontrakt tussen vormgever en opdrachtgever verkrijgt deze laatste het recht tot verveelvoudiging van het ontwerp, beperkt tot de bestemming en oplage daarbij aangegeven.
(Zie: Verveelvoudigingsrecht)

Corporate Image is de engelse en gangbare term voor „huisstijl": het totale visuele vormgevingsbeleid van een onderneming (een stad, een school, een dienst enzovoort).
Uit een doorgedreven visuele koördinatie van alle produkten van éénzelfde bedrijf resulteert een sterk impact van elk produkt afzonderlijk én een versterkt totaalbeeld van die onderneming bij het op de markt brengen van een nieuw produkt. Elk toetredend element werkt aldus kumulatief aan de „waarde" van het geheel.
Het gaat dus wel degelijk om een politiek uitspelen van het visuele. Een politiek die het publiek ontvankelijk moet stemmen voor het geboden produkt (dienst, enzovoort) en moet bijdragen tot een snelle identifikatie bij middel van een samenhangend, bevattelijk en informatierijk totaalbeeld.

Corporate Image heeft niet zozeer te maken met propaganda dan wel met een eerder neutraal patroon van konstanten. Wàt men met deze konstanten doet is, ons inziens, belangrijker dan de konstanten zelf.

Een ander, evenzeer belangrijk aspekt, van deze visuele koördinatie is haar kostenverlagende invloed op het gebruik van de produkten (tot en met formulieren voor inwendige dienst) en de vervaardiging ervan.
Het is de meest komplete opdracht die men een grafisch vormgever kan toevertrouwen, geheel ingesteld op het heden en de onmiddellijke toekomst, veelal ook gericht tot een ruim en divers publiek.
Uitgangspunt: de analyse van het betrokken bedrijf, in nauwe samenwerking met de mensen uit het bedrijf.

Het toepassen van één basiskleur, één normformaat, één lettertype en een sterk handelsmerk, wat dan toch maar een minimumprogramma is, kan enorme weerklank hebben, mits deze toepassingen oordeelkundig zijn ingeschakeld op het totale bedrijfsbeleid, gegroeid zijn uit en afgestemd op de specifieke noden van het bedrijf en uitgedragen door welbepaalde media. Een instruktieboek (design manual) dient te voorzien in het gebruik van deze konstanten en dit voor het grootst mogelijk aantal gevallen. Schema's, plannen en konstruktieaanwijzingen zullen, eerder dan beperkingen op te leggen, de strategie bepalen voor een onderling samenspel van deze konstanten en de kontinuiteit verzekeren. In veelvoud vervaardigd kunnen deze handleidingen aan de vertegenwoordigers en agenten worden meegegeven.
Bij kleine ondernemingen bijvoorbeeld, kunnen de vier hogervermelde konstanten reeds een toepassingsveld vinden op: briefhoofd, formulieren, stempels, aanmelding in de telefoongids; op de gebouwen, voertuigen, verpakkingen, produkten, enzovoort; zonder te gewagen van de direkte publiciteit.

*Op de vraag
Hoe breng ik het duidelijkst
mijn boodschap over?
geeft de huisstijl geen
volledig antwoord maar
wel een vocabularium.*

Herman Lampaert
Brochure 'Waar kan een grafisch vormgever goed voor zijn?'
(What can a graphic designer be good for?), 1980

Herman Lampaert
Poster for exhibition at Sint-Pietersabdij
(St Peter's Abbey), 1969

Herman Lampaert
Municipality of Overijse magazine, 1972-75

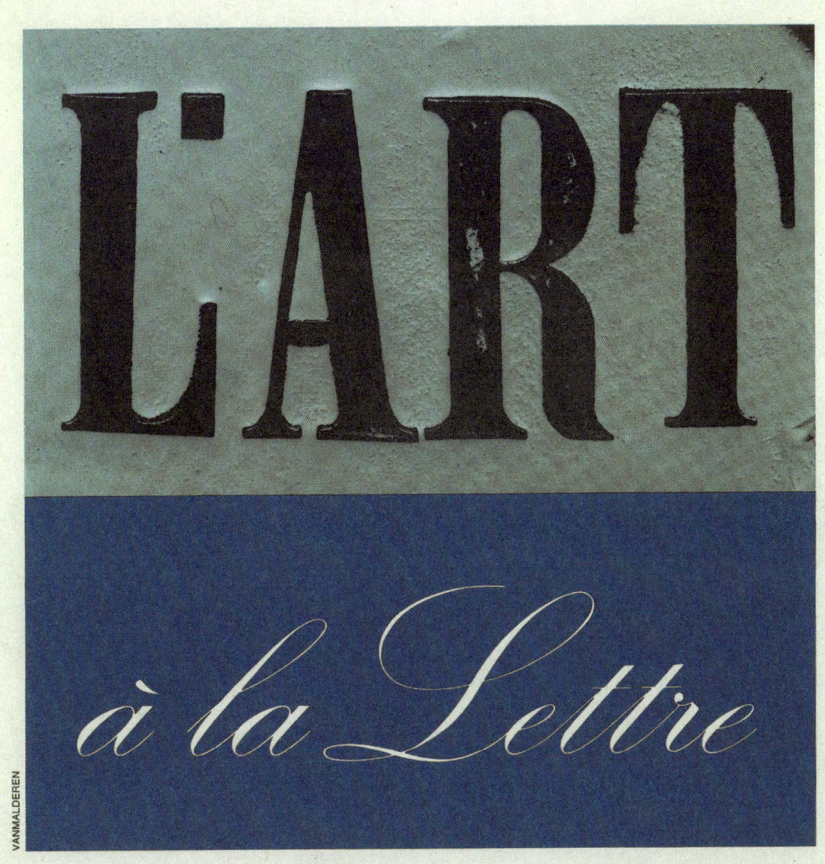

Luc van Malderen
Poster for the exhibition *L'Art à la Lettre (Art to the Letter)*, 1977

Luc van Malderen
Poster for *L'Art de la Sérigraphie (The Art of Screenprinting)*, 1972

Luk Mestdagh and Rudi Verelst (Design-Team)
Poster for Jaar van het Kind (Year of the Child), 1979

Urbain Mulkers
Poster for Servranckx Retrospectieve, 1970

May Néama
Poster for Théâtre d'essai (Experimental Theatre), 1960

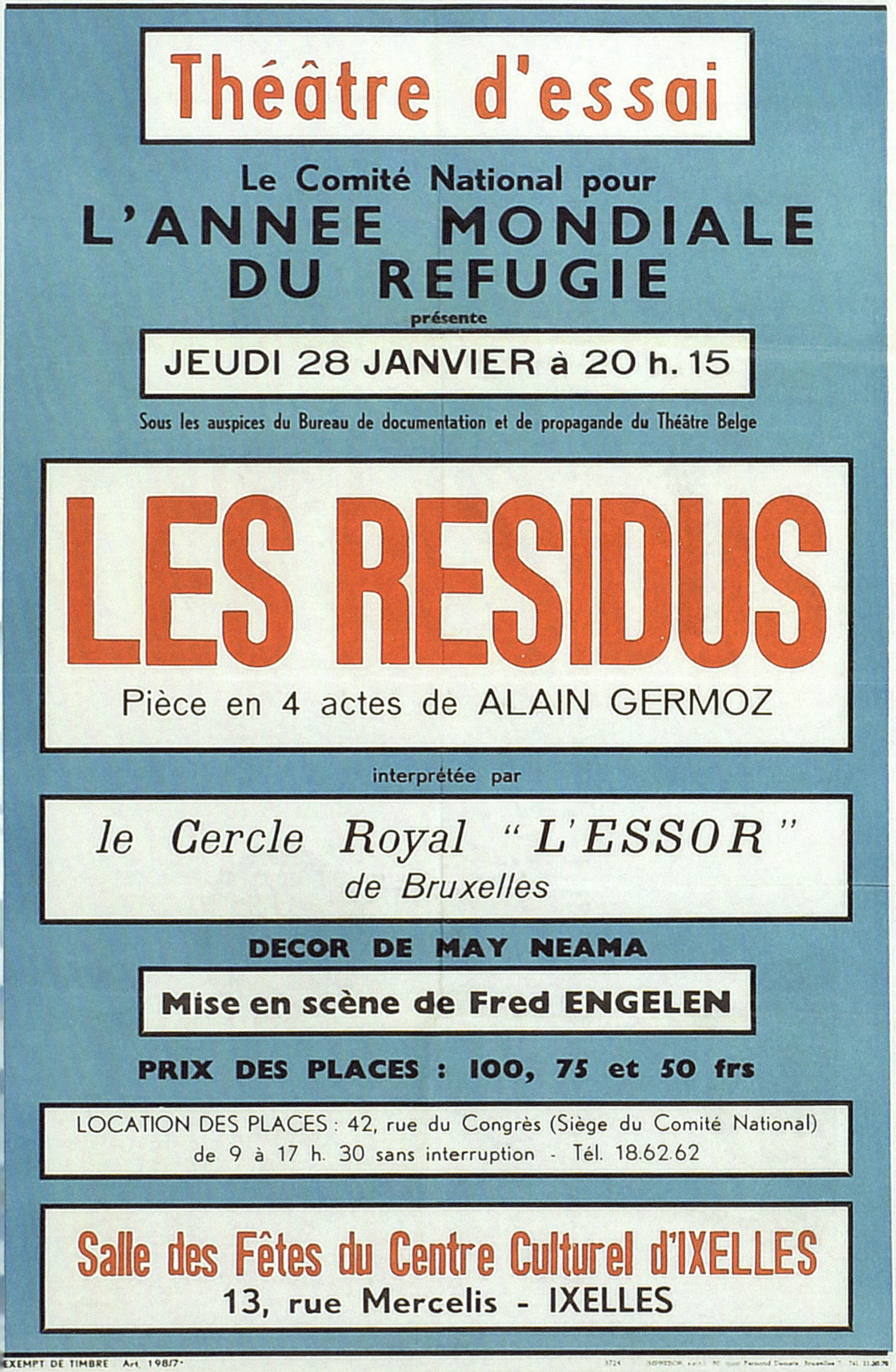

Théâtre d'essai

Le Comité National pour
L'ANNEE MONDIALE DU REFUGIE
présente

JEUDI 28 JANVIER à 20 h. 15

Sous les auspices du Bureau de documentation et de propagande du Théâtre Belge

LES RESIDUS

Pièce en 4 actes de ALAIN GERMOZ

interprétée par

le Cercle Royal "L'ESSOR"
de Bruxelles

DECOR DE MAY NEAMA

Mise en scène de Fred ENGELEN

PRIX DES PLACES : 100, 75 et 50 frs

LOCATION DES PLACES : 42, rue du Congrès (Siège du Comité National)
de 9 à 17 h. 30 sans interruption - Tél. 18.62.62

Salle des Fêtes du Centre Culturel d'IXELLES
13, rue Mercelis - IXELLES

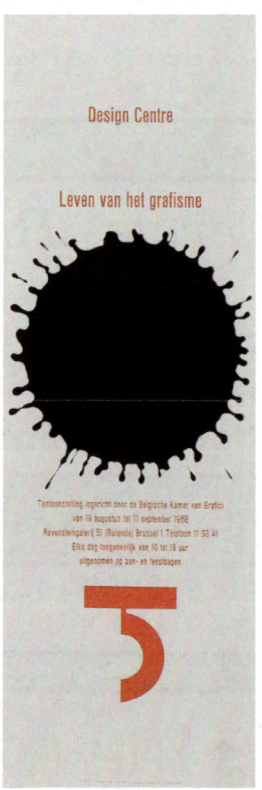

Michel Olyff
Posters for Design Centre, 1967–74

Jacqueline Ost
Book series *Comment fait-on?* (How is it made?), 1972–75

Frans Pans
Poster for Centrale voor socialistisch cultuurbeleid
(Centre for Socialist Cultural Policy), 1982

André Pasture
Poster for Nationale Maatschappij der Belgische Spoorwegen
(National Railway Company of Belgium), 1969

Jozef Peeters
Design for poster 8ᵉ Groot Nederlandsch Studentenkongres
(8th Greater Dutch Student Congress), 1922

Jacques Richez
Poster for *Esposizione belga di arazzi e di armi da caccia contemporanei*
(Belgian Exhibition of Contemporary Arms and Tapestries), 1966

Jacques Richez
L'Art graphique appliqué à la Publicité
(Graphic art applied to advertising), 1964

Piet Serneels
Poster for *Arquitecto Antonio Gaudi in Antwerpen*, 1968

Albert Setola
Poster for *Sartre: Met gesloten deuren (Huis Clos)*, 1964

Geert Setola
Poster for Jan De Wilde, 1967

S+S Alouf
Poster for Woluwe Shopping Center, 1978

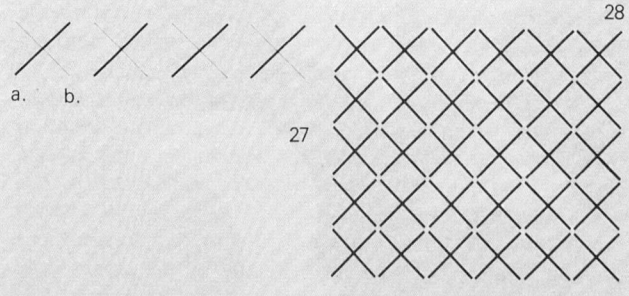

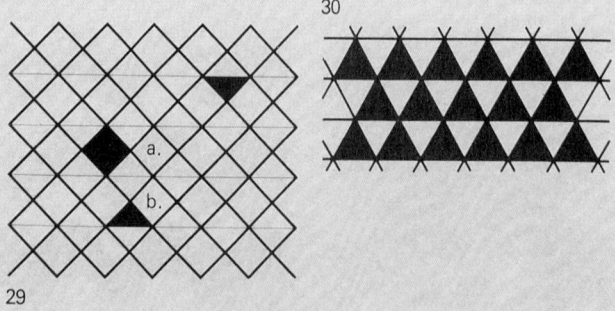

Mark Verstockt
Page from *The Genesis of Form: From Chaos to Geometry*, 1987

Michel Waxmann
Bronx typeface, ca. 1973
Michel simplifié typeface, ca. 1973

DESIGNERS

Sara De Bondt

JEANINE BEHAEGHEL

Sara De Bondt (1977) is a graphic designer, teacher, publisher, and researcher. She teaches at KASK School of Arts in Ghent. See saradebondt.com

'"No line that was not the result of violence."
Therein lies everything that I am convinced of myself.'[1]

Jeanine Behaeghel is something of an enigma. On the one hand, she is one of those rare independent female designers of 1960s Belgium about whom published documentation exists; on the other, her designs are hard to find.[2] She is often described in Dutch as a 'grafica', a gendered term that can refer to both the applied and fine arts, two fields in which she achieved success. Yet while she had a thriving practice as a designer and an artist, there is no archive preserving her collected body of work today.

Behaeghel was born in Bruges in 1940. At 16, she started her studies at its Stedelijke Akademie voor Schone Kunsten (City Academy for Fine Arts), where she was taught by teachers such as the influential designer and artist Albert Setola. In 1959, she graduated from its Decorative Arts department with the highest distinction. She decided not to stop there and enrolled in a graphic design course at the renowned Staatliche Kunstakademie für Bildende Künste (State Academy of Fine Arts) in Düsseldorf, where Setola had preceded her. In autobiographical notes, Behaeghel proudly describes how, in Germany, she learned to reduce a design to its essence by continuing to work on a single motif without losing its emotion. Her work was greatly appreciated, and long after her graduation, she maintained a correspondence with the teacher and graphic designer Walter Breker and with the rector of the Academy, the architect Hans Schwippert.

After her German studies, her eagerness to learn was still not satisfied. In 1963, she was one of the few Belgians admitted to the Graphic Design course at London's Royal College of Art. Unfortunately, this was a difficult period for her. In letters, Schwippert refers to a crisis, chaos, pills, and the police. Behaeghel struggled to get along with the dogmatic modernist teacher Anthony Froshaug: 'It seems to me that F. has a very rough way of showing! Is that because he is (unhappy) angry, because at that school, and in England generally, one is easily satisfied, satisfied with semi-achievements (semi-achievements if one sets high standards)?'[3] Froshaug wrote of this period in his autobiography: 'Huge disagreement with organisation, [I] behaved most disagreeably.'[4] Behaeghel left the school six months later and returned to Bruges.

De Korre

Despite studying abroad, Behaeghel remained active in her hometown. She was a member of De Korre, a cultural circle for young people. Meaning old Dutch for 'fishing net', it brought together talents from different creative domains. Initially, meetings took the form of sketching trips, organised by Setola and the Bruges writer René Van Houtryve, intending to teach participants how to draw. Later, this evolved into bi-monthly sessions with work discussions or creating new work such as painting, photography, or writing around a common theme.

fig. 1 (opposite)
Jeanine Behaeghel
Logo for Studio Behaeghel, ca. 1965

In 1961, De Korre found a permanent location thanks to the financial support of the Bruges patrons Fernand Simoens and Mia Cools. A medieval basement was converted into the Korrekelder (Korre Cellar). Behaeghel played a key role in its design: she gathered a team of architects and set designers and together they transformed the former storage coal cellar into a small theatre, exhibition space, and cosy bar. Above the door hung the Korrevis: the logo of a stylised fish, designed by Behaeghel (fig. 2).

In addition to the house style and signage, Behaeghel designed printed matter for the theatre performances at the Korrekelder. Today, some of these daring posters are her only applied work preserved in public archives. The series also includes work by other designers, such as Setola and Luk Mestdagh, but Behaeghel's posters stand out for their experimental and expressive typography (figs. 4). She often used her own images. Sometimes, she collaborated with Mestdagh: she created the illustrations, and he added the lettering. Later on, the duo designed printed matter for, among others, the folkloric *Kattestoet Ieper* and the Dutch-Flemish cultural magazine *Ons Erfdeel (Our Heritage)*. Despite her prolific contribution, Behaeghel is not mentioned in the Korrekelder entry on the timeline of Belgian graphic design *In koeien van letters (In Extra-Large Type*, 1993).[5]

For the exhibitions in the Korrekelder, a duotone poster template, which could be easily adapted, was designed. It was printed in two runs: a colourful large Korrevis logo was overprinted with the practical information on top in black ink (fig. 3). The format was regularly updated with a new pattern or colour. This economical solution nevertheless caught the eye.

fig. 2
Jeanine Behaeghel
Logo for Korrekelder, 1961

 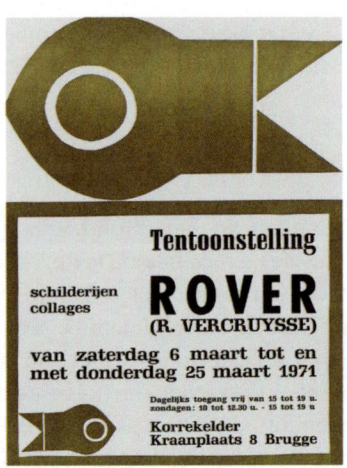

fig. 3
Jeanine Behaeghel
Posters for exhibitions at Korrekelder, 1966 and 1971

figs. 4 (clockwise from top left)
Jeanine Behaeghel
Posters for theatre plays at Korrekelder, 1977, 1969, 1966–67 and 1965–66

In a male stronghold

Exhibiting was important for Behaeghel and for her career. In 1962, she curated an exhibition featuring her Düsseldorf classmates in the Huidevettershuis in Bruges, a space for craft and applied art (fig. 5). When she returned to her hometown in 1965 to establish Studio Behaeghel, she put together a solo exhibition of her own work in various media: prints, drawings, pastels, and photography (fig. 6). The press was positive: 'I am almost certain that one is dealing here with a talent that will succeed in spite of everything.'[6] Still, one reviewer could not resist referring to her gender and expressing admiration for her 'masculine' traits, such as professionalism and modernism: 'Her black-and-white technique is definitely her strongest, but a poster such as Ferien auf Sylt makes clear that she knows how to combine colours in a delicate (and very feminine) fashion. Her occasional print work is often charmingly intimate, but otherwise one will experience how modern-professional the 'artist' can be when it comes to commercial printing.'[7]

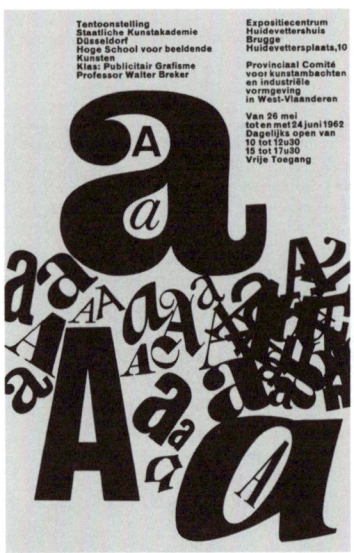 

fig. 5 (left)
Jeanine Behaeghel
Poster for Staatliche Kunstakademie Düsseldorf exhibition, 1962

fig. 6 (right)
Jeanine Behaeghel
Poster for Studio Behaeghel exhibition, 1965

The first decade of Studio Behaeghel was a success, with commissions for, among others, the city of Bruges, the publishers Lannoo and Desclée De Brouwer, and countless occasional printed matter (figs. 7). Behaeghel used a warm visual language, often drawn freehand and full of humour. In contrast to competitors such as Paul Ibou, Mestdagh, or Boudewijn Delaere, she transcended the strict Swiss style. She was aware of her subjective approach: 'The line, with its dynamic power [...] that yanks me from reality. Neither subject nor object is parsed from the outer world. They are found in an inner reality.'[8] Avoiding abstraction, her organic layouts do not fit in a grid. In an interview, she admitted that it was challenging to be a woman designer in a male stronghold:

figs. 7 (opposite, clockwise from top left)
Jeanine Behaeghel
Book cover designs, 1972, 1966, 1972, 1977

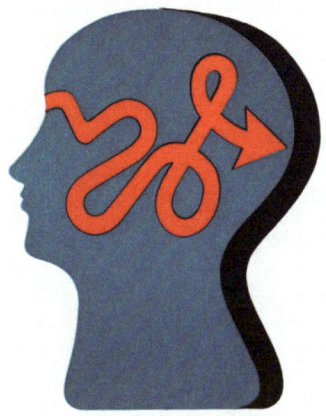

'After my studies, I started with advertising graphics in 1965. I did that for ten years and then I very deliberately stopped. For more than one reason, as it happens. Firstly, in the world of marketing, one must also be business-oriented, a businesswoman. However, I was only interested in the art. And, on top of that, as a woman, you find yourself in a man's world and you have to constantly fight for your existence. An equally important reason was that I never found real satisfaction in my work here in Belgium.'[9]

There was little support from the Belgian government and business community. For the government administration, graphic design did not exist: 'We have yet to wake up in our region, because our publicity and our graphic designers only occasionally get work and then the government or the private organisations still have to book this to exceptional expenses.'[10]

Career switch

Behaeghel did not allow herself to be pigeonholed. As early as 1965, she had exhibited work in various techniques. In the Studio Behaeghel period (1965–75), she also produced self-initiated work: photography, painting, drawings, and sculptures. There were no set boundaries between the different areas of her practice. One example is her use of her own photographs for the layout of the magazine *Ons Erfdeel*. In a letter from 1966, Breker scolded her for her interest in fine art: 'Why do you want to get out and devote yourself more to "free" art? Do you think that there are different norms there? The norm is not "what" you do, but "how" you do it?'[11]

fig. 8
Jeanine Behaeghel at work in her studio, 1975

She found it increasingly difficult to continue her design practice. In her notes, she writes about two crises and a period of rest at a convent to recover. But the sudden loss in 1975 of her son Thomas had a tremendous impact on the lives of herself, her partner Jef Gruytaert and their other son Hans. She decided to stop Studio Behaeghel and focus on fine art. Her farewell to design was announced at the Korrekelder, with an exhibition of drawings: thick, black calligraphic lines coloured in with bright felt-tip pens that she called 'plastic stenograms' (fig. 9). By the early 1980s, the female figure had taken an increasingly prominent place in her work.[12]

fig. 9
Jeanine Behaeghel
Untitled drawing, no date

The Bruges designer was not alone in making this career switch. Brussels-based Francine De Boeck graduated with high honours from La Cambre in 1971 and worked as a designer under the moniker Filigrane, for clients such as the publisher Séquoia, or the cyclist Eddy Merckx, until, after a decade, she decided to focus on illustration. Marina Ponjaert made designs for the Muziekinstrumentenmuseum (Musical Instrument Museum) in Brussels and the dancer Maurice Béjart from 1963 but decided to stop her freelance practice in 1977. And Jacqueline Ost, the internationally acclaimed author of children's books, started her career as a graphic designer for Expo 58 working alongside Lucien De Roeck.

Trailblazer

After ten years as a designer and a second decade as a figurative artist, a final period followed with a focus on sculpting. In 1985, she started working in three dimensions, in materials such as bronze and wood. An artist friend introduced her to the stonemasons in the Italian town of Carrara, who helped her produce her works in marble. She thanked them profusely at the unveiling of her work *Naiade* in 1992.[13]

The sculptures from 1989 in the exhibition at Vyncke-van Eyck, one of the few Ghent galleries at that time, had dramatic titles such as *Brandpunt (Focal Point)*, *Oorsprong (Origin)*, *Bevrijd (Liberated)* and *Geborgen (Secured)*, fig. 10). They look like logos in motion. Her past as a designer became a stigma. A journalist wrote: 'Especially in her paintings, the "decorative approach" cannot go unnoticed.'[14] She complained about the lack of success – the marble sculptures were expensive to produce and remained unsold. Behaeghel felt like an outsider: 'Flanders has a wide range of artists, each of whom experiences their passion for drawing from their own corner. I don't believe I belong to any of them.'[15]

At the end of her life, the City of Bruges bought 12 drawings and, in 1993, the year she died, a monograph was published, with collected writings about her work by loyal friends Jaak Frontier and Gaby Gysels. Since 2020, her name has graced a Bruges street, Jeanine Behaegelstraat, close to where she used to live.[16]

In her work and life, Behaeghel effortlessly crossed borders, between countries and disciplines. On the one hand, she was praised for her multidisciplinary approach. Yet her versatility was her downfall. As one observer put it, 'There is a general enthusiasm to be detected among connoisseurs and non-connoisseurs, but also a profound malaise: where to situate this work? What drawer can you store it in?'[17] Behaeghel was aware of the prejudice against women designers, and how simplicity and clarity can be repressive. She paid a steep price to follow her own voice, blazing a trail for many women designers and artists in Belgium today.

fig. 10
Jeanine Behaeghel
Geborgen (Secured),
no date

1 Annotated quote by Henry van de Velde, box Jeanine Behaeghel, Musea Brugge Archive.
2 See articles in: *Ons Erfdeel, Vlaanderen, De Bladen van Grafiek* and her monograph, *Jeanine Behaeghel* (Bruges: Stichting Kunstboek), 1993.
3 Letter from Hans Schwippert to Jeanine Behaeghel, 2 April 1964, Musea Brugge Archive.
4 Kinross, Robin, *Anthony Froshaug: Documents of a Life* (London: Hyphen Press, 2000), p.245.
5 Lampaert, Herman, 'De naoorlogse periode: Een schets' in Johan Valcke, *In koeien van letters: 50 jaar grafische vormgeving in Vlaanderen* (Brussels: VIZO, 1997), p.82: 'Albert Setola is co-founder of the Bruges theatre De Korrekelder, for which, for years, he, and later also Luk Mestdagh, did the design.'
6 Deleu, Jozef, 'Het nieuwe geluid van Jeanine Behaeghel' in *De Periscoop*, May 1965.
7 'Jeanine Behaeghel in het Brugse Huidevettershuis. Een tuil van artistiek vermogen' in *De Standaard*, 11 March 1965 (no author).
8 Gyselen, Gaby, *Jeanine Behaeghel* (Bruges: Stichting Kunstboek, 1993), p.41.
9 S.D., 'Jeanine Behaeghel. Kunst is een roeping' in unnamed newspaper cutting, (no date, no author), Musea Brugge Archive.
10 'Akademie van Düsseldorf in het Huidevettershuis' in unnamed newspaper cutting, (no date, no author), Musea Brugge Archive.
11 Breker, Walter, letter to Jeanine Behaeghel, 2 January 1966, box Jeanine Behaeghel, Musea Brugge Archive.
12 On the occasion of an exhibition at Galerij 't Leerhuys in Bruges (1983) a journalist wrote: 'Dominating her pictorial work is the stylised profile of a female face, in which the eye turned towards the viewer – pupilless – stares at the spectator.' S. B. in *Het Volk*, 12-13 November 1983.
13 Gyselen, Gaby, *Jeanine Behaeghel* (Bruges: Stichting Kunstboek), 1993, p.62.
14 R.C., *Jeanine Behaeghel: Eenheid in drie technieken* in *Het Volk*, 14 April 1989.
15 Behaeghel, Jeanine, press release *Plastische stenogrammen, recente tekeningen*, Galerij 't Leerhuys, 16-22 December 1985, p.1. Heritage Library Westflandrica via email to the author, document S-STAD215_cop_stadsarchief_0492_001.pdf.
16 https://www.brugge.be/20210125-besluitenlijst and https://www.vrt.be/vrtnws/nl/2021/02/01/twee-nieuwe-straten-in-brugge-krijgen-de-naam-van-een-vrouw/; last accessed on 7 May 2021.
17 Heritage Library Westflandrica via email to the author, document S-STAD215_cop_stadsarchief_0490_001.pdf.

Belgian Institute Graphic Design

MARLEEN DECEUKELIER

The **Belgian Institute Graphic Design** (2020) is a new platform for graphic design in and from Belgium. It curates exhibitions, researches the history of graphic design, and offers a forum to contemporary designers. Under the direction of Pia Jacques and Leroy Meyer, the institute has organised several shows, including *Focus On* (Antwerp, 2020). The poster on the opposite page was part of this window display series. See belgischinstituutgrafischontwerp.be

Marleen Deceukelier, *documenta IX* (1986)

As a full-time graphic designer at S.M.A.K., the municipal museum of contemporary art in Ghent, Deceukelier was responsible for the design of all its printed matter, including, for example, the catalogue for the famous *Chambres d'Amis* exhibition (1986) and posters for shows by artists such as Jan Vercruysse, Raoul De Keyser, Luc Tuymans, Roberte Mestdagh, Thierry De Cordier, and many others. She often worked under the pseudonym eMDé. The iconic poster design that she created with Sony Van Hoecke for *documenta IX* (1992), curated by the then S.M.A.K. director Jan Hoet, used a drawing by the artist Dietmar Guderian.

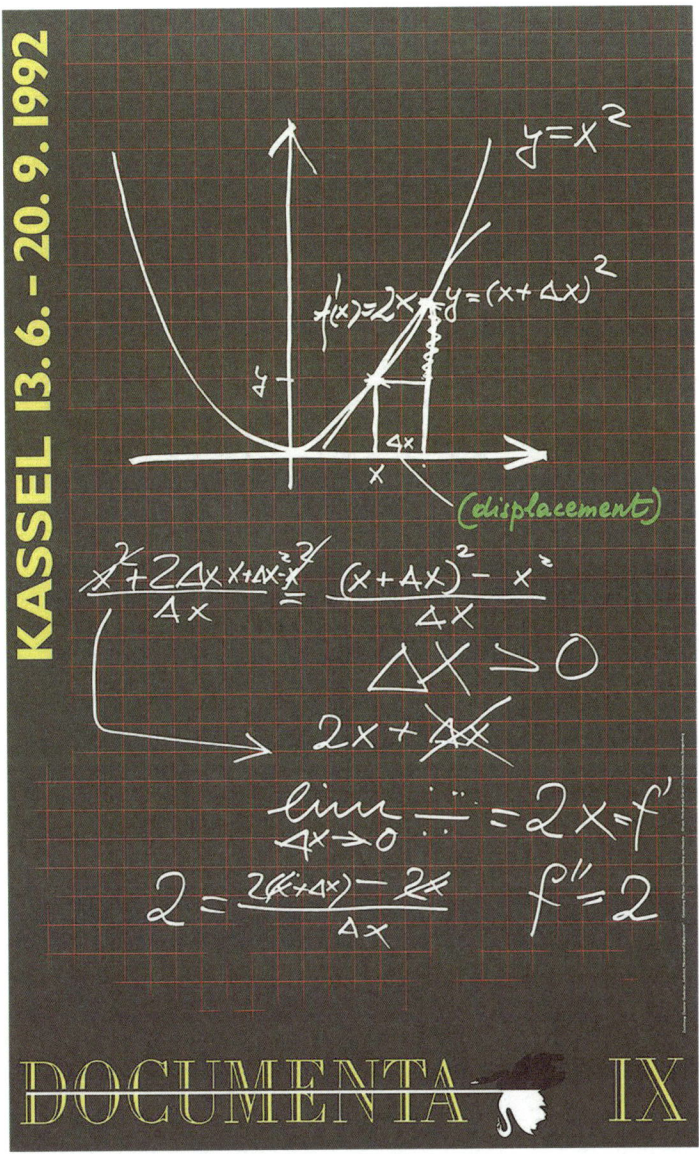

Marleen Deceukelier and Sony Van Hoecke
Poster for *documenta IX*, 1992

Belgian Institute Graphic Design

ANNE DELCOIGNE

The **Belgian Institute Graphic Design** (2020) is a new platform for graphic design in and from Belgium. It curates exhibitions, researches the history of graphic design, and offers a forum to contemporary designers. Under the direction of Pia Jacques and Leroy Meyer, the institute has organised several shows, including *Focus On* (Antwerp, 2020). The poster on the opposite page was part of this window display series. See belgischinstituutgrafischontwerp.be

Anne Delcoigne, *Der Krieg der Mumien* (1974)

Little information is available about Delcoigne's life and work. This striking poster for the movie *Der Krieg der Mumien (War of the Mummies)* – on the role played by American companies in Augusto Pinochet's coup in Chile in 1973 – is one of only two designs currently kept in public archives. In 1976, she also designed the typographic call to protest, entitled *Abortus, de vrouw beslist! (Abortion, the woman decides!)*.

Anne Delcoigne
Poster for *Der Krieg der Mumien (The war of mummies)*, 1974

Hugo Puttaert

GILLES FISZMAN: THE POWER OF NUANCE

Hugo Puttaert (1960) is a graphic designer, facilitator, professor, and editor. He trained as a visual artist at Sint-Lukas, Brussels (now LUCA) and worked for ten years as a graphic artist before founding his studio, visionandfactory, in 1990. He teaches graphic design at Sint Lucas Antwerpen. Since 2007, he has organised the biennial Integrated conference in deSingel, Antwerp. He has been a speaker at various international design conferences and symposia, worked on diverse magazines, and was the editor-in-chief of *Addmagazine*. This text is an expanded version of an article first published in *Addmagazine*.[1] See visionandfactory.be

'You hold a catalogue in your hand. That is logical because a catalogue is part of an exhibition. A monograph, however, is part of an oeuvre. If you were to hold Gilles Fiszman's monograph in your hands, it would take a lot more effort, because it would be many times heavier. That is how extensive Fiszman's oeuvre is.'

Thus began my introductory text of *Autobiographisme*, the catalogue of Fiszman's eponymous exhibition at the Huis van het Beeld/Seed Factory in Brussels. On Saturday 6 September 2014, barely three weeks before the opening, he died unexpectedly at the age of 82 and would never get to experience his self-curated exhibition. I vividly remember our pleasant conversations, in his house in Uccle, the last of which was shortly before his death.

Fiszman was one of the last survivors of his generation of graphic design pioneers in Belgium. As early as 1983, a by-then substantially yellowed book – in a fairly large square format – was published. It was a business card for Fiszman & Partners, part of the international network Axion Design Partnership, with branches in Brussels, Montreal, and San Francisco.

At that time, Belgian graphic design was already very international, something that is often forgotten. Think of the career of Paul Ibou, who was active in China and the US. From the 1960s to the 1980s, Fiszman, together with Jeanine Behaeghel, Rob Buytaert, Boudewijn Delaere, Josse Goffin, Corneille Hannoset, Julian Key, Jacqueline Ost, Jacques Richez, and others, belonged to a leading generation of Belgian graphic designers, who also enjoyed recognition beyond national borders. And let us not forget the *éminence grise* Lucien De Roeck, or the somewhat younger Luk Mestdagh, who was a visionary teacher. Fiszman also taught, between 1983 and 1989, at La Cambre, but, in his own words, it turned out not to be his greatest calling. In 2005, he officially put an end to his 50-year career. Never the less, it did not stop him from continuing to design and create, albeit at a slower pace, or, as he quipped: *'en petit comité'*. Passion can be difficult to reconcile with retirement.

I got to know Fiszman when he would visit my office in Brussels. He collaborated with Philippe Hulet, one of my employees, for the Musée Juif de Belgique (Jewish Museum of Belgium), for which he designed the beautiful tree-shaped logo with a crown of letters in 1990, a kind of symbol of united polyphony. I found him to be an amiable and thoughtful man. During our many conversations, I noticed how he combined natural charisma with a professional knowledge that would turn many a graphic designer pale. His versatility and unbiased attitude led to intelligent solutions in various projects. Fiszman was a true all-rounder with a sharp insight and that gave him a lot of credibility, not least with his clients. Nevertheless, 'design for design's sake' was by no means his thing: 'A designer analyses the assignment, questions it, researches it broadly, and then offers a relevant and personal solution', he stated. He did not like the umpteenth delving into the bag of tricks full of predetermined form and style elements. In this, Fiszman was categorical: style is irrelevant. The question takes precedence and the solution is the result. *Tout court!*

fig. 1
Gilles Fiszman
Logo for Musée Juif de Belgique (Jewish Museum of Belgium), 1990

Together with his team, Fiszman not only designed logos and complex corporate identities (many of which are still in use), such as for the Théâtre National Wallonie-Bruxelles, the Université Libre de Bruxelles, and the Communauté française de Belgique (French Community of Belgium) (figs. 2) – featuring a beautiful red cockerel – but also signage, posters, corporate brochures, packaging, and books. He even designed products (including hi-fi installations), not to speak of his talent as an illustrator.

figs. 2 (from left to right, top to bottom)
Gilles Fiszman
Logos for the Communauté française de Belgique (French Community of Belgium), Arenberg Cinemas, Théâtre National Wallonie-Bruxelles, YOR Cosmetica, STAFF Selection and Services, and UNERG

All this resulted in a huge variety in his work, although there was always the familiar, illustrative touch. Furthermore, his interest in psychology and sociology gave him insight into how companies and organisations function and what their problems are. Hence, he approached his clients in a way that was different from that of most graphic designers, and more empathically too, so that trust grew. Not that he just said what his clients wanted to hear; on the contrary. As a designer, he wanted to give them a relevant and added value. He also gave his clients strategic advice. Nevertheless, this rather analytical view never stood in the way of an intuitive solution. On the one hand, he opted for a simple, Constructivist approach (for example in the many logos). On the other, he could just as easily apply a frivolous, sometimes even anarchistic imagery, similar to, for example, the legendary French designers Grapus or Polish poster designers such as Henryk Tomaszewski. The poster for the commemoration of the 25th anniversary of the Warsaw ghetto uprising is a wonderful example (fig. 3). Fiszman designed it in 1968, commissioned by the Palais des Beaux-Arts (Centre for Fine Arts) in Brussels, where a debate about the remembrance took place. A silhouette holds a weapon above its head, like a kind of primal scream. It looks like an ancient rock carving, roaring and simple.

This intelligent broadness may have had to do with the hard times that Fiszman endured during his childhood. As the child of Jewish-Polish immigrants, he lived in hiding in Brussels during World War II. He lost his whole family and was nearly deported himself. It marked his life, but he did not give up. He started as a leatherworker, after which he studied painting, first in Brussels and later in Warsaw at the Akademia Sztuk Pięknych (Academy of Fine Arts). There, he met his wife, and subsequently, the young family moved permanently to Brussels. During

fig. 3
Gilles Fiszman
Poster for the commemoration of the 25th anniversary of the Warsaw ghetto uprising, 1968

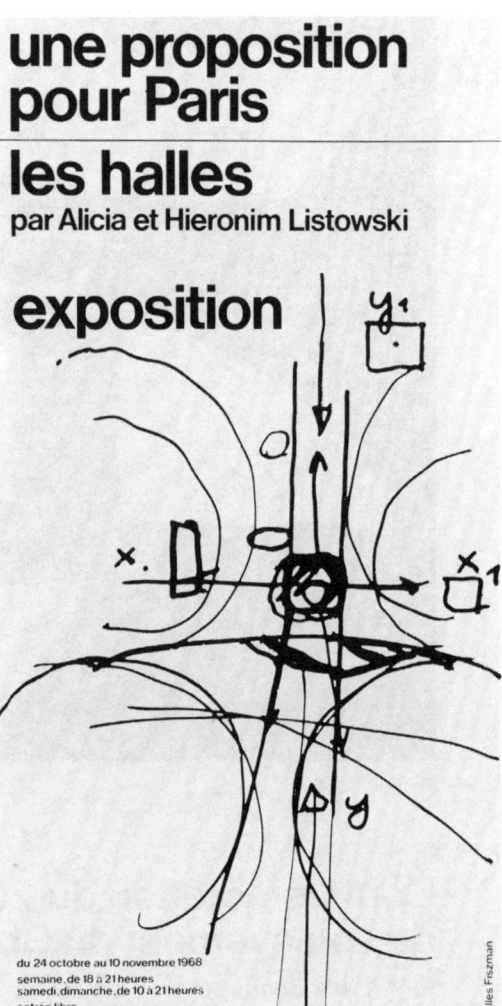

fig. 4
Gilles Fiszman
Poster for l'Ensemble dance company, 1975

fig. 5
Gilles Fiszman
Poster for *Une proposition pour Paris: Les Halles*, 1968

that time, he worked as, among other things, a window dresser, a designer at the André François advertising agency (1960–63), and as a freelance graphic artist, after which he started his own studio. Fiszman was chairman of the Chambre Belge des Graphistes (Belgian Chamber of Graphic Designers, 1975–78) and, in 1974, he was one of the few Belgians chosen to join the prestigious Alliance Graphique Internationale.

During our final conversation, Fiszman joked that he always avoided professional literature, except for three imaginary books: *Toute la typographie*, *Toute la photogravure*, and *Toute la publicité* (*Everything on Typography, Everything on Printing, and Everything on Advertising*). He was clear about the status of graphic designers: 'Graphic designers practice a different profession than advertising people. That's why I have consciously distanced myself from advertising, especially in order to position myself clearly, something that current designers or agencies rarely dare to do. This has nothing to do with a value judgement, however. It is just a reality: graphic design works more in the long term (certainly when you're talking about corporate identity and branding). Advertising, on the other hand, is very cyclical; it causes a violent response, after which it fades away again.'

It is striking how current the design and imagery of these forerunners has remained. Fiszman's work still resonates, in its pictorial power, but also in the power of its nuance.

fig. 6
Gilles Fiszman
Art direction for design furniture shop Ligne, 1972

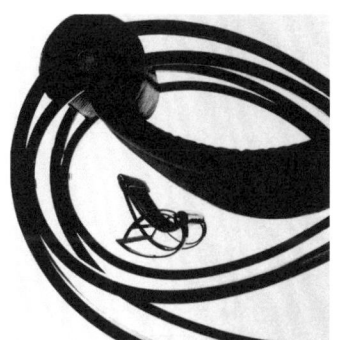

1   Puttaert, Hugo, 'Gilles Fiszman. De Kracht van de Nuance', *Addmagazine*, issue 2 (Brussels: Papyrus, 2005), pp.32–35.

Jan Ceuleers

CORNEILLE HANNOSET, CONSTANTIN BRODZKI, AND MARCEL BROODTHAERS

Jan Ceuleers (1952) was active for 30 years as an antiquarian, specialising in rare publications and archives of the avant-garde. He has published books and articles, including texts about Georges Vantongerloo and René Magritte. He facilitated the incorporation of Corneille Hannoset's archive into the Archives et Musée de la Littérature (Archives and Museum of Literature), Brussels.

The designer Corneille Hannoset's oeuvre speaks volumes about how applied art relates to architecture and visual art. His intense collaboration with the architect Constantin Brodzki in the 1950s was in line with the pursuit of *Gesamtkunstwerk*, a trend that started with Arts and Crafts, and that, through Bauhaus, determined modernist architecture and applied arts. Hannoset's brief collaboration with Marcel Broodthaers in the mid-1960s was of an entirely different order. When Broodthaers switched from a local variant of Pop Art to conceptual art, he, like his new colleagues, no longer needed a graphic designer and would play typographer himself.

The early years

Hannoset was born in Brussels in 1926. After taking evening classes at the Académie Royale des Beaux-Arts de Bruxelles (Royal Academy of Fine Arts of Brussels), he began his training at La Cambre in 1943. Together with, among others, Pierre Alechinsky, Michel Olyff, and Serge Creuze, he enrolled in advertising and illustration. After graduating in 1947, he studied book design for another year with Fernand Geersens. Hannoset's book projects from those years, mostly children's titles printed on the La Cambre presses, were illustrated with his own drawings, watercolours, and monotypes, in a style that could be called neo-romantic or *faux naïf*, with echoes of folk art and vernacular design. He shared his interest in imagery that falls outside of the canon with peers such as Alechinsky and other members of the Cobra group. He frequented their Ateliers du Marais in Brussels, but was not a full-time Cobra member. Alongside his first job at weekly newspaper *Le face à main, hebdomadaire illustré*, he produced self-initiated work such as textiles and metal sculptures (fig. 1).

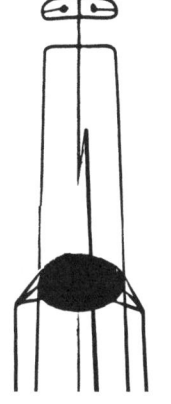

fig. 1 (above)
Corneille Hannoset
Untitled sculpture, no date

fig. 2 (below)
Corneille Hannoset
Invitation card for Cobra exhibition, 1949

Hannoset's career as a designer began in 1949. Together with Jacques Ledoux, curator of the Cinémathèque royale de Belgique (Royal Belgium Film Archive), he set up EXPRMNTL, an international festival of experimental film (fig. 3). In collaboration with Alechinsky, he designed all the printed matter until the fifth and final edition in 1974. It is no coincidence that Hannoset's career blossomed at the Palais des Beaux-Arts (Centre for Fine Arts) in Brussels. In those years, it functioned as a place where many informal contacts were made, at the intersection of art and design. Much of its revenue came from major art auctions and the sale of modern and contemporary art during exhibitions. The place offered many opportunities for Brussels' small, progressive art scene.

From 1950, Hannoset was responsible for the layout of the monthly periodical *Architecture* (fig. 4) and, in the same year, he made his debut as an interior designer with the furnishing of a bookshop. In addition to graphic design, he also designed shop windows and scenography for exhibitions.

fig. 3
Corneille Hannoset
Invitation card for
EXPRMNTL 4, 1967–68

Hannoset and Brodzki

From 1951, Hannoset worked for ten years with Brodzki – another La Cambre graduate – on dozens of larger and smaller projects: designing shops, offices, and exhibition stands at trade fairs. Several projects in this long series deserve extra attention. In 1953, they were commissioned to convert a narrow, high corridor at the Palais des Beaux-Arts into an exhibition space for new art. With a modest budget, Hannoset and Brodzki came up with a

fig. 4
Corneille Hannoset
Architecture, no.52 and
no.53, 1952 and 1953

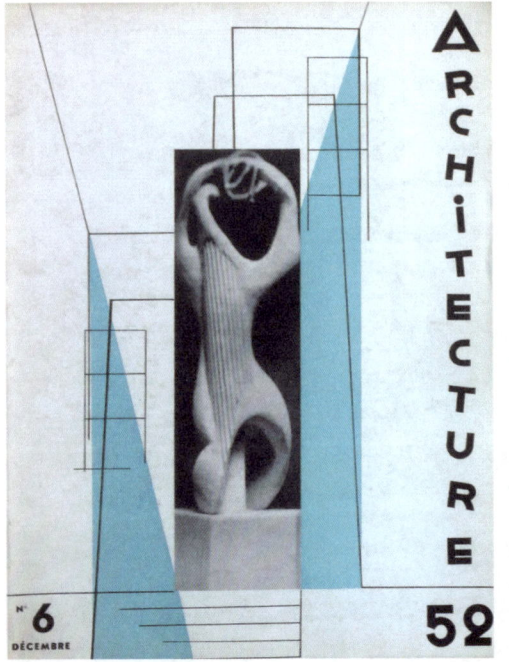

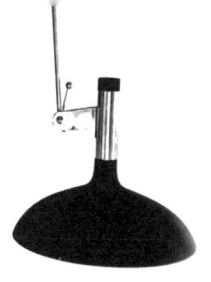

fig. 5
Corneille Hannoset
Ceiling lamp, no date

functional solution using velums, movable partitions, and adapted lighting, while at the same time creating a great sense of space. Artists who would later become famous, such as Cy Twombly and Piero Manzoni, as well as Broodthaers, exhibited their work this Galerie Aujourd'hui.

Brodzki and Hannoset designed the Congolese Fauna Pavilion for Expo 58, the Brussels World's Fair (see p.55). On the design of this, too, they collaborated with artists such as Serge Vandercam and the brothers Reinhoud and Roel d'Haese. And on the invitation of Ledoux, Hannoset produced a series of 45 announcements for film screenings by the Écran du Séminaire des Arts (Art Seminar Screenings) in the Palais des Beaux-Arts between 1955 and 1962 (figs. 6). The choice of film stills, the cut-out, and the lettering demonstrate how inventively he dealt with the principles of the Swiss Style. The fact that the result comes across as effortless and self-evident has much to do with the freedom – and not just artistic freedom – that defined Hannoset's life and work.

Craftsman and dandy

In 1962, Ledoux was finally able to set up the Musée du cinéma (Film Museum) he dreamed of at the Palais des Beaux-Arts. Hannoset and Brodzki were commissioned for the renovation and interior design. The result was a 'cinematic' installation of simple interventions with great effect, such as a bright red passage that functioned as a buffer for audiences returning to reality having watched the film. Hannoset also designed seats for the cinema, which he says were inspired by the car seats of the legendary Citroën 2CV.

Brodzki would later stress that he had certainly not been a workaholic and that he had managed to surround himself with excellent collaborators. In an interview, he said that, thanks to Hannoset and his contacts in the art world, he had escaped from his traditional vision of architecture. The fact that they worked closely for ten years was also due to the functional approach that they shared: a pragmatic preference for a minimum of resources with a maximum result, efficiency with a twist. Their work was intelligent and elegant in an unobtrusive way. Not coincidentally, they were both confident and proud personalities, with traits of the dandy.

Hannoset was a talented, versatile craftsman par excellence. He not only designed printed matter and signage, but also furniture and light fixtures; he photographed prolifically as well – repetitive motifs, random grids, and structures that he could use as a graphic designer, but that would not have been out of place in the German *Subjektive Fotografie*, a trend in the 1950s that wanted to reinvigorate photography's artistic status (figs. 12). In addition to his busy professional activities, he found time in 1955 to co-found Galerie Taptoe in Brussels, an alternative exhibition space with a bar. For two years, the gallery exhibited artists who worked on the border between figurative and informal art, such as Alechinsky, Asger Jorn, Vandercam, and Maurice Wyckaert.

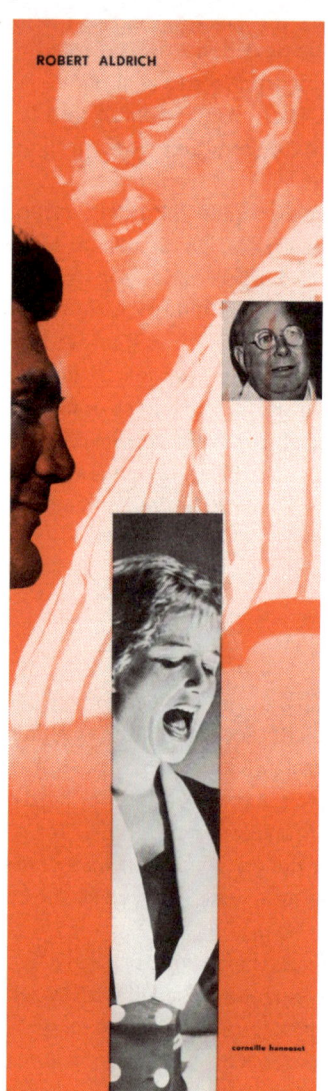
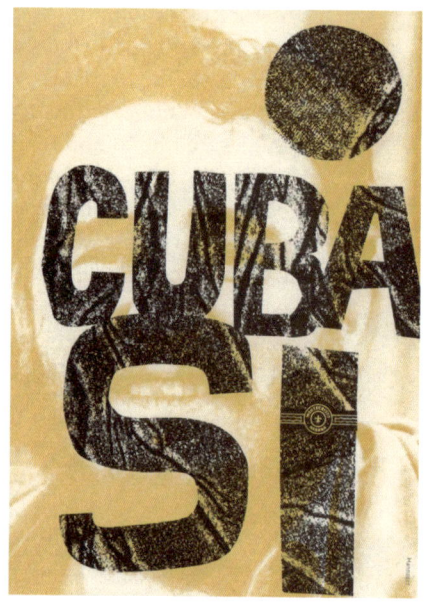

figs. 6
Corneille Hannoset
Invitation cards for Écran du Séminaire des Arts
(Art Seminar Screenings), 1955–62

figs. 7 (opposite)
Corneille Hannoset
Invitations for Musée du cinéma, 1962–82

figs. 8 (above)
Constantin Brodzki and Corneille Hannoset
Musée Lapidaire, 1960

The pinnacle of Hannoset and Brodzki's oeuvre – and also the only surviving result of their collaboration – is the Musée Lapidaire (Gallo-Roman stone museum) at Montauban-Buzenol, in the middle of the forests of the Belgian province of Luxembourg (figs. 8). It was completed in 1960 and is among the few cultural buildings of significance in Belgium from those years. In 1968, it was selected for the Museum of Modern Art in New York's *Architecture of Museums* exhibition. The museum displays fragments of Roman funerary monuments, excavated on site, which were reused in the Merovingian era to build fortifications. The variation of blank walls and large glass expanses allows the objects and the environment to come into their own. By burying the building in a hill, Hannoset and Brodzki were able to make optimal use of its location in a forest with a capricious terrain. Hannoset's now-disappeared signage brought visitors to a well on top of a hill. A mysterious, narrow underground staircase leads to the entrance: the visitors dig themselves, as it were, back in time. Together, the location, the building, and the history provide a total experience.

The collaboration between Hannoset and Brodzki came to an end with the Musée du cinéma. Hannoset went his own way. In addition to numerous graphic design commissions, he was responsible for the design of shops and offices, the scenography for exhibitions, and, in 1967, the expansion of the Musée du cinéma (figs. 7). Traces of all this work are still preserved in his archive, but – in an irony of history – his most depicted work, a design for Broodthaers, is rarely attributed to him, although his name is clearly stated on it. One of the reasons why is that it emerged in the twilight zone between fine and applied art.

Collaboration with Broodthaers

Broodthaers also belonged to the milieu of Palais des Beaux-Arts. In the margins of post-war Surrealism, he published in magazines and brought out a few volumes of poetry, which were barely noticed. He lived from hand to mouth, occasionally working as a freelance journalist, giving tours of Palais des Beaux-Arts, and receiving financial support from friends and acquaintances – including Brodzki; they were the same age and had known each other from early on.

In 1964, Broodthaers, who was 40 at the time, decided to step into the art world with a Belgian take on Pop Art. He launched his first exhibition, at the small Saint Laurent gallery in Brussels, with an announcement that, with hindsight, could serve as an explanation of his entire oeuvre (figs. 9):

> 'I, too, wondered whether I could not sell something to succeed in life. I have been good for nothing for a long time now. I am already forty years old ... Finally, I came up with the idea of inventing something insincere and I immediately got to work.'

Of course, that text itself had an impact, as a cynical, *faux-naïf* self-introduction, but it only became truly effective through Hannoset's design. The text, in the typeface Mercator Bold, in black or in red and black, is printed on both sides of existing pages from *Elle* or *Marie-Claire* magazines. Each copy of the invitation is unique. Notable are the Pop Art motifs, such as household appliances, that have been overprinted with text. But the brash demeanour of the would-be artist Broodthaers, who announced that he would use everyday things to acquire a new status, is also striking. In this context, the chronology of Broodthaers' early printed matter is important. The announcement of his next exhibition was also designed by Hannoset, printed on both sides of the pages from a telephone directory. And at the end of 1964, Broodthaers sent New Year's greetings using stencilled letters and silver paint on the financial pages of the Belgian newspaper *Le Soir*. It is closely related to the previous two announcements in terms of effect.

The design of Broodthaers' first volumes of poetry was not particularly striking. His fourth and final volume, *Pense-Bête (Memory Aid*, 1963), has a large format for a collection of poems and is printed in the same sans-serif typeface – perhaps on the advice of Hannoset. *Pense-Bête* is well known because in most copies the author covered parts of the text with glossy paper and signed the volumes using his fingerprints. For one of his first assemblages, he encased the unsold copies in plaster. The iconoclastic way in which he dealt with this last poetry volume marked his entry into the visual arts.

In May 1966, Broodthaers held his first exhibition in the Wide White Space gallery in Antwerp. He had the small catalogue produced by a local commercial printer. The typeface was a surprising swash script, usually employed for formal announcements such as marriages. The following year, he held a solo exhibition, *Court Circuit* (1967), at Palais des Beaux-Arts, with a catalogue designed by Hannoset

figs. 9
Marcel Broodthaers and Corneille Hannoset
Invitation to *Moi aussi, je me suis demandé si je ne pouvais pas vendre quelque chose et réussir dans la vie...*, 1964

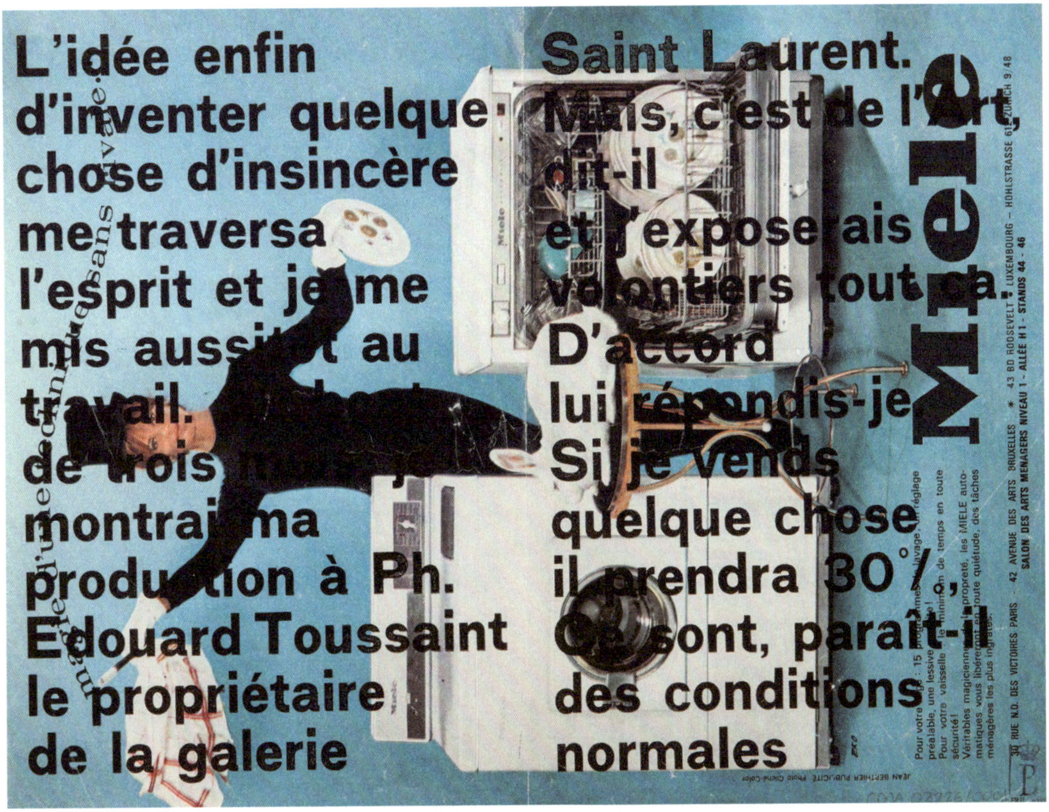

L'idée enfin d'inventer quelque chose d'insincère me traversa l'esprit et je me mis aussitôt au travail. Au bout de trois mois, je montrai ma production à Ph. Edouard Toussaint le propriétaire de la galerie Saint Laurent. Mais, c'est de l'Art, dit-il et j'exposerais volontiers tout ça. D'accord lui répondis-je. Si je vends quelque chose il prendra 30%. Ce sont, paraît-il des conditions normales certaines galeries prenant 75%. Ce que c'est ? En fait, des objets. Marcel Broodthaers

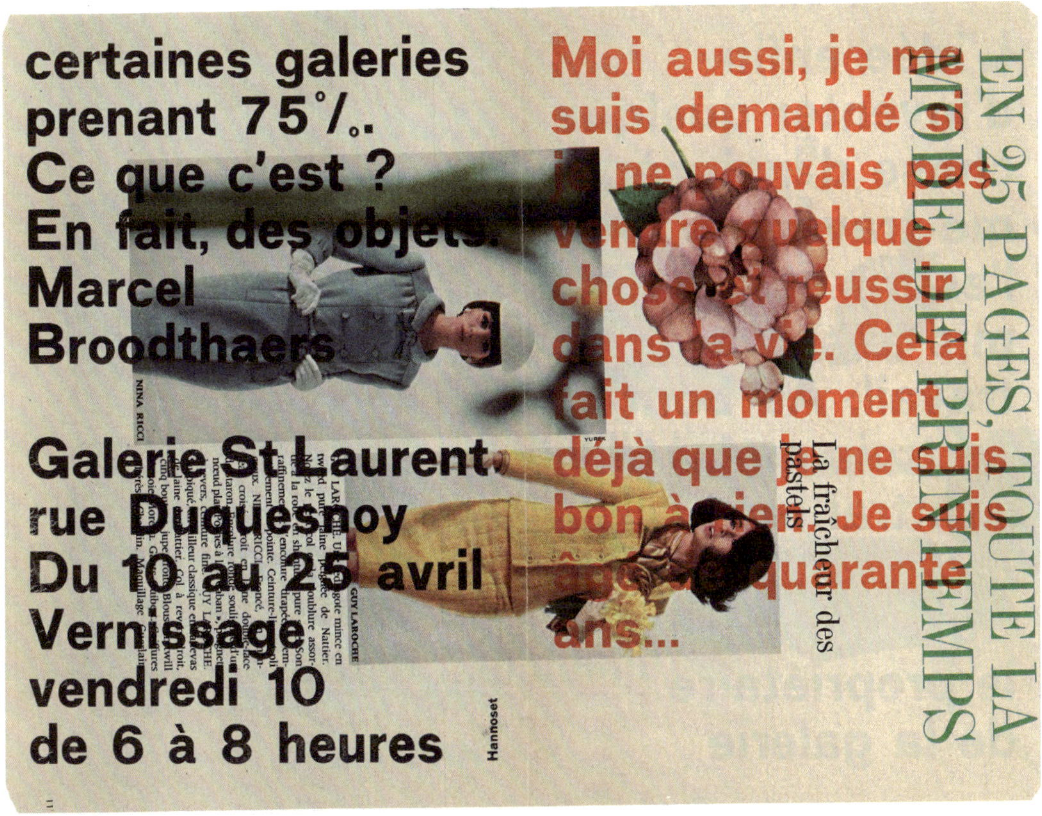

Galerie St Laurent
rue Duquesnoy
Du 10 au 25 avril
Vernissage vendredi 10
de 6 à 8 heures

Moi aussi, je me suis demandé si je ne pouvais pas vendre quelque chose et réussir dans la vie. Cela fait un moment déjà que je ne suis bon à rien. Je suis âgé de quarante ans...

(fig. 10). A swash typeface was used here too, presumably on Broodthaers' suggestion, but this time in combination with sans serifs. While the Wide White Space catalogue of 1966 looks unadventurous by today's standards, the design in this case is much bolder, with an asymmetrical page layout and unconventional combinations of text and image.

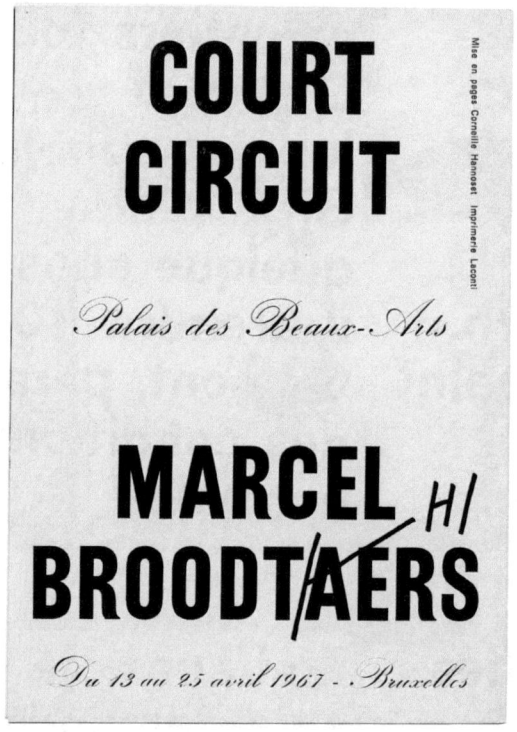

fig. 10
Corneille Hannoset
Back cover of
Court Circuit, 1967

The aesthetic of administration

This catalogue put an end to the collaboration between the artist and designer. From this point on, Broodthaers alone would determine the appearance of his invitations, catalogues, and books. Through the collaboration with Hannoset and his friendship with Jacques Darche, the French book designer and artistic director of the Club français du livre (French Book Club), Broodthaers understood well that language has little impact without effective typography, and that this impact could be magnified by combining word and image. He also quickly understood that he had to distinguish himself from the contemporary art world with a house style, a sort of corporate identity. In the context of his fictional museum – the *Musée d'art moderne, département des Aigles* – which he started in 1968, the script typeface became a permanent a feature in his work. It suited the ex-poet and self-made artist that text was the main medium of the conceptual trend. Using simple means – such as the design of his printed matter – he was able

fig. 11
Corneille Hannoset
Invitation card for
Carlo Carlotti, 1966

Si vous aimez Michel Ange, l'art Khmèr, Phidias, Coysevox,
la sculpture monumentale Maya et Riemenschneider, alors

CARLOTTI
PRIX JEUNE SCULPTURE PARIS MILLE NEUF CENT SOIXANTE QUATRE

« Le Moyen-Age a fait la petite Eve d'Autun et ce fut
Ghisbelert. Et la Grèce a fait le Panthéon,
et dès lors pouvait disparaître. Et notre culture con-
temporaine, elle, à son tour, devant les
« Son et lumière » du futur, pourra présenter Carlotti... »
André Malraux

Carlo **TTI**

CARLOtti

ITTOLRAC

A PARTIR DU SEIZE DECEMBRE MILLE NEUF CENT SOIXANTE SIX
A DIX NEUF HEURES A L'ESTRO ARMONICO
CENT SEPTANTE SIX AVENUE DEFRÉ UCCLE
EXPOSITION : DEUX MOIS A PARTIR DE QUATORZE HEURES ET LE SOIR

to distinguish himself from colleagues such as Lawrence Weiner or Joseph Kosuth, who, each in their own way, turned texts into art without the intervention of professional designers.

The art theorist Benjamin Buchloh coined the phrase 'aesthetic of administration' for the business-like look of most conceptual meta-art. But Broodthaers rejected this aesthetic: instead of the usual pseudo-philosophical discourse, he made paradoxical statements in a rather literary language. He distinguished himself sufficiently, but also not too much, in an effort to create 'pure' art. The covers of his artist's books are pristine white, but the layout differs profoundly from the no-nonsense style of his colleagues. Like the numerous quotations from nineteenth-century literature in his work, Broodthaers' typography refers to a distant, pre-conceptual past. It is often inspired by the layout of French literary publications, notably Stéphane Mallarmé's *Un coup de dés*. Broodthaers turned his literary origins to his advantage; as a former poet, he was perhaps better read and better with language than the others.

Just as the style of Brodzki's early work is inconceivable without Hannoset's contribution, so is the latter's influence visible in Broodthaers' artistic oeuvre. One example of many: in 1967, Broodthaers produced an ambitious multimedia work of film, collage, and graphics, *Le corbeau et le renard* (*The crow and the fox*). The film harks back to the famous first invitation, with bold sans-serif capitals across the screen and shots in which text almost completely covers the everyday imagery.

The last word belonged to Hannoset. A month after Broodthaers' death on 28 January 1976, the designer published an in memoriam in the magazine of Palais des Beaux-Arts. A fragment:

> 'You haunt a lot of minds, without them even realising it. One day, you opened the door for them by placing a mussel pot in the corner. It was in Palais des Beaux-Arts, in the first room on the left. Real sacrilege. Everyone laughed. But now, no one laughs anymore, it's all become standard fare. Your calling as an angel of deception was rewarded ten years later. Then you were allowed to fill the halls. Your laughter was long gone. "You can't shock them in any way anymore", you told me, in a naïve tone, you who were anything but naïve.'

figs. 12
Corneille Hannoset
Travel photographs, no date

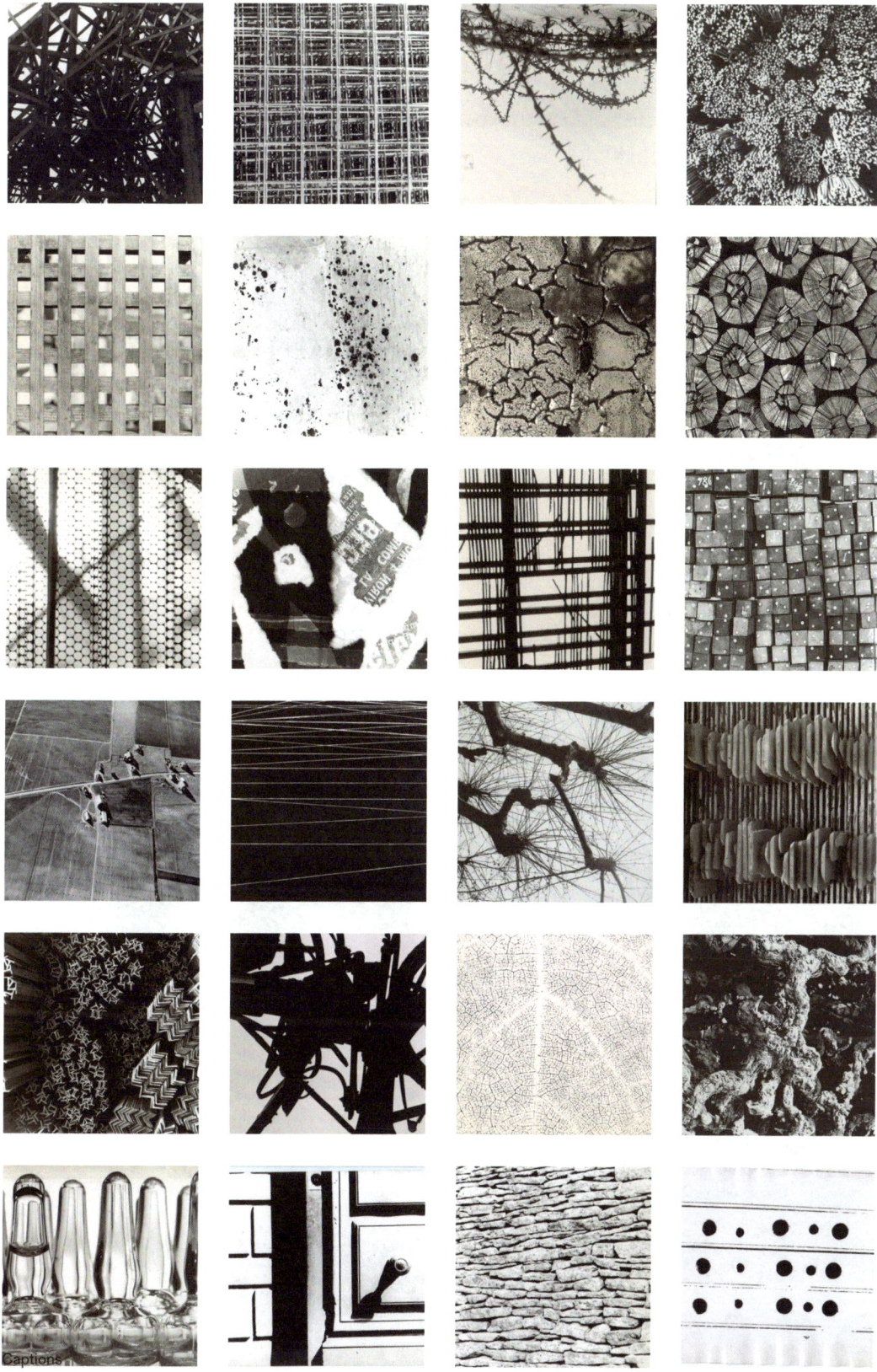

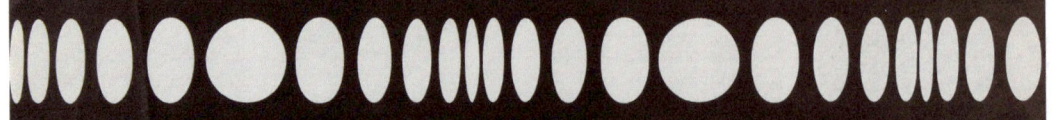

figs. 13 (top and bottom left)
Corneille Hannoset
Posters for Festival du court métrage Belge (Belgian Short Film Festival), 1960

fig. 14 (bottom right)
Corneille Hannoset
Poster for *Candid Shots*, 1961

fig. 15
Corneille Hannoset
Poster for Roland Kirk Quintet concert, 1963

Hugo Puttaert

LUK MESTDAGH: AN AMIABLE TROUBLE-MAKER

Hugo Puttaert (1960) is a graphic designer, facilitator, professor, and editor. He trained as a visual artist at Sint-Lukas, Brussels (now LUCA) and worked for ten years as a graphic artist before founding his studio, visionandfactory, in 1990. He teaches graphic design at Sint Lucas Antwerpen. Since 2007, he has organised the biennial Integrated conference in deSingel, Antwerp. He has been a speaker at various international design conferences and symposia, worked on diverse magazines, and was the editor-in-chief of *Addmagazine*. This text is an expanded version of an article first published in *Addmagazine*.[1] See visionandfactory.be

FontShop, Maaltecenter Ghent, a strange office complex, autumn 1992: a celebratory evening was taking place with the presentation of the FontFont Awards. FontFont was the legendary type foundry of FontShop, at the time one of the largest and most diverse font distributors in the world.[2] An animated public discussion was underway between a male speaker and Neville Brody, the graphic design superstar, just back from a lecture in Tokyo and visibly tired. Terms like plagiarism and epigonism were being used. Suddenly, the speaker abandoned the debate and began a monologue. He presented slides in which he compared Brody's work with that of the Bauhaus. Image after image, he juxtaposed Brody's work with a possible source of inspiration. The similarities were very striking. Brody, visibly embarrassed, began to shift back and forth in his chair, and then – with a jaundiced smile – leaned forward and clasped his hands around the speaker's neck. He did not strangle him, however. Young bloods, like me back then, watched in awe as the star suddenly became human. The speaker in question was Luk Mestdagh and I have considered him an amiable troublemaker ever since, a title by which he was always honoured to be known.

Mestdagh, born in Bruges, studied printing, typesetting, and decorative arts at the Koninklijke Academie voor Schone Kunsten (Royal Academy for Fine Arts) in Ghent, after which he continued in applied graphics at the Kunstakademie Düsseldorf (Art Academy Dusseldorf). For a while he was assistant to professor Walter Breker. In 1967, he started as a freelance graphic designer and, in 1970, he joined Design-Team in Antwerp, one of the first Belgian design studios. He became a figurehead, alongside Rob Buytaert, Antoon De Vylder, and Rudi Verelst. Mestdagh was also a teacher, first at Sint Lucas Antwerpen and later at the Provinciale Hogeschool Limburg (Provincial High School Limburg) in Hasselt. In the last years of his life, together with Anton de Haan, he curated *Type an Sich*, a series of exhibitions about type design at Catapult gallery in Antwerp. He moved into the basement, in the shadow of the city park. His immense archive is now housed there.

Mestdagh's work shows incisiveness. He designed the logo and corporate identity for Antwerpen 93, Cultural Capital of Europe and worked for, among others, the King Baudouin Foundation, the National Bank of Belgium, IBM, the newspaper *Gazet van Antwerpen*, and Shell. He created many logos, posters, signage systems, and typefaces. There is always a fresh and inspiring interaction between type and image in his work. Mestdagh got along well with industrial clients, and created iconic logos for, among other Belgian companies, J. Gatz paper factory, Die Keure printers, Debbaut cabinetmakers, Belovo, Blondé Printing, Boss Paints, and Brugse Zeevaartmaatschappij (Bruges Shipping Company) (figs. 1). Many of these logos were created between 1967 and 1977, a period in which most designers worked directly with clients. The majority of the logos have since been replaced, which is a shame, because they belong to Belgium's cultural heritage.

A strong example of editorial design is issue 04/1994 of *Kwintessens*, the magazine of Design Vlaanderen, each issue of which

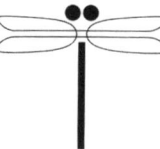

was handled by a different designer (figs. 2). The issue on the theme of 'new technologies' was designed by Mestdagh, with photographs by Lieven Herreman. The cover is functional and does not stand out, in contrast to the inside, which is more special. He combined a Constructivist approach (inspired by compositions by Bauhaus and the Dutch designer Piet Zwart) with the imminent twenty-first century: throughout the issue, swathes of fluorescent blue and pink and titles are printed on the text and photographs. Mestdagh – unruly as he was – made a connection with a younger generation with this atypical layout. The issue remains one of the most eye-catching in *Kwintessens*' fascinating history and shows how influential Mestdagh's work still is.

figs. 1 (top left)
Luk Mestdagh
Logo designs, 1969–79

figs. 2 (opposite)
Luk Mestdagh
Layouts of *Kwintessens* magazine, issue 04/1994

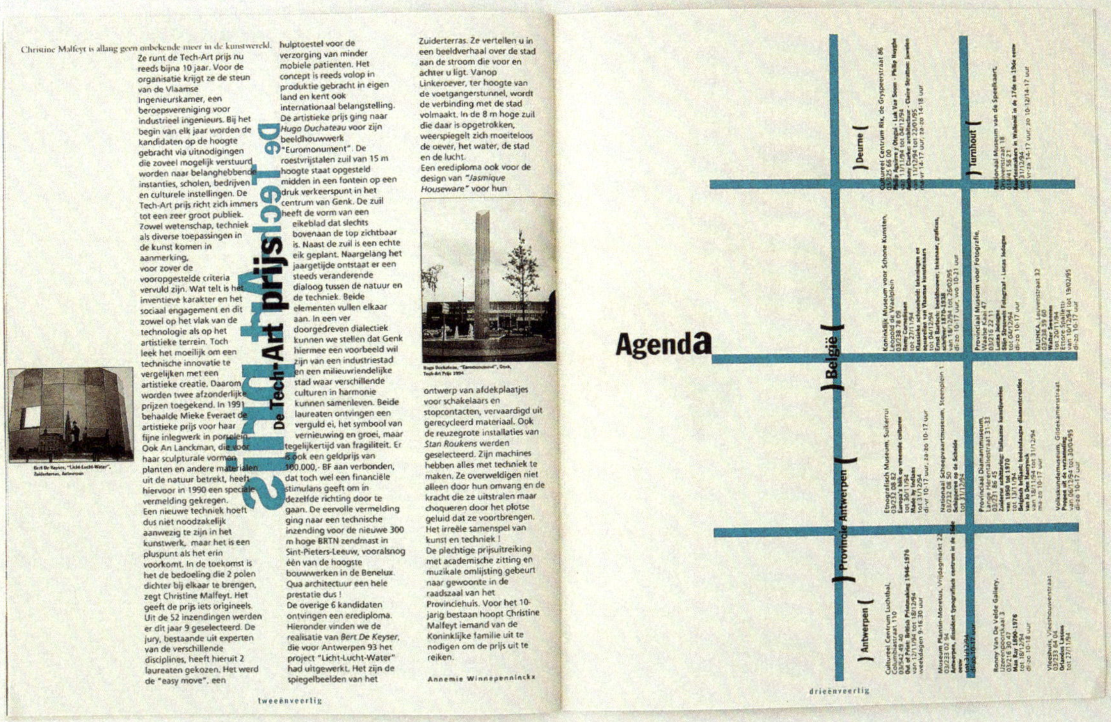

De Tech-Art prijs 1994

Christine Malfeyt is allang geen onbekende meer in de kunstwereld. Ze runt de Tech-Art prijs nu reeds bijna 10 jaar. Voor de organisatie krijgt ze de steun van de Vlaamse Ingenieurskamer, een beroepsvereniging voor industrieel ingenieurs. Bij het begin van elk jaar worden de kandidaten op de hoogte gebracht via uitnodigingen die zowel mogelijk verstuurd worden naar belanghebbende instanties, scholen, bedrijven en culturele instellingen. De Tech-Art prijs richt zich immers tot een zeer groot publiek. Zowel wetenschap, techniek als diverse toepassingen in de kunst komen in aanmerking, voor zover de vooropgestelde criteria vervuld zijn. Wat telt is het inventieve karakter en het sociaal engagement en dit zowel op het vlak van de technologie als op het artistieke terrein. Toch leek het moeilijk om een technische innovatie te vergelijken met een artistieke creatie. Daarom worden twee afzonderlijke prijzen toegekend. In 1991 behaalde Mieke Everaert de artistieke prijs voor haar fijne inlegwerk in porselein. Maar sculpturale vormen uit de natuur betrekt, heeft hiervoor in 1990 een speciale vermelding gekregen.

Een nieuwe techniek hoeft dus niet noodzakelijk aanwezig te zijn in het kunstwerk, maar het is een pluspunt als het erin voorkomt. In de toekomst is het de bedoeling deze 2 polen dichter bij elkaar te brengen, zegt Christine Malfeyt. Het geeft de prijs iets origineels. Uit de 52 inzendingen werden er dit jaar 9 geselekteerd. De jury, bestaande uit experten van de verschillende disciplines, heeft hieruit 2 laureaten gekozen. Er werd de "easy move", een

Bert De Nayers, "Licht-Lucht-Water", Tentoonsteling, Antwerpen

hulptoestel voor de verzorging van minder mobiele patiënten. Het concept is reeds volop in produktie gebracht in eigen land en kent ook internationale belangstelling. De artistieke prijs ging naar Hugo Duchateau voor zijn beeldhouwwerk "Euromonument". De roestvrijstalen zuil van 15 m hoogte staat opgesteld midden in een fontein op een druk verkeerspunt in het centrum van Genk. De zuil heeft de vorm van een eikeblad dat slechts bovenaan de top zichtbaar is. Naast de zuil is een echte eik geplant. Naargelang het jaargetijde ontstaat er een steeds veranderende dialoog tussen de natuur en de techniek. Beide elementen vullen elkaar aan. In een ver doorgedreven dialectiek kunnen we stellen dat Genk hiermee een voorbeeld wil zijn een een milieuvriendelijke stad waar verschillende culturen in harmonie kunnen samenleven. Beide laureaten ontvingen een verguld ei, het symbool van vernieuwing en groei, maar tegelijkertijd van fragiliteit. Er is ook een geldprijs van 300.000,- BF aan verbonden, dat toch wel een financiële stimulans geeft om in dezelfde richting door te gaan. De eervolle vermelding ging naar de technische inzending voor de nieuwe 300 m hoge BRTN zendmast in Sint-Pieters-Leeuw, vooralsnog één van de hoogste bouwwerken in de Benelux. Qua architectuur een hele prestatie dus ! De overige 6 kandidaten ontvingen een erediploma. Hieronder vinden we de realisatie van Bert De Keyser, die voor Antwerpen 93 het project "Licht-Lucht-Water" had uitgewerkt. Het zijn de spiegelbeelden van het

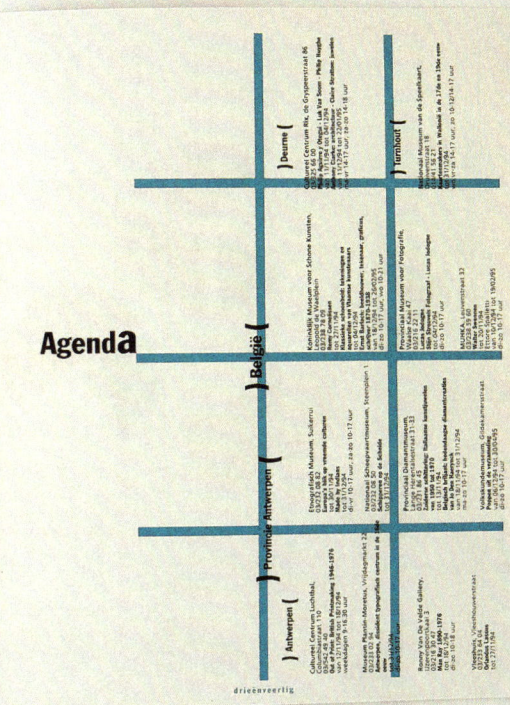
Hugo Duchateau, "Euromonument", Genk, Tech-Art Prijs 1994

Zuiderterras. Ze vertellen u in een beeldverhaal over de stad aan de stroom die voor en achter u ligt. Vanop Linkeroever, ter hoogte van de voetgangerstunnel, wordt de verbinding met de stad volmaakt. In de 8 m hoge zuil die daar is opgetrokken, weerspiegelt zich moeiteloos de oever, het water, de stad en de lucht.

Een eredipoma ook voor de design van "Jasmique Houseware" voor hun ontwerp van afdekplaatjes voor schakelaars en stopcontacten, vervaardigd uit gerecycleerd materiaal. Ook de reuzegrote installaties van Stan Roukens werden geselecteerd. Zijn machines hebben alles met techniek te maken. Ze overweldigen niet alleen door hun omvang en de kracht die ze uitstralen maar choqueren door het plotse geluid dat ze voortbrengen. Het irreële samenspel van kunst en techniek !

De plechtige prijsuitreiking met academische zitting en muzikale omlijsting gebeurt naar gewoonte ook naar de raadszaal van het Provinciehuis. Voor het 10-jarig bestaan hoopt Christine Malfeyt iemand van de Koninklijke familie uit te nodigen om de prijs uit te reiken.

Annemie Winnepenninckx

Agenda

België

Antwerpen

Cultureel Centrum, Luchtbal,
Groenendaallaan 68
03/542 49 48
Man-Vrouw Photovisies 1968–1976
van 13/11/94 tot 18/12/94
di-vr 14-17 uur, za-zo 10-18 uur

Museum voor Plastische Artsen, Vrijdagmarkt 22
03/231 60 94
Rustrum: Stadion Typografisch naaktheid in de zilveren eeuw
van 12/11/94 tot 15/01/95
di-vr 10-17 uur, za-zo 10-18 uur

Ronny van de Velde Gallery, IJzerenpoortkaai 3
03/238 92 59
Man Ray 1890–1976
van 11/11/94 tot 21/01/95
di-zo 14-18 uur

Provincie Antwerpen

Etnografisch Museum, Suikerrui
Europa's blik op vreemde culturen
Made by Indians
van 26/11/94 tot 12/03/95
di-zo 10-17 uur

Provinciaal Diamantmuseum
Langse Herentalsestraat 31-33
03/202 48 90
Zaderen verlichting: Italiaanse kunstsieraden
van 19/11/94 tot 15/01/95
Van de Wee Naamrijk
van 12/11/94 tot 15/01/95
di-zo 10-17 uur

Volkskundemuseum, Gildekamersstraat 2-6
Volkskundig prentenkabinet
van 03/12/94 tot 30/04/95
di-zo 10-17 uur

Vleeshuis, Vleeshouwersstraat
03/233 64 04
Orgelpark Vlaamse
vol.t 231794

Deurne

Cultureel Centrum Rix, de Groperstraat 86
03/324 68 03
Vijftiger: Luk Van Soom + Philip Aguirre
03/11/94 tot 04/12/94
di-zo 10-17 uur

Sterckshof, Hooftvunderlei 160
03/324 02 11
Schoon verchijnsel: textielen, jewelen, grafieken,
sculptuur 1875–1920
van 09/11/94 tot 12/02/95
di-zo 10-17 uur

Provinciaal Museum voor Fotografie,
Vlaskaai 47
03/232 47 17
Louis Julio Fotograaf - Lucas Samaras
van 18/11/94 tot 29/01/95
di-zo 10-17 uur

Turnhout

Nationaal Museum van de Speelkaart,
Druivenstraat 18
014/41 56 21
Kleurstaalen in Wallonië in de 17de en 19de eeuw
van 14/11/94 tot 12/14/17 uur

In Memoriam Dominique Van Heddegem

Dominique van Heddegem overleed op 28 juli 1994. Een auto-ongeval in Bayonne, aan de grens tussen Spanje en Frankrijk werd haar en Hans, haar jongste zoontje, fataal. De familie was op weg naar huis.

Ik kende Dominique Knockaert zo afzijdelijk in 1981, tijdens Nationaal Hoger Kunsten te Antwerpen, afdeling keramiekkunst. Haar verblijf in Antwerpen werd door haar huwelijk met Johan Knockaert onderbroken. Ze vertrokken naar Vlissingen om door hun huwelijk onder meer. Ondertussen kwam de wijk waar in Antwerpen waar zij sindsdien woonden. Dominique volgde de opleiding ceramiek in de juwelzaak Sterckshof en Dominique kwam op de vestigingszaak. Een jeugdig wonen, een vaste onderzoeksposten.

Joinette vroeg Typenhoffers in 1983, die programmaonderwijs in de CC. Schoppeniek waartin de recenteworden werken was.

Borstvank, 1994
(Pail Inaas Schulp)

Vlaamse Kunstgemeenschap Gent/
Voor deze tentoonstelling op 11 tot en met 6/25 van 1994 onder voorzitterschap van Maurice Van Essche nodigen uitnodigingen bij 3 december 1994, Zaal Hessenhuis, in de CC de Spil (Roeselare), bij Maria Simoen in Sint-Idesbald, in Brouwerij Binks te Turnhout, in Museum Turnhout en in de Galerij Sint-Rochus 9, Gosselies, bij Gert Vande Vijver, Lange Molenstraat 11, Oudenaarde, Vanessa Vlaeminck in Kalmthout en nu binnenkort in de Sterckshof en het Museumbezoek van Vlaanderen. Ook is zij vertegenwoordigd in de privé-collectie Dr. De Bisscher. Van 04/12/84 tot 27/01/95.

Liveart - Art Content
03/236 55 98
Leigestraat 5, Antwerpen
02/233/35/17 34

Nieuws

Korte Berichten

Het Beeld
Wetstraat 50 1040 Brussel
Wetstraat 50 heeft ontwerpen vereiste van Maria
Cabo Van Houten gemaakt. Ze werken er
voornamelijk met hout, rottan-materiaal,
leven, touwen, kaarten, enz.
Heidenbergstraat 9, 2470 Retie.
Tel.: 014/37.94.11 - Fax: 014/37.94.21.
van 3/12/94 tot 29/11/94
di-zo 14-17 uur

Quatrième Biennale "Forme Triëste 1994"
Voor deze biënnale heeft een tentoonstelling
van hedendaagse kunst georganiseerd in de
kathedraal, Triëste, met deelnemers uit de hele
wereld. Keramieken kunstenaars uit volgende
landen: Duitsland, Frankrijk, Italië, Joegoslavië,
Kroatië en Slovenië.
Pnr. Oudenaardseweg 4, 2500 Lier.
Tel.: 03/248.80.58
Fax: 03/248.80.59

Nieuwe bedrijfjes

Les Linens Contemporains
2002–1994 werkgevoerd geconstrueerde 1995.
Het 1 december 1994 verschijnt 1 jaar volgende
nieuwsbrief van de Europese Commissie voor Kunst,
de Linens - Rue St-André des Arts - F 75006 Paris.
Tel.: 0/43.54.19.23
Tel.: 03/248.90.25

Internationale Kunstbeurs
van vrij 20 januari 1995 te Miami
De Internationale Kunstbeurs geeft beurs van
150.000,- voor een 45-tal gerenommeerde
galeries, musea en kunstcentra uit de hele
wereld toezien. Initiatief is afgebakend door
Cultuurcentra & Koning Boudewijnstichting.
Rue Ravenstein, 23, 1000 Brussel.
Tel.: 02/507.82.00 - Fax: 02/507.84.72.
van 1-5/02/95

Prijzen en wedstrijden

Tech-Art Prijs 1995
Aan de Tech-Art Prijs bestaan diverse vereisten.
Gevraagd worden werken van artiesten die
gebruik maken van industriële en technologische
technieken. Ze ontvangen hiervoor een
prijzenpot van BF 100.000,- Art heeft ook de
erepijs voor 500.000,- BF en de kleine prijs van
300.000,- BF, met verder nog 10 eervolle
vermeldingen 15 maart 1995 sluiting van de
inzendingen 9 mei de opening van de
tentoonstelling in het Provinciehuis.
Vlaamse Ingenieurskamer van:
Broederminstraat 9, 2018 Antwerpen.
Tel.: 03/216.55.04

Internationale Prijs Triënaal '95
Na grote plaatsspanen van de buitengewone
triënaal voor de hedendaagse plastische
kunst in België ontsluit tentoonstelling zich
Beeldende Kunstcentrum Bulle-Mistat-Jebus,
1 mei 1995 onder. Dertig kandidaten
van verenigingen van Zuid-Lieve in aanmerking
voor het tentoonstellen in een uitnodiging
van Bouchbal, Turnhout, Slechte Tielen,
Parkoers 350

Beurzen

Art Cannes
De internationale kunstbeurs "Art Cannes"
gaat van 15 tot 22 februari 1995 door. Er worden
exposanten van meer dan 40 landen verwacht.
In zijn opzet staat enorm
ondersteunt. Een driedaags progromma 26-27
mei met in Cannes, dat pays -
Palais des Festivals - 06403 Cannes.
Tel.: 933-74-13-74

Textiel

Internationale Kunstwedstrijd
voor Textiele Kunsten "Alphyl '95"
Op 16 juli 1995 moeten alle gegevens binnen
zijn, op 7 september heeft de selectie plaats.
Inzendingen moet naar: Mr. Jos Fluijs-Puympen
(directeur van de textielafdeling van de Antwerpse
Academie), Franklin Rooseveltpl 18, 2060 Antwerpen.
Tel.: 03/226.88.88 - Fax: 03/226.93.50.

Grafiek

Biënnale Internationale d'Estampes
La Charité-sur-Loire heeft voor 1995 een
biënnale van grafische kunst georganiseerd.
Kunstenaars kunnen deelnemen door
zich in te schrijven met maximaal 3 werken.
Inschrijvingen tot 28 februari 1995.
Details bij Marie-Paule Deville, secrétariat
général, 48 rue Guynemer, 58200 La Charité-sur-Loire (F).

Glas

Third Glass Prize 24 Concorso
Internationale d'Arte Vetraria 1995.
Uit de gegevens zelf kunt u dan ook vaststellen
hoe professioneel men ingeschreven heeft.
Naam, 1995, ni. 1995. 15 maart laatste
inschrijving bij: Associazione Arti di Venezia,
Gotzborg, Sant Gombo 1299 - 30125 Venezia.
Tel.: 041/528.12.44 - Fax: 041/520.68.86.

Keramiek

Steinzeug-Keramik-Prijs
Dit is een biennale van keramiek georganiseerd
door de Städtische Galerie Höhr-Grenzhausen.
De aanmelding kan tot 1 februari 1995 doorgaan.
Kandidaten tussen 18 en 45 jaar kunnen
deelnemen met steenaar en ingevolgd formulier
en ten ten dia's van hun werk. Zowel
sierobjecten als gebruiksvoorwerpen komen
in aanmerking. Nadere informatie bij: Steinzeug-
Keramik-Preis 1995 - Der Westerwaldkreis -
Peter-Altmeier-Platz 1 - 56410 Montabaur (D).

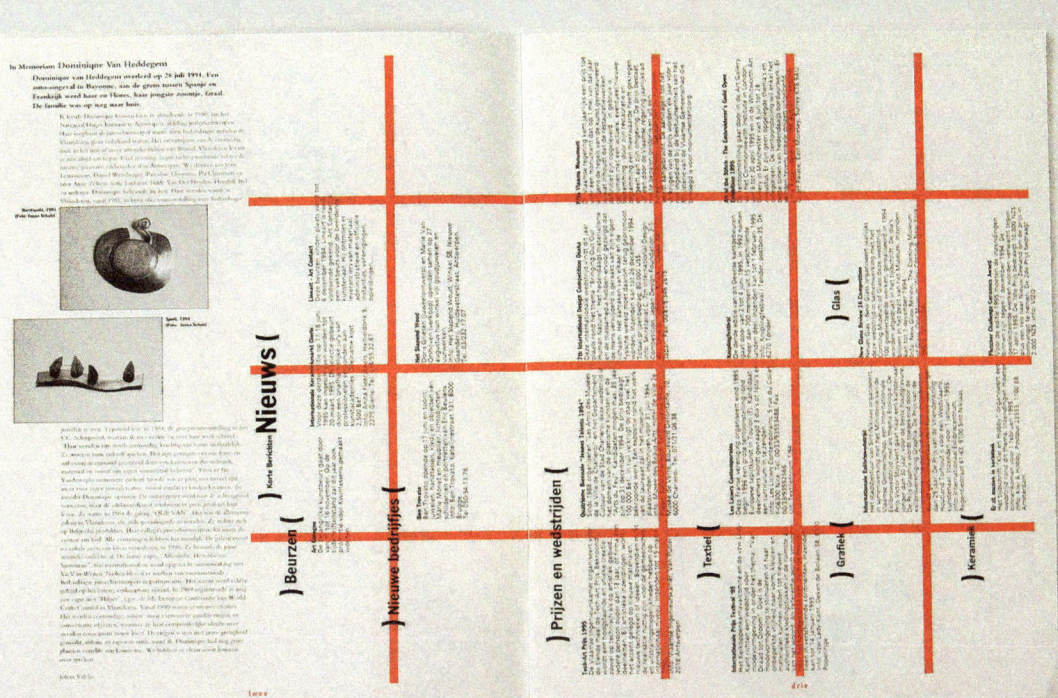

Johan Valcke

fig. 3 (top and bottom left)
Luk Mestdagh
Game to teach fractions to schoolchildren, no date

fig. 4 (right)
Design-Team
Flyer for Jaar van het Kind (Year of the Child), 1979

Mestdagh was known as a critical figure. He was not gentle with his own work either. He approached commissions in an idiosyncratic manner, as an intelligent pictorialist, with clear and sometimes unruly, but always balanced designs. 'As a client, you are better off with an intelligent bad designer than a stupid good one', he once said, laconically. With his comment, 'Did you know that the graphics on Belgian TV are BBC cast-offs?', he denounced the blind trust that clients placed in foreign agencies. In the years that followed, the Vlaamse Radio- en Televisieomroeporganisatie (the public broadcaster of the Flemish Community in Belgium) would repeatedly consult British design studios to restyle their channels – to the frustration of good design studios in Belgium. It annoyed Mestdagh, although he respected some big international studios, like MetaDesign in Berlin or Total Design in Amsterdam.[3]

Convinced that a good designer is a problem solver who dares to question the assignment, Mestdagh was honest and always willing to have an in-depth discussion, especially in his job as a teacher. 'Today, designers are often driven solely by marketing and clients are quickly satisfied with bland, pre-chewed concepts', he said.

> 'Designers must learn to organise themselves better by looking for solutions across disciplinary boundaries. Not easy, because the chair in front of the computer is so safe. Education plays a crucial role in this: rather than opting for a slick design, a course should stimulate students to learn to think in a process-based way and to teach them how to deal with failures. Because it is okay for things to be difficult. That said, as a designer you can stand your ground, unless you choose to be a servile, well-executing, yes-nodding slave. But it can be different, if you have a personality. A solid education can help you to become more alert.'

Are these statements still current? Judge for yourself. Several years ago, a young job applicant turned up to meet him with design that he had plagiarised without batting an eyelid. 'Think a bit more about your work and always sign with your own name', Mestdagh advised him.

---

1   Puttaert, Hugo, 'Michel Olyff – Een beeld als beeltenis', *Addmagazine,* issue 3 (Brussels: Papyrus, 2005), pp.22-24.

2   FontShop International was taken over by Monotype Imaging in 2014.

3   MetaDesign was founded by Erik Spiekermann in Berlin in 1973, and Total Design by Wim Crouwel in Amsterdam in 1963.

Sara De Bondt

MULTI-ART BY LILIANE-EMMA STAAL AND PAUL IBOU

Sara De Bondt (1977) is a graphic designer, teacher, publisher, and researcher. She teaches at KASK School of Arts in Ghent. A version of this text was first published in *Le livre & l'estampe*.[1] See saradebondt.com

The work of Paul Ibou, one of Belgium's most prolific designers, is little-known beyond national borders. Yet his extraordinarily varied output – over 400 logos and more than 250 posters since the late 1950s – deserves wider recognition. Over the course of numerous meetings with Ibou in his home and studio over the past few years, I have come to appreciate his passionate commitment to his practice, and to share his concerns for its legacy. What comes across as particularly relevant for designers today is Ibou's ability to shift between two- and three-dimensional design, his carefree transgressions of the line separating art and design, and his steadfast belief in non-linguistic communication. As he likes to say, quoting Confucius: 'Signs and symbols rule the world, not words or laws'.

As Ibou points out in the video interview I made with him (see pp.104–08), he was recently made honorary citizen of Zoersel, a small town outside Antwerp, where he has lived for five years. During the award ceremony, his life-long partner, Liliane-Emma Staal was referenced several times as someone who helped shape his career.[2] Their brainchild, Multi-Art – an artists' book publishing company, gallery space and bookshop that they co-founded in 1969 – was an exceptional experiment in bridging art and design, and in developing new forms of distribution for hybrid art-design objects. Multi-Art ignored hierarchical publishing structures and invented its own world, where artists and designers worked closely together on printed matter. Alongside Ibou's own radical graphic design, Multi-Art remains, I would argue, a rich source of inspiration for contemporary practitioners (myself included) interested in blurring disciplinary borders.

Staal had graduated with high distinction in Trade Science,[3] was fluent in four languages and was working as a senior executive secretary at the Bunge Institute in Antwerp,[4] when late one night in 1962, she and some friends stumbled into a party at Ibou's studio. The pair were immediately smitten with each other – Ibou describes Staal as 'silent but deep water' – and became inseparable ever since, marrying one year later.[5] In a recent interview, Ibou stresses that Staal was his partner on all levels, in 'creation, business, spirit and being' and that he has had trouble creating new work since she passed away in 2015.[6]

In 1965, when Ibou was appointed as designer for the sculpture exhibition Biënnale Middelheim (Middelheim Biennial), and business started taking off, Staal decided to quit her day job and join his studio as its general manager. The couple were eager travellers from the start, first to the Côte d'Azur and then further afield: Switzerland, Malta, Czech Republic, the US, Mexico, Russia, Egypt, India, Taiwan and China, always trying to reach out to like-minded people, including artists, graphic designers, and writers. Their home archive is brimming with personal correspondence from international designers, such as Hermann Zapf, Saul Bass, Jacques Garamond, Takenobu Igarashi, Wim Crouwel, Josef Müller-Brockmann, and Milton Glaser.

Two years later, Ibou visited Montreal Expo 67, which included architectural icons such as Richard Buckminster Fuller's geodesic US pavilion and the Canadian rainbow-patterned Kaleidoscope Pavilion. He also attended the landmark conference *Vision 67 – Survival and*

Growth in New York, with lectures by Jean Tinguely, Umberto Eco, Victor Vasarely, and Ken Garland, among others. Ibou was on the lookout for business opportunities. He met with George Wallace, owner of Fitchburg Paper Company, and Domenico Mortellito, owner of Dupont de Nemours, who produced coloured films in Wilmington. Both companies would later on provide financial support.

Metamorphosis

The nom de plume 'Ibou' (Paul's real last name is Vermeersch) is a reference to the French word for owl (*hibou*), a symbol for solitary, bookish people who live at night. When Staal and Ibou moved to a countryside farm in Nijlen, outside of Antwerp, they baptised it Uilenhoeve (Owl Farm). It was there that *Metamorphosis: illegible color variation book* (1967, figs. 2) was born. 'Like a baby', Ibou has said, 'it was unstoppable'.[7]

Ibou calls himself a 'multi-artist', someone who simultaneously produces art and design. The two fields feed each other; in the evenings at Uilenhoeve, he started experimenting with paper samples and offcuts from his design studio, trying out new ways of folding, scoring and cutting. He discovered the magic of overlaying colours of Letraset films, and the first result was the geometric *Sun Calendar* (1963, figs. 1), a stunning explosion of colour.

From the start, grids featured prominently in Ibou's designs, and this structure influenced *Metamorphosis,* a large, square, blank artist's book, each page die-cut into different geometric shapes, interlaid with transparent coloured films. What makes the book so special is these films, which allow 'readers' to layer colours, thereby creating a feeling of depth and allowing for an active role in the book's discovery. As Ibou explains:

figs. 1 (below)
Paul Ibou
Sun Calendar, 1963

figs. 2 (opposite)
Paul Ibou
Metamorphosis, 1967

'Thanks to the die-cut shapes, flat tints can become three-dimensional. A red plane leans against a blue plane and creates a visual line, and that is where I start my incision. I place different die-cut planes of colour on top of each other, which creates movement and three-dimensionality. People can interact with it and become participant in the subject. It somehow entices play.'[8]

Or, as the artist Anne-Mie Van Kerckhoven recently put it, after selecting *Metamorphosis* as her favourite artist's book: 'a slow animated movie (...) free, playful, sexy, smooth and intelligent'.[9] Emphasising his interest in communicating with geometric forms instead of letters, Ibou wrote that with '*Metamorphosis* the idea of the book is completely re-thought. The word has been replaced by a changing game of shapes and symbols, the alphabet is refreshed, enriched, rendered inexhaustible.'[10]

Ibou acknowledges the influence of the *libri illeggibili* (1949–50) by Bruno Munari, whose work he had seen at the *Vision in Motion / Motion in Vision* (1958) exhibition by G58 at the Hessenhuis, Antwerp, a few houses down from Photogravure De Schutter where he was working at the time.[11] But *Metamorphosis* also betrays Ibou's admiration for the artists Josef Albers, Sol Lewitt, Dieter Rot, and Vasarely, many of whom he and Staal had met during their travels.[12]

It was a school friend, the artist Jef Verheyen, together with author Ivo Michiels, who urged Staal and Ibou to get *Metamorphosis* published, and suggested Monas, 'the one-man publishing house of the poet Henri-Floris Jespers'.[13] On 9 May 1968, the book was launched in the Ostheriet House in Antwerp. Each of the 1,000 copies was lavishly packaged in a patterned, silver-foil box, inlaid with purple velvet. Ibou's former employer, Photogravure De Schutter, helped fund production. It was printed by De Bièvre on the outskirts of Antwerp and the colour

fig. 3
Paul Ibou at work in his studio, 1969

films were supplied by Dupont de Nemours.[14] Monas eventually went bankrupt, and its successor Mercator lost most of the copies of the book in a storage flooding. Unsurprisingly, therefore, *Metamorphosis* has become a highly sought-after collector's item.

Multi-Art Press

In 1969, during another trip to New York, Staal and Ibou opened a business address on Fifth Avenue,[15] and their agent André Wouters, cultural advisor of the Belgian embassy, donated a copy of *Metamorphosis* to the library of the Museum of Modern Art.[16] It was in a lunch meeting with Richard E. Oldenburg, the Head of Publications at MoMA,[17] that the idea of Multi-Art Press was born.[18]

The idea behind Multi-Art Press was to 'publish paper or cardboard artworks in collaboration with artists and designers'. As Staal and Ibou made clear to a journalist at the time, Multi-Art aimed to democratise access to art and design, and render it more participative:

> 'Paper or cardboard artworks are blank, die-cut, scored or folded sculptures. This form of expression is a reaction against highly expensive paintings and objects. They come in a handy size, and people can carry them in their suitcase. The art moves and viewers can interact with it: through folding, gluing, participating. (...) The contemporary notion comes full circle: democratisation, consumption, participation.'[19]

The company Multi-Art Press was legally registered on 4 June 1970 under 50/50 co-ownership of Paul Vermeersch (Ibou's given name) and Jozef De Wolf, owner of Grafo Printers.[20] Grafo had been one of the businesses owned by Ibou's father, and as a child he had found a second home there, playing with paper cuttings on the printshop floor. Grafo not only became a regular client but also a sponsor of Staal and Ibou's many publishing projects, together with paper merchants such as Scaldia, Bührmann Papier and Epacar. Multi-Art Press also received financial support from Georges Plouvier (successor of Staal's uncle at one of Antwerp's oldest and wealthiest companies, Kreglinger Holding) and Fernand Bertrand (Director of Bank van Parijs en de Nederlanden).[21]

Even though she was not a co-owner, Staal was the driving force behind Multi-Art Press, unpaid and full-time.[22] She is listed as 'Managing' on Multi-Art's promotional material, and press coverage from the time is unambiguous about Staal's leading role in the venture.[2] Photographic documentation shows her surrounded by dignitaries at openings, giving speeches during launches, or presenting works to journalists (figs. 6).

Paper Art

In its first six months, Multi-Art produced a series of 14 multiples entitled *Paper Art*, commissioned from artists, architects and designers, including Verheyen (fig. 5), Paul Van Hoeydonck, Slothouber & Graatsma, Günther Kirchberger (fig. 4), Ibou, Gilles Fiszman, Ad Dekkers, Marinus Boezem and César Bailleux. In an interview, Staal specified that all those who were contacted 'reacted enthusiastically. They were immediately able to integrate working with paper and cardboard into their way of thinking'.[24] She goes on to describe the personal approaches taken by each invited artist or designer: 'Someone like Kirchberger, who is professor at the Werkkunstschule (School of Applied Arts) in Krefeld, can supply a prototype that is worked out in detail and ready for production. Sometimes, however, an artist just submits a drawing, a project, an idea.'[25]

Multi-Art's first series set the tone for its radical agenda: it dared to bring together very different practitioners (although most of them men) and did not shy away from conceptual or production-related challenges. Verheyen, who had represented Belgium at the 1970 Venice Biennial, produced the interactive object *Multiple AB=BC*, a 'variable, tri-dimensional multiple which can be arranged in an endless configuration.'[26] For his part, conceptual Dutch artist Boezem made *Paper Events*, a 'curious booklet in white paper',[27] packaged in a small, transparent plastic bag and designed to be destroyed. Boezem pushed Paper Art to its limits by inviting the reader-user to 'cut; wrinkle and throw away; cut; tear; soak in water; hang in open window; burn rest of book and keep in plastic bag'.[28]

fig. 4 (opposite, top)
Günther Kirchberger
Folding Object I, 1971

fig. 5 (opposite, bottom)
Jef Verheyen
Multiple AB=BC, 1971

figs. 6 (below)
Liliane-Emma Staal at Multi-Art events, 1969–72

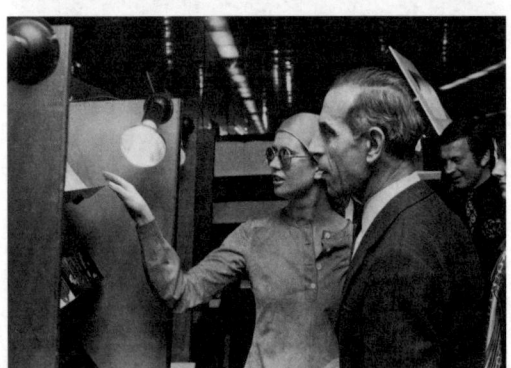

Paper Art met with considerable success. Thanks to Staal and Ibou's connections, the series was launched at several venues in Belgium and the Netherlands, with over 600 people attending the Antwerp event, according to a newsletter. To encourage distribution, the series was presented in a small catalogue titled *Prospectus 1*, designed by Multi-Art Press.[29] Most editions were produced in small print runs, with the exception of Verheyen's, which came in an edition of 500 copies. It was Ibou's own *12 Owl Variations* (1970, fig. 7) – a figurative, owl-inspired take on *Metamorphosis* – that won Paper Art its first prize, the prestigious Italian Diano Marina book award in 1971.

fig. 7 (previous spread)
Paul Ibou
12 Owl Variations, 1970

Multi-Art Gallery

In her September 1971 newsletter, Staal announced the opening of 'an exclusive Multiple Gallery & Bookshop' on Groendalstraat in Antwerp.[30] The announcement includes images of the renovation of a restaurant into a shopfront, with a gallery on the left and bookstore on the right. According to Ibou, it was the first art book shop in Flanders.

One excited journalist contrasted Multi-Art Gallery to 'a cold exhibition space', comparing it to a 'bazar, where wide-ranging objects will be on display: multiples (paper and others), small original artworks, sculptures, catalogues, brochures, posters, art magazines, litho prints, screen prints, etc.' The same journalist noted the pedagogical and democratising potential of the Gallery: 'The arrangement has a big informative value. All catalogues of modern art manifestations in Europe and the US will be available for perusal in the gallery. Young people cannot afford to visit all important exhibitions abroad. One has to ask a friend to import a catalogue, because it cannot be purchased in one's own country. This becomes possible now.'[31]

For the Gallery's first exhibition, *24 Originals + Paper Art* (1971), original artworks were combined with multiples from the Paper Art series. Meanwhile, the team was expanding: Erik Claus designed a poster of a three-dimensional number 24 (fig. 10), Patrick Conrad manned the desk, Theo Bonné helped out with public relations and Danielle Engelen acted as shop manager.[32]

Of Bruno Munari's contribution – *3 Paper Sculptures* (fig. 8) – only photographic documentation seems to remain. The object is similar to his travel sculptures, which he started making in the late 1940s and which had inspired Staal and Ibou to produce paper objects in the first place.[33] Another contribution of which no physical trace remains is *Ultraviolet* by Roberte Mestdagh, despite its relatively high print run of 120 copies. Albert Szukalski's contribution, on the other hand, did survive: for *Neuzen/Neuzen (Noses/Noses*, 1971) he glued a small nose sculpture in the middle of the catalogue for his exhibition at the Koninklijk Museum voor Schone Kunsten Antwerp (Royal Museum of Fine Arts Antwerp). Spiral-bound around each copy are photographs of different faces (including Ibou's), which are cut into three horizontal strips, inviting the reader to combine them to create new portraits.

fig. 8
Bruno Munari
3 Paper Sculptures, 1971

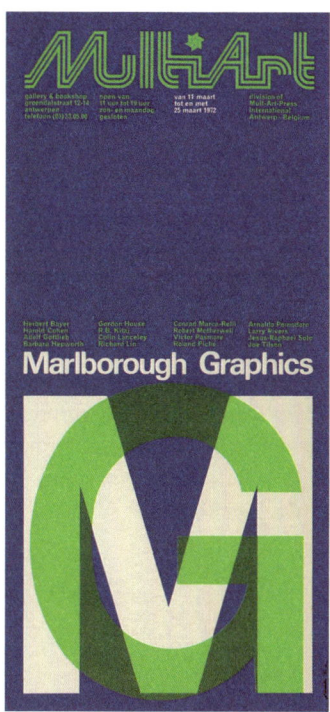
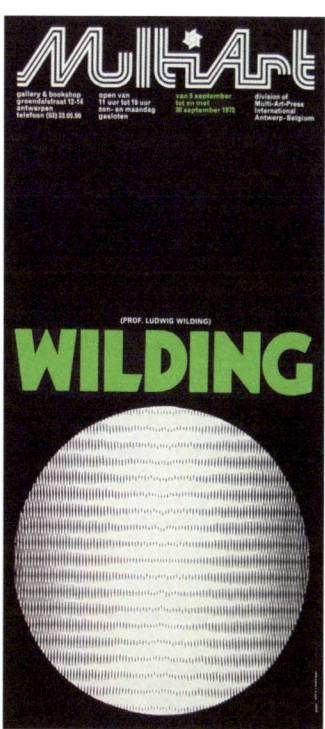

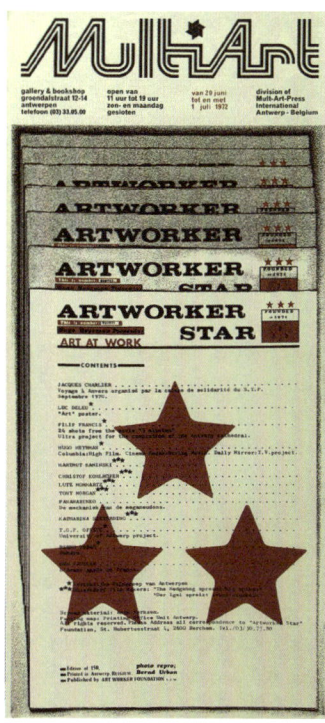

figs. 9
Paul Ibou
Posters for exhibitions at Multi-Art Gallery, 1970–72

fig. 10 (bottom right)
Paul Ibou and Erik Claus
Poster for Paper Art exhibition Multi-Art Gallery, 1971

At this time, Multi-Art's own editions decreased in print run and increased in price. Among the artists who created Paper Art for the second series were Cel Overberghe, Walter Leblanc, Pierre Heyvaert, Hermann Goepfert, Jo Delahaut and Herman Devries, Michael Michaeledes, and Mark Verstockt. Yet it is clear that Multi-Art was beginning to show signs of financial strain. Staal started importing editions published by others, in swap agreements with partners such as Marlborough Graphics (London), Edition Olympia 1972 (Munich) and Edition der Spiegel (Cologne). Multi-Art Gallery's second newsletter includes an expanded sales catalogue from these other presses with prints by the likes of Albers, Herbert Bayer, Max Bill, Robert Filliou, Karl Gerstner, Barbara Hepworth, and Willem Sandberg. In a further sign that the Gallery was facing financial headwinds, one newsletter resembles an annual report, emphasising Multi-Art's popular openings, attended by ambassadors and politicians, and coverage on national television.

The last chapter

In July 1972, Multi-Art produced an over-the-top publication to celebrate Verheyen's 40th birthday. Not only was it oversized, but it also carried an inflated price tag of 28,000 Belgian Francs. It was launched with a lavish reception at the Museum Plantin-Moretus in Antwerp with speeches by Staal and local dignitaries.

Two months later, Multi-Art's story came to an abrupt end. On 1 September 1972, one of the company's backers, Georges Plouvier, died in a car crash. Unable to secure additional funding, Multi-Art was closed on 27 February 1973. Plans for a pocket-book series and several titles with artist Pol Mara had to be shelved, as did Staal's intention to produce at least four more series of Paper Art. The ending was painful. She returned to her job as Ibou's manager, which she continued until her retirement in 2002.[34]

Many years later, at the opening of the exhibition *Collectie Paul Ibou van Creatieve en Alternatieve Boek-Vorm-Realisaties (Paul Ibou's Collection of Creative and Alternative Book-Object-Realisations)* at Limburgs Universitair Centrum in Diepenbeek in 1983, Ibou gave a speech about the future of the book, where he pre-empted today's flurry of independent artist's book making:

> 'Design is an instrument for the message. It needs to be a clear announcement in the most remarkable shape. (...) Book designers need to be given more chances, and recognised better as specialists who will make the book survive, especially when we are talking about the cultural identity of tomorrow's book. (...) I plead for more freedom for book designers (...) I plead for publishers and commissioners to take more risks, so that the conventions and the conventional can be shattered, in order to create a new way of reading, looking and feeling.'[35]

1. Pas, Johan; Colpaert, Rika; Dockx, Nico (eds.), *Le livre & l'estampe*, n.190, 2019, pp.30–47.
2. Paulus, Camille, *Laudatio* and Ibou, Paul, *Dankwoord*, both unpublished, 2019, p.1 and p.3.
3. *Curriculum vitae: Liliane Emma Staal 73*, unpublished, undated, Paul Ibou Archive.
4. Ibou, Paul, *Hommage: Liliane-Emma Staal, 2.09.1939–10.01.2015*, unpublished, 2016, p.2, Paul Ibou Archive.
5. Conversation by the author with Paul Ibou, 31 August 2017.
6. Claeys, Guinevere, 'Paul Ibou, Verzamelaar van vormen' in *dS Weekblad*, 14 April 2018, n.343, p.30.
7. Conversation by the author with Paul Ibou, 31 August 2017.
8. Vandermeerschen, Rafaël, 'Design is nog assepoes in ons gezegend landje' in *Spectator*, 23 August 1975, no.34, pp.21–25.
9. http://kunstenaarsboeken.kunsten.be/nl; last accessed on 15 April 2019.
10. Ibou, Paul, *Iboubook* (self-published, 1974), unpaginated.
11. De Bruyn, Frans, 'Paper Art Multiples' in *Delta International*, date unknown, p.105.
12. Conversation by the author with Paul Ibou, 21 September 2018.
13. De Bruyn, 'Paper Art Multiples', p.105.
14. Ibou, Paul, *Aan wijlen mijn vriend Jef Verheyen: Terugblik op Metamorphosis, 25 jaar geleden*, unpublished manuscript, 1993, p.2.
15. Stuyck, Raymond, *De Winners: Gesprekken met suksesmensen* (Antwerp: Brito, 1972), p.79.
16. Letter from librarian acknowledging receipt, 1969, Paul Ibou Archive.
17. Vogel, Carol, 'Oldenburg Quits as Head of Modern' in *New York Times*, 10 September 1993.
18. Email from Paul Ibou to the author, 8 October 2017.
19. De Bruyn, 'Paper Art Multiples', p.108.
20. Staatsblad, no.1704–4, 1970.
21. Depuydt, Piet, 'Ik ben geen dinosaurus die met uitsterven is bedreigd in *De Tijd*, 30 August 2014.
22. Staal, Liliane-Emma, letter, 7 March 1973, Paul Ibou Archive.
23. Professor Van Jole, Marcel, opening speech, Gallerit Center, 1 December 1970, Paul Ibou Archive.
24. De Bruyn, 'Paper Art Multiples', p.106.
25. *Ibid.*
26. Staal, Liliane-Emma, *Prospectus 1*.
27. *Ibid.*
28. Boezem, *Paper Events* (Antwerp: Multi-Art Press, 1970), cover.
29. Staal, Liliane-Emma, *Prospectus 1*, pp.12 & 14.
30. Staal, Liliane-Emma, *News 1* (Antwerp: Multi-Art Press, September 1971).
31. Sterckx, Piet, 'Liliane E. Staal; de eerste multipel-galerij voor Antwerpen' in *De Nieuwe Gazet*, 15 October 1971.
32. Sterckx, Piet, 'MultiArt gallery maakt internationale furore' in *De Nieuwe Gazet*, 1972.
33. http://www.munart.org/index.php?p=19; last accessed on 24 April 2019.
34. Staal, Liliane-Emma, 'Overzicht', unpublished letter, September 1973, Paul Ibou Archive.
35. Ibou, Paul, *Collectie Paul Ibou: Van creatieve en alternatieve boek-vorm-realisaties, 24 March–24 April 1983* (Diepenbeek: Limburgs Universitair Centrum, 1983), pp.1–10.

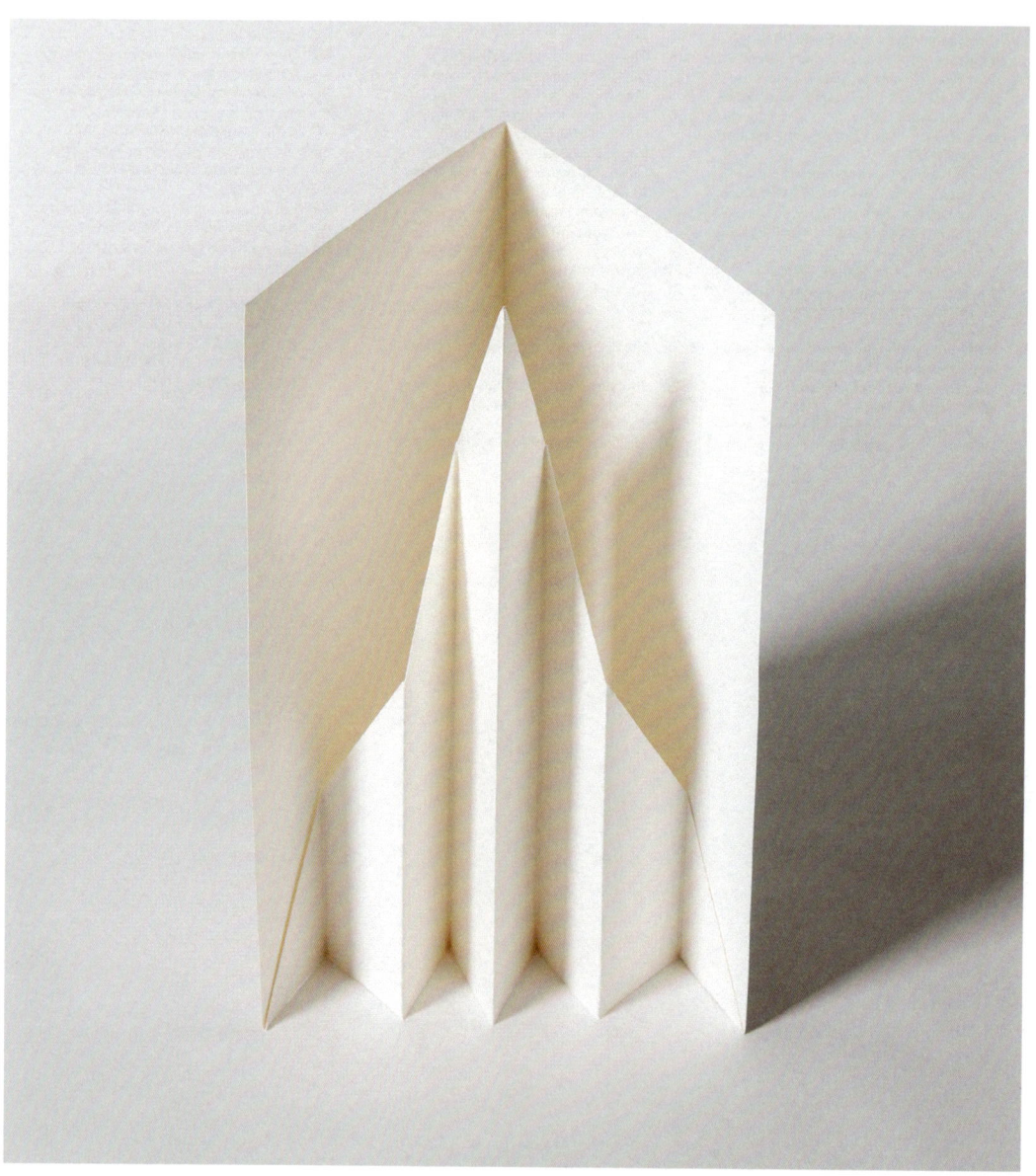

fig. 11
Gilles Fiszman
Cathedral Card, 1971

fig. 12
Albert Szukalski
Neuzen/Neuzen (Noses/Noses), 1971

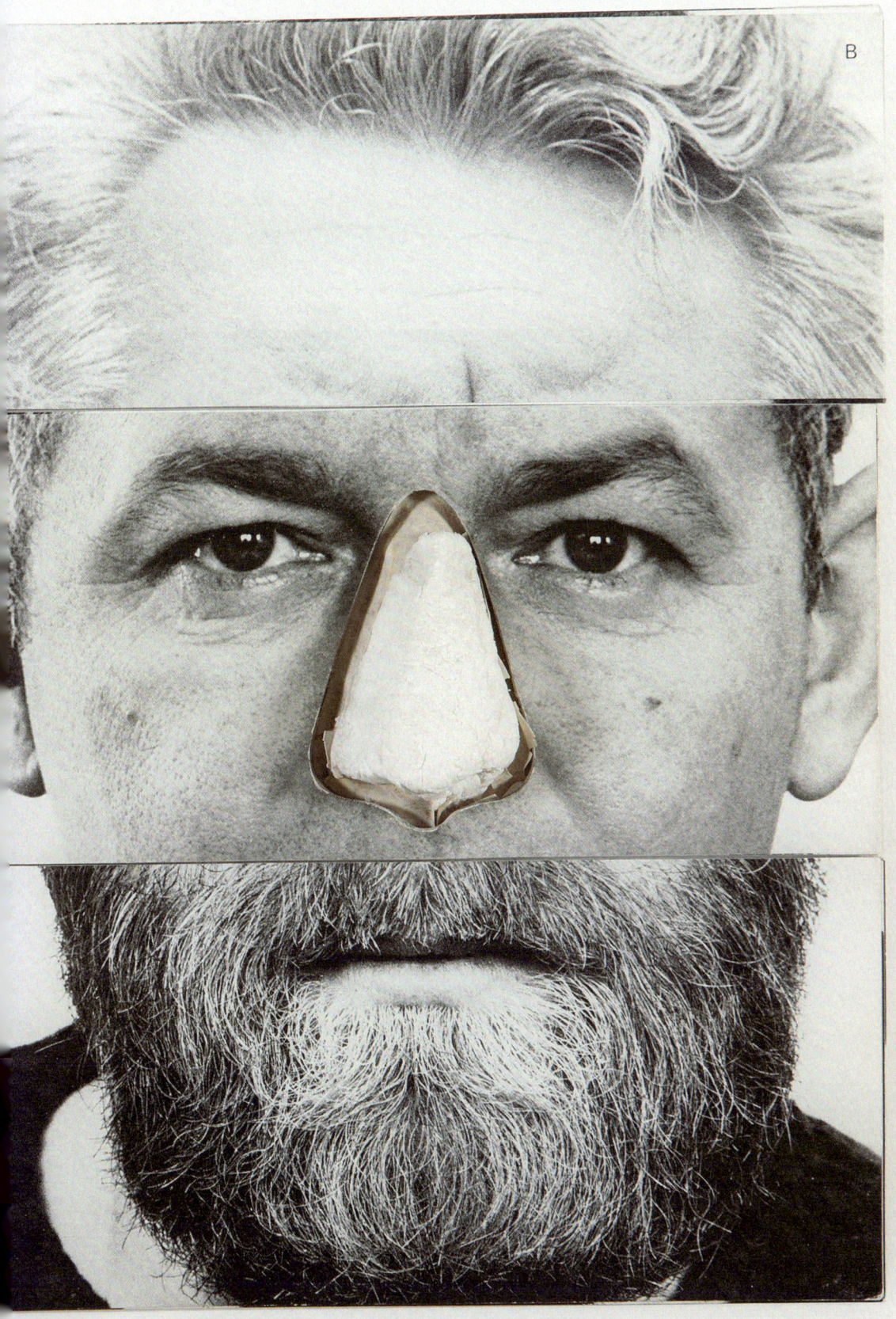

Multi-Art Press	zal met medewerking van internationaal bekende kunstenaars en designers uit verschillende landen, op basis van papier en karton, multiples realiseren en publiceren, onder de vorm van speciale boeken, portfolios, kalenders, wenskaarten, plooikaarten, enz. bedrukt en onbedrukt, in reliëf en uitgekapt met doorzichtige en kinetische effecten. enz.
Multi-Art Press	zal regelmatig een publicitaire promotie met reprodukties van de uitgaven laten verschijnen. Bestellingen kunnen per post gebeuren. Kunstgalerijen, boekwinkels, uitgevers, kulturele organisaties, e.a. zullen als medeverdeler optreden.
Multi-Art Press	kan, en dit op verzoek, naam en wensen opdrukken op voornoemde uitgaven.
Multi-Art Press	zal een hoofdbureau in Antwerpen en New York hebben en postadressen in Amsterdam, Frankfurt, Londen, Milaan, Parijs, Zürich, enz.
Multi-Art Press	heeft de bedoeling beperkte oplagen met hoge standing en kwaliteit te verzorgen, die als kunst-objecten of relatiegeschenken kunnen beschouwd worden, en dit voor de moderne kunstliefhebber van vandaag.
Multi-Art Press	dankt U voor uw bijzondere belangstelling en hoopt op uw medewerking te mogen rekenen.

Multi-Art Press   Antwerpen/New York

fig. 12
Paul Ibou
Promotion for Multi-Art Press, no date

fig. 13
Paul Van Hoeydonck
Silver City, 1971

fig. 14
César Bailleux
Moon Project I, 1971

fig. 15
Slothouber & Graatsma
Changeable Cubic Color, 1971

Hugo Puttaert

MICHEL OLYFF: IMAGE AS EFFIGY

Hugo Puttaert (1960) is a graphic designer, facilitator, professor, and editor. He trained as a visual artist at Sint-Lukas, Brussels (now LUCA) and worked for ten years as a graphic artist before founding his studio, visionandfactory, in 1990. He teaches graphic design at Sint Lucas Antwerpen. Since 2007, he has organised the biennial Integrated conference in deSingel, Antwerp. He has been a speaker at various international design conferences and symposia, worked on diverse magazines, and was the editor-in-chief of *Addmagazine*. This text is an expanded version of an article first published in *Addmagazine*.[1]
See visionandfactory.be

A smiling, grey-haired man stood in the doorway of a stately townhouse in Haut-Ittre, Belgium. Inside, the warmth of the interior welcomed us. It was immediately clear that we had all the ingredients for an inspiring studio visit.

Michel Olyff was born in Antwerp, in 1927, the son of an engineer, Hubert Olyff, and Claire De Vigne, a descendant of a well-known artist family. In his spare time, Olyff senior was an illustrator, poster maker, and notorious antagonist. In 1949, he published the book *ULB 20-26*, with caricatures of all the professors at the Université Libre de Bruxelles, which he had secretly made during his studies. Consequently, a degree of contradiction is in Olyff junior's blood.

In the winter of 1945, at barely 18 years old, Olyff left high school to join the Brigade Piron, an infantry group under Allied command during World War II. He was soon injured during a campaign in the Netherlands, in an accident with an armored vehicle. In 1947, he began a course in book illustration at La Cambre. While studying, he founded Les Ateliers du Marais in Brussels in 1948, with Pierre Alechinsky. It was a community centre where artists such as Jan Cox, Luc de Heusch, Reinhoud d'Haese, Olivier Strebelle, and Asger Jorn were frequent guests. Between 1953 and 1963, he lived with his family in Nieuwpoort, on the Belgian coast, and later settled in Haut-Ittre on the outskirts of Brussels. Many years later, his daughter Clotilde followed in his footsteps as a graphic and typeface designer.

A thorough analysis of Olyff's work requires more room than the limited space of this text. His studio houses a multitude of objects, posters, drawings, and all kinds of graphic elements. The many drawers, cupboards, and piles of files hide an even greater wealth. As a sort of multi-designer, like many of his contemporaries, Olyff not only designed logos (some of which are still in use), including for Radio-télévision belge de la Communauté française (Belgian Radio-television of the French Community, RTBF), Europalia, the Loterie Nationale (National Lottery), and Musées royaux des Beaux-Arts de Belgique (Royal Museum of Fine Arts of Belgium) (figs. 1), but also designed countless typefaces, posters, and books, and produced paintings, linocuts, woodcuts, and lithographs. During our conversation, he dug up a document in which he explained in minute detail the difference between pictograms, ideograms, monograms, logotypes, emblems, and symbols. He regards this as required knowledge to be able to understand and apply these elements and techniques. In 2007, his 80th birthday was celebrated with exhibitions in La Maison de la Culture in Namur, and during the renowned *Rencontres Internationales de Lure (International meetings of Lure)*, in Provence, where he was a frequent guest.

figs. 1
Michel Olyff
Logos for RTBF, 1967; Europalia, 1969; Loterie Nationale, 1969; and Musées royaux des Beaux-Arts de Belgique, 1973

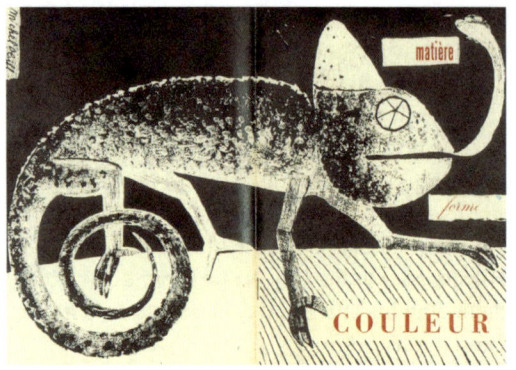 

Olyff's career thus started in Les Ateliers du Marais, where the international Cobra movement also settled. These influences are visible in his work. He points to a drawing in washed Indian ink: 'I don't paint the tree, I paint the surroundings. The tree emerges spontaneously.' It seems like a witticism, but it typifies his working method and attitude. He studies the image from outside, until it takes on a certain shape. This allows him to abstract – a technique designers use when stylising. Drawing and painting enable him to search for different ways of image-making. Sometimes this filters through in his design work.

figs. 2
Michel Olyff
Illustrations, no date

That is why Olyff is difficult to sum up as an artist/designer in a single description. He is a maximalist who can also be very minimalist, and vice versa. Previously, figures such as Wim Crouwel and Josef Müller-Brockmann developed their work from a Constructivist idea, based on grids and a strict typography. Their oeuvre is strongly linked to the possibilities offered by the new reproduction and printing techniques of that period. Olyff's work, by contrast, especially in the early period, is more in the tradition of figures such as Lucien De Roeck, his teacher at La Cambre (see p.230–39). It is about a visual language that arose from an interaction between artists, painters, and illustrators, with graphic stylisations that emerge, for example, from the woodcarving technique. Letters, often hand-drawn, were intertwined in and part of the image. This shows the influence of Raymond Savignac and Julien Keymolen (or Julian Key), known for their advertising posters. It must be said that Olyff's later work evolved significantly. His logos are distinguished by their geometric configuration and simplicity, a style characteristic of the 1960s and 1970s, without losing their illustrative aspect.

fig. 3
Michel Olyff
Illustration of Les Ateliers du Marais, Brussels, *Cobra* magazine, no.7, 1950

There is a fascinating anecdote about one of his iconic logos. In 1971, Olyff received an unexpected call from designer Peter Kneebone – co-founder of the International Council of Graphic Design Associations (Icograda, then based in London) – asking if he would like to design the logo for UNESCO's International Year of the Book (fig. 4). The fee was next to nothing, so initially Olyff was sceptical. But during the phone call, the two came to an agreement – and by the time Olyff was on board, he had already sketched a rough draft of the logo. It illustrates that the work of a driven and smart designer sometimes emerges quickly, but only takes its final shape after a thorough process. In 1978, Olyff, together with Gilles Fiszman, would develop another UNESCO logo, this time for the protection of world heritage (fig. 5).

fig. 4 (left)
Michel Olyff
Logo for UNESCO's International Year of the Book, 1971

fig. 5 (right)
Gilles Fiszman and Michel Olyff
Logo for UNESCO World Heritage, 1978

Olyff was always particular when it came to fees. In 1972, for example, he contributed to the drafting of pay scales for the Chambre Belge des Graphistes (Belgian Chamber of Graphic Designers, see p.69), of which he was the chairman between 1972 and 1974. He had good links with designers abroad, such as Crouwel and Ben Bos in the Netherlands. In 1966, at the invitation of his British colleague Henri Kay Henrion, he was nominated as a member of the Alliance Graphique Internationale.

In 1982, Olyff designed the somewhat bizarre poster for the Saint-Martin festivities in Tourinnes-la-Grosse, a picturesque village nestling in the slopes of Walloon Brabant (fig. 6). The iconic work is reminiscent of the famous later designs of the American Stefan Sagmeister. This has to do with the approach. Olyff wanted to design a poster according to a traditional crochet technique. He drew horizontal and vertical lines, free-handed with a Rotring pen, on large sheets of paper. He then filled in with thread pattern here and there, until a figure became visible. He did this with bold line drawing, without a single addition, except for his own signature. The design was then transferred to film and printed in two colours, with a stunning result.

fig. 6
Michel Olyff
Poster for Saint-Martin festivities in Tourinnes-la-Grosse, 1982 (detail)

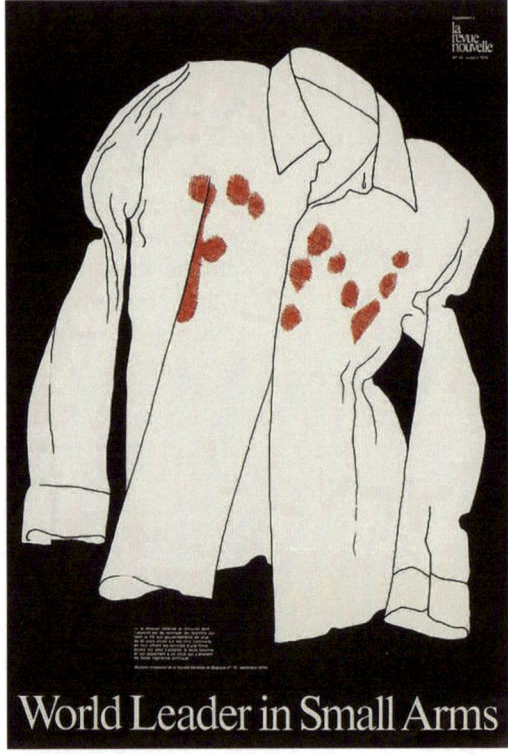

figs. 7 (clockwise from top left)
Michel Olyff
Illustration, no date
Magazine supplement, protest against arms producer Fabrique Nationale Herstal, 1974
Advert for Tigra cigarettes, no date
Invitation for screening at Les mardis de l'écran du Séminaire des Arts, Brussels, 1958

This design demonstrates Olyff's approach. He was able to combine ideas, technical skills, and experiment in a decisive way. Designers like him, who often still worked in an analogue manner, could visualise the end result in their heads and estimate the effect of various techniques. Everything had to be thought out in advance, because the execution was complex and expensive. Once a design was prepared for print by the repro- or lithographer, there was little room for turning back, unless you started all over again.

At the start of his career, Olyff also designed iconic advertising posters – a fusion of stylised illustrations, graphic elements such as grids, and hand-drawn typefaces. He also used transfer or adhesive letters, but only the photocopies of them (he left the original sheets in pristine condition). The grids were also drawn on with a pen.

During my visit, a laptop in the corner of his studio caught my eye. When I hesitantly asked him if he had any digital files, he sat down immediately and copied the files onto a USB stick. Like others of his generation, his work spans a time period in which graphic design evolved from the artisanal/analogue to the digital in just a few decades. It therefore does not seem inappropriate to qualify him as a 'genuine multimedia professional'.

fig. 8
Michel Olyff
Woodcut, 1950

1 Puttaert, Hugo, 'Michel Olyff – Een beeld als beeltenis', *Addmagazine,* issue 4 (Brussels: Papyrus, 2007), pp.32–37.

Jean-Michel Meyers

LUCIEN DE ROECK

Jean-Michel Meyers (1974) is an independent graphic designer. Born in Brussels, he studied at Sint Lucas Antwerpen. He has made book designs for, among others, Nico Dockx, Jules Wabbes, Anton Cotteleer, Caroline Coolen, and Frank Wagemans. Meyers has also designed comic books for François Avril, Philippe Berthet, Yves Chaland, and others. His practice includes the design of posters, magazines, records, catalogues, flyers, and illustrations. He is the director of the Lucien De Roeck Foundation. See jeanmichelmeyers.be and lucienderoeck.be

Lucien De Roeck was a Belgian graphic designer, typographer, set designer, illustrator, poster designer, draughtsman, teacher – and my grandfather. He was born in 1915 and wanted to become an architect, but that was not financially feasible for his parents. In 1933, he went on to study publicity and display at La Cambre. It was during his studies in Brussels that he developed an admiration for the artist and architect Henry van de Velde, the founder and director of the school. Inspired by his work, De Roeck developed his mantra: 'Go to the essence'. One of the teachers there, the etcher and artist Joris Minne, also had a great influence on him.

Expo 58

During an extra year at La Cambre, he immersed himself further in typography. De Roeck soon started designing lettering by drawing unique letterforms for each job. After winning a competition, he created two important designs at the age of 19: 'Antwerpen' (1934, see p.41) and 'O(o)stende-Dover 3 Heures Uur' (1935, fig. 1). Both were hand-drawn and airbrushed, including the letters. As a result of the recognition he received for them, he already had loyal customers by the time he graduated, such as the Nationaal Instituut voor de Radio-omroep (National Institute for Radio Broadcast) and the Palais des Beaux-Arts (Centre for Fine Arts) in Brussels. In 1939, De Roeck designed the typographical poster for the Concours international de danse (International Dance Competition, fig. 2). He used Peignot, the typeface designed by his other great role model, the French designer Cassandre.

fig. 1
Lucien De Roeck
Poster O(o)stende-Dover, 1935

fig. 2
Lucien De Roeck
Poster for Concours international de danse (International Dance Competition), 1939

In 1941, at the invitation of van de Velde, De Roeck started teaching at La Cambre. He taught typography to, among others, Michel Olyff, Jean-Michel Folon, Boudewijn Delaere, and Pierre Alechinsky. He was very proud that he was asked to design the poster for the 25th anniversary of the Palais des Beaux-Arts, and that his former student, Alechinsky, was later asked to do the same for the 50th anniversary.

LA LANTERNE
LE PHARE
LE QUOTIDIEN

At the start of his career, De Roeck worked for numerous Belgian newspapers; he drew portraits, plans, logos, and designed layouts (figs. 2). In 1954, he won a professional competition to design the logo for the World's Fair in Brussels, a first round of the contest having ended without success. The star he drew is now his most famous achievement. It was De Roeck's choice to only use the figures 58, and not the full year, 1958. As a result, we still talk about Expo 58. He also designed one of the four official posters, a green field with a blue sky and the geometric lettering 'Brussel 58 Algemene Wereldtentoonstelling' (Brussels 58 General World's Fair) (fig. 4).

figs. 2
Lucien De Roeck
Newspaper logos, 1940s

fig. 3 (left)
Lucien De Roeck
Exhibition stand for *L'eau (Water)*, late 1930s

fig. 4 (opposite)
Lucien De Roeck
Poster for *Expo 58*, 1956

New Year's greetings

In the years that followed, De Roeck continued to work steadily on many typographical posters. Playing with letters and numbers had become a passion for him, in sharp contrast to the many photographic designs popular at that time. Sometimes, he combined this with his own illustrations, for example for charities such as UNICEF.

In 1966, he took part in a competition to design the 20 and 50 Belgian Franc banknotes. His designs were not selected. On the back of a drawing De Roeck wrote: 'Declined for reasons of technique and taste, I have enjoyed working on these projects.' Later, he told me that the jury found his designs 'too modern'.

De Roeck occasionally provided graphic design for commercial clients, but he did so with less enthusiasm (fig. 6 and figs. 9). From 1945 onwards, he mainly earned a living as a teacher at three higher education colleges: La Cambre, Sint Lucas Antwerpen, and L'école technique féminine (Women's Technical Academy) in Saint-Ghislain.

fig. 5
Lucien De Roeck
Illustration of La Cambre, no date

fig. 6
Lucien De Roeck
Advert for Ucemine Becum, no date

figs. 7
Lucien De Roeck
New year's greeting cards, 1977, 1964, 1968 and 1972

Partly because of his teaching, De Roeck was able to focus more on interesting and unexpected projects. His work evolved towards abstraction, and his working methods became increasingly personal. One of his pet projects was New Year's greetings cards (figs. 7), which he sent to his circle of friends and acquaintances, many of whom were designers. He worked out a different idea into a unique design every year, with great attention and precision. For 1964, he used an asymmetrical composition of overlapping black number fours. He also signed a personalised envelope for each addressee. If they had ever designed a stamp, as had Olyff, De Roeck invariably used it for the envelope. Many recipients kept these objects, which looked like little artworks. 'When we eat a banana, we throw away the peel,' joked his designer and artist friend Luc Van Malderen, 'but the opposite is true with Lucien. The postman brings a beautifully decorated envelope with your name on it, with a finely worked out composition and embellished with colours!'

Craftsman, not artist

De Roeck was obsessed with his craft. He worked constantly. When he wasn't teaching, he was designing a poster, painting letters, or creating illustrations for newspapers. In addition to his professional activities, he was a passionate draughtsman. With one or more sketchbooks under his arm, he would draw at weddings, openings, and dinners. When he was driving somewhere, he would stop along the way to sketch or paint a building. He was a fan of parades, architecture, ships, and people. He filled 485 sketchbooks over his career. I took his advice to make one drawing a day to heart. I was allowed to start drawing with him in sketchbooks, bound and compiled by him. So, he, my two brothers, and I would sit in a row along the Scheldt river or on a wall in Tournai, drawing the scenery.

De Roeck considered himself a craftsman, never an artist. He was too modest for that. Any result was preceded by an intense work process. He was never looking for recognition; he saw it as a waste of time. His work had to shine, not him. He also seemed to think it was unnecessary to submit invoices in order to receive his fee. The cartoonist Hergé once asked him in a greetings card when he would finally send his invoice for an illustration. After his retirement, he continued to teach unpaid at La Cambre for another year, until his successor was found.

Besides his work, his passion, my grandfather was a chaotic man. He collected all kinds of stuff: miniature cars, books, posters, antique and plastic toys, trains and soldiers, all sorts of knick-knacks. After he died in 2002, I spent six months at his home tidying up, listing and organising everything. This became the basis of the Lucien De Roeck Foundation, which aims to promote and conserve his work. I am still making discoveries. I dream of creating a database of his creations, including the more than 40,000 studies and drawings from his countless sketchbooks. A valuable oeuvre.

fig. 8
Lucien De Roeck in his home office, Brussels, 1950s

figs. 9
Lucien De Roeck
Adverts, no date

figs. 10
Lucien De Roeck
Lettering, 1933–34

Belgian Institute Graphic Design

FRIE SOOMERS

The **Belgian Institute Graphic Design** (2020) is a new platform for graphic design in and from Belgium. It curates exhibitions, researches the history of graphic design, and offers a forum to contemporary designers. Under the direction of Pia Jacques and Leroy Meyer, the institute has organised several shows, including *Focus On* (Antwerp, 2020). The poster on the opposite page was part of this window display series. See belgischinstituutgrafischontwerp.be

Frie Soomers, *Jazz Middelheim* (1979)

Frie Soomers was hired as a graphic designer for the Antwerp festival Jazz Middelheim in 1974, succeeding Frans de Jonck. The visual identity remained the same for 15 years: only a few elements, like the year and the sponsors, changed with each edition. Soomers' idiosyncratic logo, which uses musical notes to form the initials of Jazz Middelheim, became an icon. The green tones reflect Den Brandt Park, where the performances take place.

Frie Soomers
Poster for Jazz Middelheim, 1979

Hilde Pauwels

JEAN-JACQUES STIEFENHOFER: IN DESIGN WE TRUST

Creative laziness   Creative stress

Hilde Pauwels (1952) studied philosophy, is a freelance translator and taught Dutch to non-native speakers. From 1975 till his death in 2013, she was the partner and occasional assistant of Jean-Jacques Stiefenhofer.

The client was supposed to come at two o'clock. It was noon, and outside, the heatwave of 1976 was in full swing. Jean-Jacques Stiefenhofer had been a freelance designer for a few months and was still musing in the bath. I had only been living with him for a little over a year and was worried, because I knew that nothing of the promised design had materialised. At half past twelve, the master rose from the water, dressed, cleared his drawing table, with no sense of urgency, unrolled a large sheet of tracing paper and began to draw. A quarter of an hour before the client, puffing from the heat, arrived at our tiny house in Bosvoorde in his made-to-measure suit, the design was on paper – a barrier for Urbis, a street furniture company. I was witnessing for the first time a typical example of Stiefenhofer's creative method.

Like many creatives, he was a monomaniac, totally absorbed by his assignments, which were constantly buzzing around in his head, even when he was apparently doing nothing. He called his method creative laziness, combined with creative stress. The first phase, in which everything had to mature slowly, took a long time. The second was brief and powerful. Under pressure of time, the volcano erupted, sometimes producing violent sparks (fig. 1).

Creative ingenuity

Stiefenhofer (hereafter JJS) was born, an afterthought, on 27 September 1943 in Mechelen, in the middle of the war. In his first year of life, his family regularly had to hide in the basement from flying bombs. He later claimed that this is where his need for so much sleep originated. While studying at the Hochschule für Gestaltung Ulm (Ulm School of Design, HfG), he wrote to his mother: 'Now I have to make something I detest more than anything: an alarm clock.'

His mother Alice van Eelen had a sewing workshop. It was from her that he inherited his love for beautiful fabrics and motifs. He always brought textiles back from his travels, fascinated by their techniques, colours, and patterns.

His father Fernand Stiefenhofer was a carpenter and worked in Paris at the beginning of the twentieth century. After his return to Belgium, he started working as a carpenter at Belgium's national airline Sabca (later Sabena). From him, JJS inherited his creative ingenuity. His father could work magic with wood. In his attic workshop, he made vases and ashtrays with marquetry of precious woods, model aircraft, and even a nearly life-sized wooden horse that could gallop.

In high school, JJS attended the technical publicity department. He didn't like the school, but he did become acquainted with printing techniques. Fortunately, he could enjoy himself in the evenings and on Saturdays at Academie Mechelen, where teachers such as Geert Reusens saw his talent and encouraged him. Every year, he won first prizes and, even before he was of legal age, he was allowed to draw 'from the nude', quite an experience for an adolescent. He was also fascinated by Stanislas Van der Brempt's art history lessons. This enthusiastic teacher, who taught at many Flemish academies, and who encouraged young

fig. 1 (opposite)
Jean-Jacques Stiefenhofer's creative method

people to look with an open mind, inspired a lasting curiosity about art in him, from ancient Egyptian to Greek to contemporary art. As a 17- and 18-year-old adolescent, he designed posters and leaflets for the City of Mechelen and interned in Sabena's advertising department.

In Mechelen, he was in close contact with Raymond Gilles, a painter and cartoonist with an idiosyncratic style, and also a theorist who developed his own colour theory. As a mentor, he introduced JJS to Gestalt and art philosophy. Gilles also taught at, among others, the Akademie Industriële Vormgeving (Academy for Industrial Design) in Eindhoven.

In the monastery

It was obvious that JJS would become a painter. His father, however, was against this, because he had seen in Paris what poverty awaited most artists. Perhaps stunned by his father's sudden death, the son obeyed, and chose a different direction. In 1962, he moved to Eindhoven, where, during the day, he interned at Philips' design department and, in the evenings, he attended the Akademie Industriële Vormgeving. He didn't enjoy the course, writing to a friend: 'The school – and in particular the evening school – is very depleted and is on its last legs. And at Philips you're just a number. As far as design is concerned, a lot of crap is produced, and the rest is copied. There are still a few interesting teachers, such as Karel Elno, who teaches Spatial Design.'

In 1963, he swapped Eindhoven for the Product Design department at the Hochschule für Gestaltung Ulm (fig. 2).[1] A fascinating new world opened up for him. The school had a multidisciplinary approach, with a strong cross-fertilisation between the different departments – product design, visual communication, industrial architecture, information design, and film. Design was not regarded as a non-committal activity, but required social engagement. In addition, there was great emphasis on practical training with workshops for metal, wood, plastic, and photography, as well as a print shop. JJS immediately felt at home and loved this multidisciplinary approach (fig. 3). Here, he sharpened his critical thinking and learned skills that would serve him for the rest of his career.

fig. 2 (left)
Hochschule für Gestaltung Ulm, 1955

fig. 3 (right)
Hans Gugelot and students discussing a walkie-talkie assignment, ca. 1962. JJS is first left.

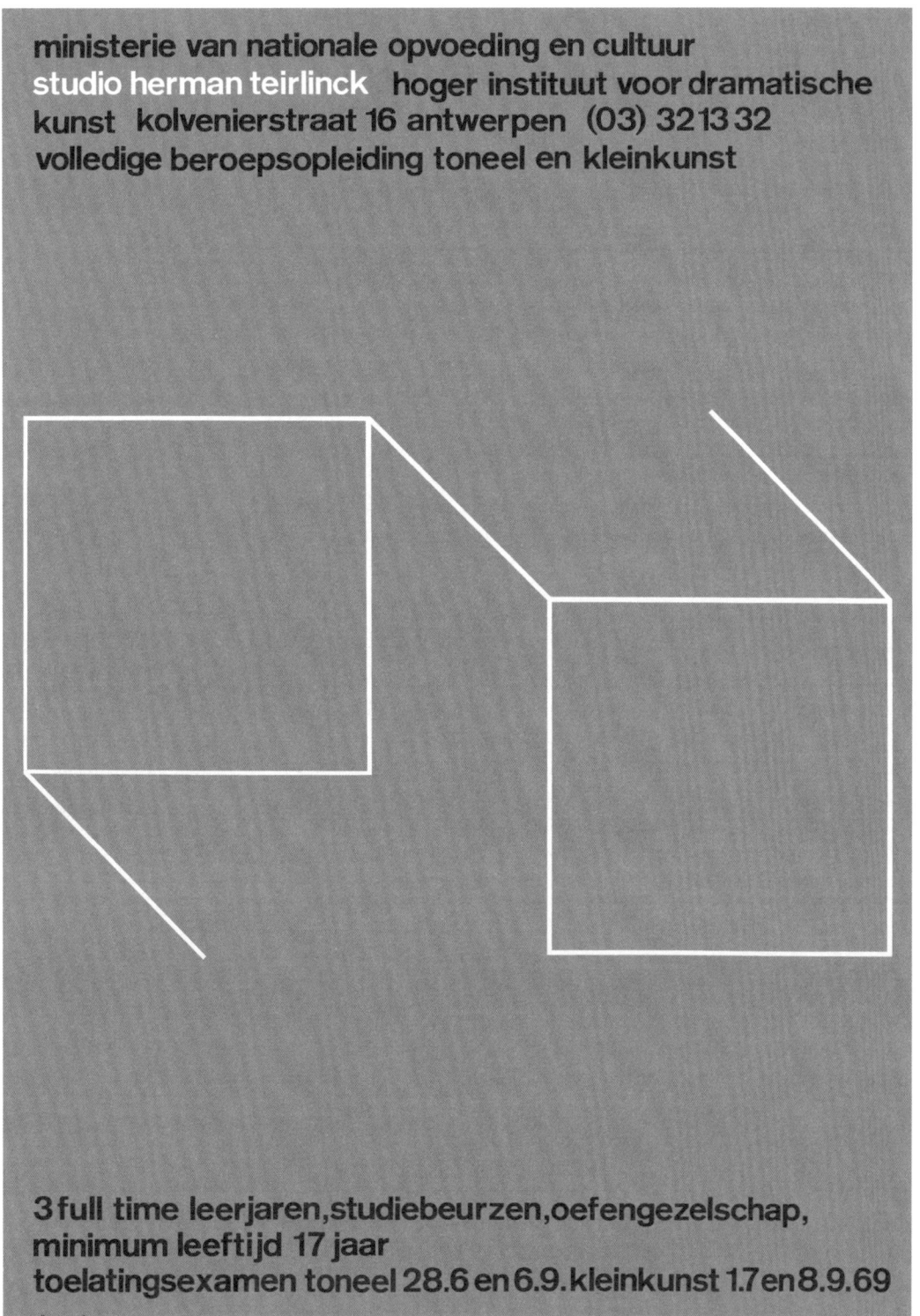

fig. 4
Jean-Jacques Stiefenhofer
Poster for Studio Herman Teirlinck, 1969

The HfG campus, designed by Max Bill in 1955 on a hill just outside the city of Ulm, combined classrooms, workshops, a canteen with a bar, and a residential building for student and teacher accommodation. In the city, the school was called 'the monastery'. This excerpt from a letter from JJS to his mother proves that it was anything but monastic:

> '... now it really is time. It is two o'clock and here they come. Because that's when [Peter] Raacke goes to sleep.[2] Raacke is a new professor who hasn't been here long and doesn't know us well yet, but the man is good, one can describe him generally as being a "cordon bleu". [...] and he doesn't quite know the habits of the house yet. He has now bought a barrel of most (most is a young wine made from apples that is not very strong, but which likes to be drunk). He has placed that barrel under the protruding living room, next to his house. He thinks that it looks good there, nice and fresh, but of course that is stupid ... to put a barrel of wine, so exposed, next to his house, so stupid ... He goes to sleep at half past one, and then the procession starts to the other side of the carpark with coffee pots, milk jugs, empty bottles, and other receptacles ...'

In terms of graphics, the HfG aligned itself with the International Typographic Style,[3] which sought objective visual communication with clear and powerful geometric shapes, asymmetrical layouts, and simple sans-serif typefaces. These principles can be found in countless of JJS's designs. During his studies, he designed the house style for Provinciale en Intercommunale Drinkwatermaatschappij Antwerpen (Provincial and Intercommunal Drinking Water Company Antwerp, fig. 5) and posters for cultural centres and galleries, entirely in the spirit of HfG principles. He graduated with a design for an X-ray machine and an essay about industrial design and economics.

fig. 5
Jean-Jacques Stiefenhofer
Logo for Provincial and Intercommunal Drinking Water Company Antwerp, late 1960s

Studio Herman Teirlinck

JJS returned to Belgium at the end of 1967. In Antwerp, he came into contact with Fons Goris, director of the Studio Herman Teirlinck, which was the start of many years of collaboration. Goris trusted him entirely. Still imbued with influences from Ulm, JJS designed invitations, programmes, posters, and photo books for the Studio.

He always came up with a new image for the book covers, while the inside remained unchanged – sloping black-and-white photos with minimal text. When it was announced that the Studio would close down, Goris wrote in the last publication: 'These photo books, conceived in their delightful form by Jean-Jacques Stiefenhofer, have become part of our pride. They show how the Studio functioned.' For the celebration of Teirlinck's 100th birthday, JJS designed a poster with his portrait, comprised of the letters of a text he had written. By setting the text in different thicknesses and colour separations, he 'digitised' the photo by hand (fig. 6).

fig. 6
Jean-Jacques Stiefenhofer
Poster for the celebration of
Herman Teirlinck's centenary, 1979

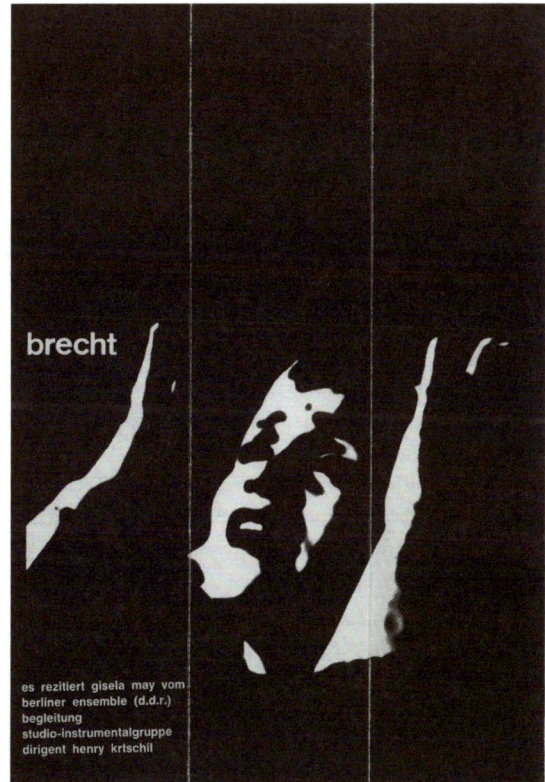

fig. 7
Jean-Jacques Stiefenhofer
Leaflet for a performance by Gisela May
at Palais des Beaux-Arts, 1967

Product development

In 1967, Gilles put JJS in contact with Walter van de Maele from the Kunst- en Kultuurverbond (Art and Culture Alliance, KKV) of the Palais des Beaux-Arts in Brussels (Centre for Fine Arts), which resulted in another close collaboration. In 1968, the KKV organised the *Nederlandse Dagen (Dutch Days)* event, for which JJS designed the promotional material. For its travelling exhibition on Flemish and Dutch literature in translation, JJS devised a concertina system of stapled cardboard walls that were foldable and extendable, making them easy to move (fig. 8). Large prints of photographs and texts were pasted on the panels. The result was long, undulating walls, which were easy to fit into a space. He subsequently used this system several times. The *Nederlandse Dagen* exhibition opened on 15 May. It was taken over and occupied by students and artists three days later – the infamous occupation of the Palais des Beaux-Arts in May 1968 – but that is another story.

fig. 8
Jean-Jacques Stiefenhofer
Exhibition design for *Nederlandse Dagen (Dutch Days)* at Palais des Beaux-Arts (Centre for Fine Arts), Brussels, 1968

In 1967, the Ministry of Culture asked JJS to set up an industrial design department at the Nationaal Hoger Instituut voor Bouwkunde en Stedenbouw (National Higher Institute for Architecture and Urban Planning) in Antwerp. He named the department Productontwikkeling (Product Development) and introduced HfG's multidisciplinary design approach and academic underpinnings there (figs. 9). Seminars by visiting professors were a key component, often former students from Ulm. The department was allocated a building, which JJS had furnished. But he soon clashed with Frans de Groot, the school's director, who interfered too much and imposed his friends as teachers. In 1971, JJS resigned in protest.

After a period of travelling to India and Thailand, in 1972 JJS was appointed director of the Belgisch Instituut voor Industriële Vormgeving (Belgian Institute for Industrial Design). The institution was financed

figs. 9
JJS teaching at Productontwikkeling (Product Development), Antwerp, late 1960s

by the Belgische Dienst voor de Opvoering van de Productiviteit (Belgian Service for Productivity Enhancement, created under the impulse of the Marshall Plan) and worked closely with the Design Centre, which was led by Josine des Cressonnières. As the institute's director, JJS was a member of the Design Education work group of the International Council of Societies of Industrial Designers (ICSID) and participated in several conferences. He was also a regular member of the Design Centre jury to select products eligible for exhibition.

In 1975, he organised the ICSID seminar 'Urban traffic on a human scale', in Bruges, for which he also designed the logo. Designers from all over the world spent a busy week thinking about traffic in a historic city.

Self-employed designer

The Institute's activities were suspended in 1976 and so JJS began the tough life of a self-employed designer. Initially, he tried to work as a designer for industry. He designed a barrier for a street furniture business and a sink for the Belgian ceramics factory Warneton, but most of the time the contacts came to nothing. With the exception of a few companies, Belgian industry was little interested in contemporary functional design in the 1970s and 1980s. The Design Centre's efforts received a marginal response.

After a few years, JJS increasingly began to focus on exhibition graphics and scenography for museums. He once wrote to a friend: 'I have made a virtue of necessity, have followed my love for art history, and have thrown myself cautiously on the museums, and all that with great satisfaction. Like a kind of homo universalis, it all seemed to flow out of me, from labels, paintings, carpentry, and everything in between to catalogues and posters.'

fig. 10
Jean-Jacques Stiefenhofer
Poster for *Kerkelijke kunst uit Rome* (*Ecclesiastical art from Rome*) exhibition, Kultureel Centrum Melaan, 1963

fig. 11
Jean-Jacques Stiefenhofer
Poster for Privaat Lustrumgalabal (Private lustrum gala ball), Salons van Dijck, 1967

In the 1980s and 1990s, JJS worked closely with Robert Hoozee, director of the Museum voor Schone Kunsten (Museum for Fine Arts, MSK) in Ghent, providing the scenography for several exhibitions.[4] He frequently designed the accompanying catalogue and poster. Several other museums followed, such as the Koninklijk Museum voor Schone Kunsten Antwerpen (Royal Museum of Fine Arts Antwerp, KMSKA), the former Etnografisch Museum (Ethnographic Museum), Europalia, the Instituut voor Sociale Geschiedenis (Institute of Social History), and many others.[5]

JJS devised the scenography for these exhibitions down to the last details, all in a traditional way. He designed pedestals and display cases, determined the colour of walls, the way works were arranged, the layout of room texts and captions. He kept tight control and did much of the work himself (often with my helping hand), including hammering labels into the wall. He was not interested in fanfares, he preferred subtlety and had a talent for bringing artworks together, in the right tone. For example, a reviewer writing about the George Minne exhibition at MSK in Ghent (1982) remarked that it was 'as if Minne's hand had placed the statues'. And at an exhibition on Pieter Breughel the Younger and Jan Brueghel the Elder in the KMSKA (1998), the Viennese and Cologne curators expressed great admiration for 'die Hängung' – the way in which the paintings were hung.

In design we trust

JJS also designed many exhibition catalogues, art books, and posters. In consultation with the client, he would begin each book by laying out what he called a 'chemin de fer' (a flat plan – literally a railroad, though sometimes it did indeed become a 'chemin d'enfer', a road to hell, fig. 12). Every 'wagon' on this 'railroad' had 16 pages, which corresponds to a section. He would sketch the whole 'scenario' of the book, giving himself a good overview of the distribution of illustrations and colour pages. He worked manually, without a computer, until almost the end of the 1990s. This way of working requires mental gymnastics and imagination. Layout, typeface, size and paragraph width for different types of text and the format of illustrations and captions all had to be determined in advance. The instructions went to the typesetter, who then supplied galleys, long strips of typeset text. The format of the images, then still delivered in the form of Ektachromes or printed photographs, had to be decided before they went to photogravure. With a lot of cutting and pasting, the strips of typesetting and illustration proofs were then combined into a maquette – a thick pack of paper. This was then sent to the printers, where technicians merged the elements and transferred them onto film. In the 1990s, this was already partly done with computers, but there was no question of submitting PDFs yet.

Covers got extra attention, of course. JJS always worked them out very meticulously with all the instructions for the printer. Through his collaboration with museums, his graphic design had evolved into

fig. 12 (next spread)
Jean-Jacques Stiefenhofer
Flat plan for Bernd Lohaus catalogue, 1995

MUHKA   BERND LOHAUS   128 p?

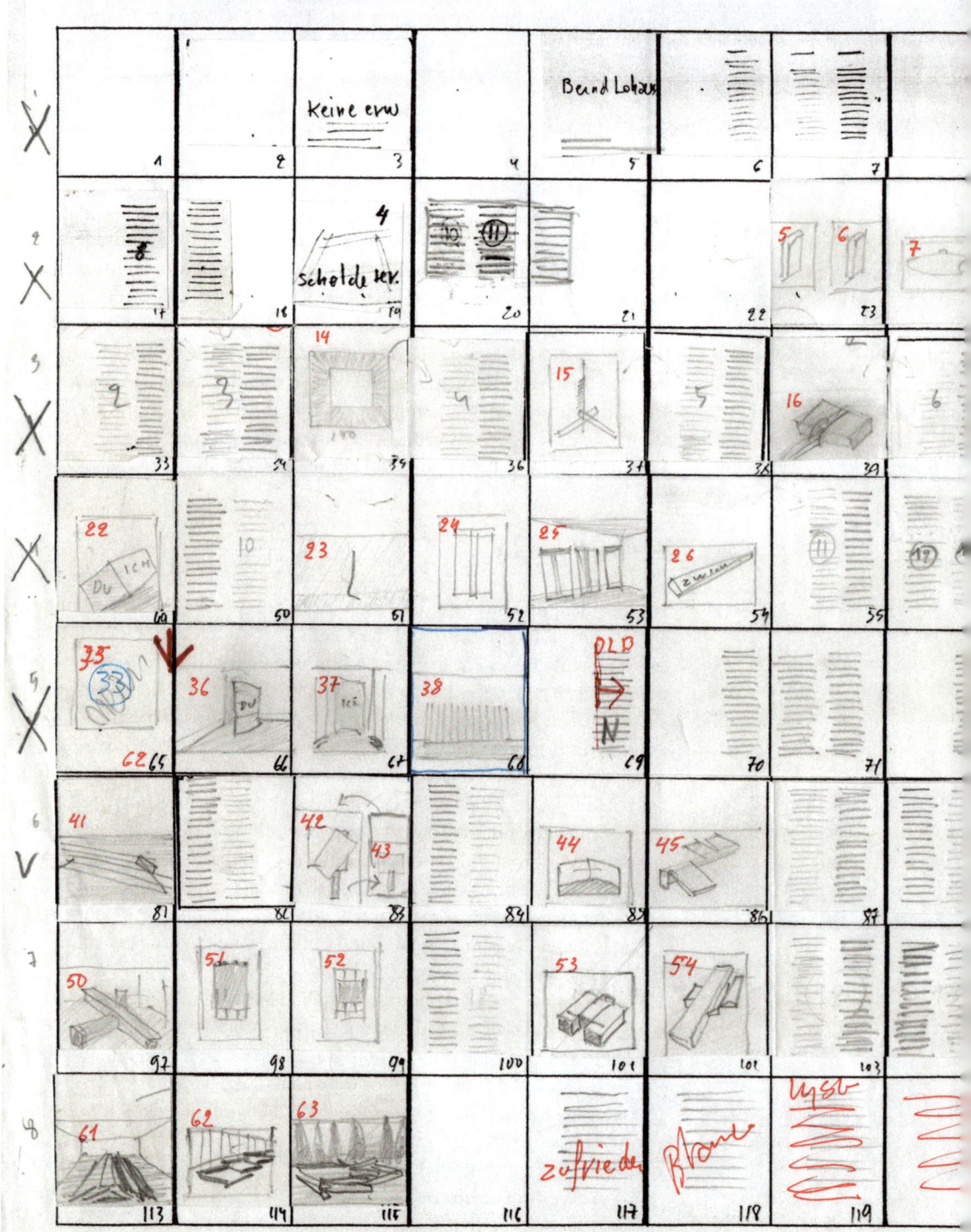

chronie

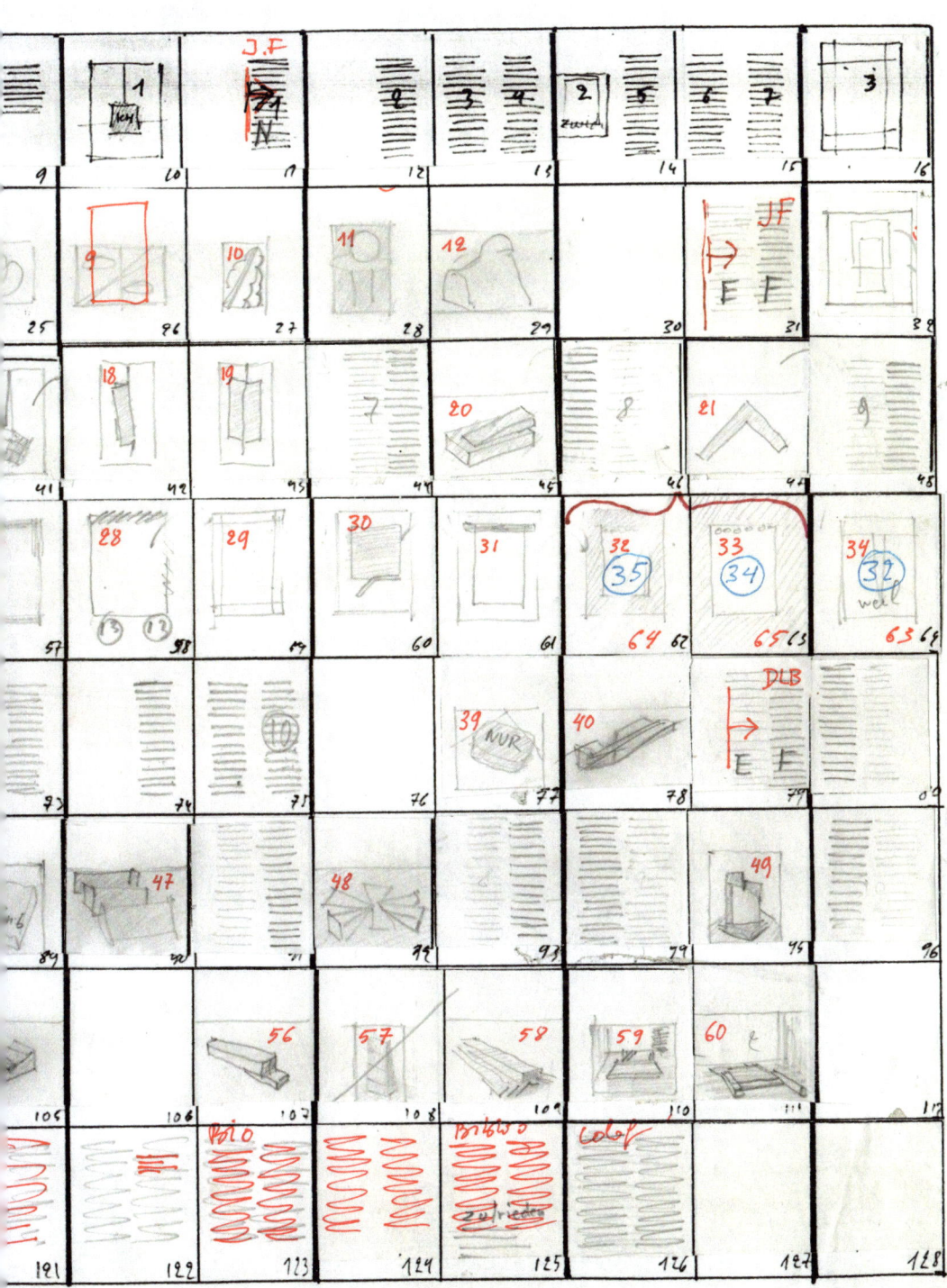

a more 'classic' design, with restrained and calm page layouts, which did, however, remain true to the HfG principles of paired-down design. He detested book designs with a 'glitzy' look. A good example of his design philosophy is the 1992 book *Moderne kunst in België 1900–1945 (Modern Art in Belgium 1900–1945)*. He also often collaborated with contemporary artists, commissioned by, among others, Annie Gentils Gallery, Middelheim Museum, and Museum van Hedendaagse Kunst Antwerpen (Museum of Contemporary Art Antwerp). This required a different approach, which sometimes caused tensions, but it also led to close friendships, such as with the artist Kati Heck, for whom JJS also became a beloved model.

Jacques, Jean-Jacques, JéJé, Jean-Pleure de la Misère, was a man of many names who sometimes signed off his letters with the provocative and combative 'In design we trust'. He was bursting with talent and always viewed life with a special humour, but as is often the case with creative minds, he was uncompromising and inflexible when it came to his designs. More than once he burned all his bridges, when the client wanted to interfere too much. Better bust than bend.

In the novel *Over het water (Across the Water*, 1998), author Hans Maarten van den Brink writes that there are people who try their best to excel, but that they often do not understand that 'the best rise above everything and do not experience work as work, but rather as a confirmation of their possibilities.' JJS never tried his best.

---

1 Hochschule für Gestaltung Ulm (Ulm School of Design) was a leading school for industrial design between 1953 and 1968. See https://hfg-archiv.museum ulm.de (last accessed on 2 December 2021).
2 Peter Raacke is a German product designer who designed the Mono-A cutlery set, and pioneered in cardboard furniture design.
3 Also known as Swiss Style.
4 These include: *Het Landschap in de Belgische kunst*, 1980; *George Minne en de kunst rond 1900*, 1982; *Frans Masereel*, 1986; *Minne-Lehmbruck-Beuys*, 1991; *Laat-gotische beeldhouwkunst*, 1994; en *Parijs-Brussel / Brussel-Parijs*, 1997.
5 With exhibitions such as: *Breughel-Brueghel*, 1998; *Elck zijn Waerom*, 2000; *Kinderen op hun mooist*, 2001; *Venus een vergeten mythe*, 2001; *Korea*, 1993; *Enku*, 1999; *Paul van Ostaijen*, 1996; *Praag, art nouveau*, 1998; *Louis Major*, 1988; *100 jaar 1 mei*, 1990.

fig. 13
Jean-Jacques Stiefenhofer
Poster for *Monique Destrebecq, Victor Govaerts, Hugo de Clercq*
Galerie le vendôme, 1964

Graphic design archives in Belgian public institutions
Flanders Architecture Institute

Currently, there is not a single public institution dedicated to collecting and preserving graphic design in Belgium. This precarious situation means that archives can have difficulty finding a home, and the research and study of graphic design can be challenging. The Flanders Architecture Institute has recently started recording such archives in public institutions in response to this problem. The list below focuses on those after 1945, including related fields such as illustration, printmaking, printing, and animation. We hope it will offer a starting point to explore this rich material further.

Graphic designers

Fernand Baudin
Université Libre de Bruxelles (ULB), Brussels

August Boschmans
KADOC / Documentation and Centre on Religion, Culture and Society at KU Leuven, Leuven

Rob Buytaert
Letterenhuis, Antwerp

Elza Courtoit
Letterenhuis, Antwerp

(Lodewijk) Albert Daenens
Letterenhuis, Antwerp

André Delbaere
Letterenhuis, Antwerp

Corneille Hannoset
Archives et Musée de la Literature (AML), Brussels

Hugoké (Hugo De Kempeneer)
KADOC / Documentation and Research Centre on Religion, Culture and Society at KU Leuven, Leuven
Archive and Museum for the Flemish Living in Brussels (AMVB), Brussels

Paul Ibou
Letterenhuis, Antwerp
Museum of Modern Art (M HKA) library, Antwerp
Museum Plantin-Moretus, Antwerp
Design Museum Gent

Julian Key (Julien Keymolen)
Letterenhuis, Antwerp

Gorik Lindemans
Archive and Museum for the Flemish Living in Brussels (AMVB), Brussels

Marc Mendelson
Archives of Contemporary Art in Belgium (ACAB), Brussels

Luk Mestdagh
Letterenhuis, Antwerp

Leo Meurrens
KADOC / Documentation and Research Centre on Religion, Culture and Society at KU Leuven, Leuven

May Néama
M – Museum, Leuven
Royal Library of Belgium (KBR), Brussels
Archives et Musée de la Littérature (AML), Brussels
Université Libre de Bruxelles (ULB), Brussels
Letterenhuis, Antwerp

Jozef Peeters
Letterenhuis, Antwerp

Lode Sebregts
Letterenhuis, Antwerp

Elza Severin
Felixarchief, Antwerp
Renaat Braem house, Antwerp

Joris Snaet
KADOC / Documentation and Research Centre on Religion, Culture and Society at KU Leuven, Leuven

Jean-Jacques Stiefenhofer
Flanders Architecture Institute, Antwerp

Eduard Van Ballaer
Flanders Architecture Institute, Antwerp

Hélène van Coppenolle
Letterenhuis, Antwerp

Martha van Coppenolle
Letterenhuis, Antwerp

Nicole Van Goethem
Letterenhuis, Antwerp

Berthe Van Regemorter
Letterenhuis, Antwerp

Roger Vansevenant
City Archive, Poperinge

Stef Vanstiphout
KADOC / Documentation and Research Centre on Religion, Culture and Society at KU Leuven, Leuven

Herman Verbaere
Letterenhuis, Antwerp

Margot Weemaes
Archives of Contemporary Art in Belgium (ACAB), Brussels
M – Museum, Leuven
Royal Library of Belgium (KBR), Brussels
British Museum, London
Boijmans Van Beuningen, Rotterdam
Centre de la Gravure et de l'Image Imprimée, La Louvière
Fashion Museum (MoMu), Antwerp

Publishers and printers

Christelijk Vlaams Kunstenaarsverbond (CVKV)
KADOC / Documentation and Research Centre on Religion, Culture and Society at KU Leuven, Leuven

Davidsfonds
KADOC / Documentation and Research Centre on Religion, Culture and Society at KU Leuven, Leuven

De Sikkel
Letterenhuis, Antwerp

Drukkerij De Voorzorg
Institute of Social History (AMSAB), Ghent

Drukkerij Strobbe
City Archive, Izegem

Zeemeeuw
Archive for National Movements (ADVN), Antwerp

Educational institutions

Ecole nationale supérieure des arts visuels de La Cambre
Library and collections of ENSAV – La Cambre, Brussels

Hogeschool Sint-Lukas Brussel
KADOC / Documentation and Research Centre on Religion, Culture and Society at KU Leuven, Leuven

Hogeschool voor Wetenschap en Kunst Sint-Lucas Gent
KADOC / Documentation and Research Centre on Religion, Culture and Society at KU Leuven, Leuven
Documentation for Local History, Sint-Amandsberg

Instituut voor Kunstambachten / De Vrije Academie
Letterenhuis, Antwerp
Heritage Library Hendrik Conscience, Antwerp
Royal Conservatorium, Antwerp
Archives et Musée de la Littérature (AML), Brussels

Provinciaal Hoger Instituut voor Architectuur en Toegepaste Kunsten
Provincial Archives Limburg, Hasselt
KADOC / Documentation and Research Centre on Religion, Culture and Society at KU Leuven, Leuven

Intermediary organisations and individuals

Design Centre
National Archives of Belgium, Brussels
Letterenhuis, Antwerp
Belgian Foreign Trade Agency, Brussels
Belgian Productivity Service, Brussels

Design Vlaanderen
Coordinating archives service Flanders, Brussels

Documentation series Moniek E. Bucquoye
Design Museum Gent

National Documentation Centre for the Arts and Crafts
Design Museum Gent

Sub-collections and documentation (selection)

Graphic matter and ephemera can be found in numerous archives and collections. Many city archives and the six Flemish heritage libraries also have rich sub-collections related to graphic design. Below is a selection.

Artevelde Hogeschool (Campus Mariakerke), Ghent
Includes collection first started in the 1930s, classified by type of printing: lace printing, New Year cards, tin prints or prints on plastic, posters and religious printed matter. A special sub-collection is the work of Charles Doudelet, a book illustrator.

Design Museum Gent
Designs by Boudewijn Delaere for Interieur Kortrijk; poster collection by Michel Olyff; poster collection by former director Adelbert Van de Walle; logo objects, calendars and books by Paul Ibou and book bindings of Rob Aerts

Frans Masereel Centre, Kasterlee
Mainly printmaking by artists with an increasing number of graphic design objects, with a focus on typography, in the last 10–15 years

Ghent Industry Museum
Objects related to the graphic industry as well as graphic magazines, advertising leaflets, letter proofs, posters, adverts, oral history

KADOC / Documentation and Research Centre on Religion, Culture and Society at KU Leuven, Leuven
Contains numerous sub-collections related to graphic design, such as a collection of didactic prints, prayer cards and political cartoons, work by François Gianolla and Marc Sleen, and a collection of children's magazines *Zonneland* and *Vlaamse Filmpjes*. Also holds interviews about Averbode publishers and an extensive poster collection.

Letterenhuis, Antwerp
A collection of about 50,000 posters which is searchable via its online database at letterenhuis.be

Royal Academy of Fine Arts Antwerp (KASKA)
Small collection of works by Leo Marfurt

Museum Plantin-Moretus, Antwerp
Mainly includes illustrations, prints and posters as well as a large collection of works by Jos Léonard.

Royal Library of Belgium (KBR), Brussels
The national scientific library and legal deposit collects all publications published on Belgian territory and all publications by authors of Belgian nationality abroad. Its print cabinet also manages a collection of 2,000 posters.

Royal Museums of Fine Arts of Belgium (KMSK), Brussels
One of the most important collections of post-war poster art with works by Julien Key, André Pasture, Charles Rohonyi, and Leo Marfurt. Partly digitised at opac-fabritius.be

Poster collections

Archive for National Movements (ADVN), Antwerp

Le Centre de la Gravure et de l'Image Imprimée, La Louvière

Cinematek / Filmmuseum, Brussels

Institute of Social History (AMSAB), Ghent

Ghent University Library

Gin Museum, Hasselt

KADOC / Documentation and Research Centre on Religion, Culture and Society at KU Leuven, Leuven

Liberal Archive vzw (Liberas), Ghent

Mundaneum, Mons

Museum of Ixelles, Ixelles

Museum of Walloon Life, Liège

Royal Museum of the Armed Forces and Military History, Brussels

State Archives (Cegesoma), Anderlecht

Bibliography

Compiled by Sara De Bondt with input from Jo De Baerdemaeker, Katrien Van Haute, Herman Lampaert, Leroy Meyer, Stéphane de Schrevel, and Katarina Serulus

Books

Lucas, Robert; Scheerlinck, Karl, *Antwerpen lonkt...: Culturele en toeristische affiches van 1940 tot nu uit de collectie van het Letterenhuis* (Antwerp: AMVC-Letterenhuis, 2005).

Arenbergschouwburg, *May Néama: toneelontwerp, boekillustratie* (Antwerp: Provinciebestuur, 1974).

BASE, *Base: Works from 06.00 to 03.03* (Brussels: BASE, 2003).

Baudin, Fernand, *À la lettre: Digressions à propos d'écriture et de typographie* (Brussels: Erasmushuis, 2003).

Baudin, Fernand, *De drukletter: vorm, vervaardiging, indeling, toepassing* (Brussels: Établissements Plantin, 1965).

Baudin, Fernand, *How Typography Works: And why it is Important* (London: Lund Humphries, 1988).

Baudin, Fernand, *L'effet Gutenberg* (Brussels: Éditions du Cercle de la Librairie, 1994).

Baudin, Fernand, *La typographie au tableau noir* (Paris: Retz, 1984).

Baudin, Fernand; Liliane, Baudin-Tytgat, *Créer, c'est ma joie* (Brussels: Labor, 1977).

Baudin, Fernand; Dreyfus, John; Magermans, Rémy, *Dossier A–Z 73: Association Typographique Internationale* (Andenne: Rémy Magermans, 1973).

Baudin, Fernand; Durand, Ben, *Fernand Baudin: Conversation avec Ben Durand* (Gerpinnes: Éditions Tandem, 2004).

Baudouin, Anne, *The Power of Print: Culturele affiche- en folderwedstrijd* (Antwerp: Prospekta, 2008).

Baudoux, Vincent, *Fortuna: 80 jaar Nationale Loterij* (Brussels: Seed Factory, 2014).

Baudson, Pierre, *Affichistes de Wallonie et de Bruxelles* (Paris: Centre Culturel de la Communauté française de Belgique, 1982).

Baudson, Pierre, *De affiche als kunstvorm in België 1900–1980* (Brussels: Galerij A.S.L.K., 1980).

Baudson, Pierre, *Julian Key* (Tielt: Lannoo, 1981).

Baudson, Pierre, *L'Affiche en Belgique 1880–1980* (Paris: Musée de l'Affiche, 1980).

Baudson, Pierre, *L'Art de l'affiche en Belgique 1900–1980* (Brussels: Galerie C.G.E.R., 1980).

Baudson, Pierre, *Van Beeld tot Grafiek (Aspekten van de affiche en de grafiek in België van de jaren twintig tot heden)* (Brussels: Koninklijke Musea van Schone Kunsten van België, 1957).

Bekaert, Johnny; Michiels, Michel; Bos, Ben; Devroye, Luc; Huftier, Arnaud, *Font Design: Johnny Bekaert* (Brussels: Seed Factory, 2018).

Bekaert, Johnny; Michiels, Michel; Olyff, Clotilde; Regout, Patrick, *Typo* (Brussels: Seed Factory, 2013).

Bernard, Marie-Laurence; Dumont, Fabienne, *Affiches Sportives en Belgique : 1890–1940* (Brussels: Crédit Communal, 1981).

Bernard, Marie-Laurence; Florizoone, Roland, *Affiches van de Belgische Kust 1890–1950* (Bruges: Marc Van de Wiele, 1992).

Bex, Flor, *Jozef Peeters (1985–1960)* (Antwerp: ICC / Esco Books, 1978).

Bilked, Marits; Delahaut, Jo; Peeters, Jozef, *De eerste abstracten in België: Hulde aan de pioniers* (Antwerp: G58 Hessenhuis, 1959).

Bivort, Valérie; Vandevivere, Ignace, *Le graphiste Jacques Richez (1918–1994)* (Louvain-la-Neuve: UCL, 2000).

Block, Jane, *Homage to Brussels: The art of Belgian posters 1895–1915* (New Jersey: Zimmerli Art Museum, 1992).

Block Jane; Combaz, Gisbert, *Gisbert Combaz (1869–1941): Fin de siècle Artist* (Ghent: Snoeck-Ducaju, 1999).

Bodenstein, Wulf; Debbaut, Ann; Danckaert, Lisette; Gryseels, Guido; de Moerloose, Philippe; e.a., *Kaarten van Afrika* (Tervuren: Koninklijk Museum voor Midden-Afrika, 2017).

Boudens, Pierre; Dacquin Hedwig; Setola, Albert, *Twintig jaar Korrekelder* (Bruges: De Korre, 1980).

Boudens, Paul; Debo, Kaat, *Paul Boudens: Invitations* (London, Zegris, 2020).

Boudens, Paul; Esch, Gerdi; Blanchard, Tamsin; e.a. *Paul Boudens: Works* (Ghent: Ludion, 2003).

Brepoels, Jaak, *Toen de muren spraken: Een halve eeuw politieke affiches (1918–1968), gesprokkeld uit het Leuvense Stadsarchief* (Leuven: Salsa!-Cahier, 2016).

Bruyninckx, Robert; Koninklijke bibliotheek van België, *Leven met letters: Wim Platteborze: tentoonstelling Nassaukapel Koninklijke Bibliotheek van België* (Brussels: Wim Platteborze, 1999).

Bucquoye, Monique; Daenens, Lieven; Poulain, Norbert, *Forms from Flanders. From Henry van de Velde to Maarten van Severen 1900–2000* (Ghent: Ludion, 2001).

Canonne, Xavier; Van de Velde, Jessy; Van de Velde, Ronny, *Dada in Knokke* (Knokke-Zoute: Galerie Ronny Van de Velde, 2016).

Carre, Anne; Scheerlinck, Karl; Puttaert, Hugo; Meyers, Jean-Michel, *Lucien De Roeck: Van affiche tot letter* (Tielt: Lannoo, 2015).

Charron, Frédéric, *Alechinsky: les affiches: catalogue raisonné* (Neuchâtel: Ides et Callendes, 2007).

Cleeren, Steven; Vandenhoudt, Ingrid; Mombaerts, Marc; Sarah Daeleman; Capelle, Marleen, *Vormgeven doe je niet alleen: de meerwaarde van boekverzorging* (Brussels: Design Vlaanderen, 2009).

Cockx-Indestege, Elly, *Berthe van Regemorter: Een Antwerpse Kunstboekbindster (1897–1964)* (Brussels: Bibliotheca Wittockiana, 2014).

Cockx-Indestege, Elly, *Fernand Baudin: typograaf, typographiste, book designer* (Amsterdam: Uitgeverij De Buitenkant, 2002).

Cockx-Indestege, Elly; Colin, Georges, *Fernand Baudin ou la typographie au service du lecteur – Fernand Baudin,* typograaf: een leven in dienst van de lezer (Brussels: Royal Library of Belgium, 2000).

Colenbier, Hendrik; Van Den Haute, Herman, *België huppelt Nederland achterna: of Belgische grafische vormgeving versus Nederlandse grafische vormgeving* (Ghent: Hoger Instituut voor Beeldende Kunsten Sint-Lucas, Afdeling Functionele Grafiek, 1993).

Coppens, Bob; Adriaens-Pannier, Anne; Mertens, Phil, *Jozef Peeters en zijn tijdgenoten, tekeningen en grafisch werk, tentoonstellingen, catalogi* (Brussels: Museum voor Schone Kunsten, 1986).

Couvreur, Daniel; Olyff, Michel; Scheerlinck, Karl, *Lucien De Roeck* (Ghent: Borgerhoff & Lamberigts, 2008).

Cox, Ines, *Save* (Antwerp: Koninklijke Academie voor Schone Kunsten Antwerpen, 2019).

Cultureel Centrum, *Van A tot Z: Grafische Vormgevers in Vlaanderen* (Leopoldsburg: Cultureel Centrum, 2000).

De Baere, Bart; Cleppe, Birgit; Pas, Johan; Teigeler, Piet; de Pauw, Josse; e.a., *Ercola. Experimental Research Center of Liberal Arts. 1968–2018* (Tielt: Lannoo, 2018).

De Bondt, Sara, *Het ontstaan van een visuele identiteit* (Brussels: WIELS, 2008).

De Bondt, Sara, *Off The Grid: Belgian Graphic Design from the 1960s and the 1970s as Seen by Sara De Bondt* (Ghent: Design Museum, 2019).

De Braekeleer, Catherine; Van Bosterhaut, Marie; Van der Vrecken, Julie, *Mai 68: L'imagination au pouvoir* (La Louvière: Centre de la gravure et de l'image imprimée de la Communauté française de Belgique, 2008).

De Croës, Cathérine; Weill Alain; e.a., *L'art de l'affiche en Belgique 1880-1980* (Liège: Musée de la Vie Wallonne, 1980).

De Meyer, Erik, *20 jaar grafiek* (Antwerp: Erik De Meyer, 1989).

De Mont, Wim; De Graef, Sarah; Van den Bossche, Geert, *De best vormgegeven boeken 2011: Plantin-Moretusprijs* (Borgerhout: Vlaamse Uitgevers Vereniging, 2011).

De Palmenaer, Els; Madjedo, Nsayi, Nadia; e.a., *100 X Congo: Een eeuw Congolese kunst in Antwerpen* (Antwerp: BAI, 2020).

De Roeck, Lucien; Marissal-Bertot, Lou; Brocorens, André; Bouquiaux, Louise; Schel, Louis, *Graphisme 50 : Publicité – Publiciteit* (Antwerp: Éditions du Lion Assis, 1951).

De Vijlder, Antoon; Lampaert, Herman, *Embleem en huisstijl van de Vlaamse Gemeenschap* (Brussels: Ministerie van de Vlaamse Gemeenschap, 1989).

De Winter, Roland; Van den Eede, Louis, *Illustratietechnieken: traditionele grafische technieken en hun toepassingen in de boekdrukkunst* (Antwerp: Museum Plantin-Moretus, 2004).

Delaere, Boudewijn; Huysentruyt, André, *Graphic Design: Boudewijn Delaere* (Kortrijk: Boudewijn Delaere, 2020).

Delfosse, Antoine, *The underground press in Belgium* (London: Lincolns-Prager, 1944).

Delsaerdt, Pierre; Dhaese, Tonia; e.a., *Louis Van den Eede: Een halve eeuw typografie in Vlaanderen* (Antwerp: Mercatorfonds, 1999).

Demeure De Beaumont, Alexandre, *L'affiche belge : essai critique, biographie des artistes* (Toulouse: Chez l'Auteur, 1897).

den Boef, August Hans; van Faassen, Sjoerd, *Van De Stijl en Het Overzicht tot De Driehoek: Belgisch-Nederlandse netwerken in het modernistische interbellum* (Antwerp: Garant, 2013).

Dooreman, Gert, *Dooreman* (Tielt: Lannoo, 2009).

Duchesne, Jean-Patrick, *L'affiche en Belgique: Art & Pouvoir* (Brussels: Éditions Labor, 1989).

Duchesne, Jean-Patrick, *L'Affiche en Wallonie* (Liège: Musée de la Vie Wallonne, 1979).

Duchesne, Jean-Patrick, *Belgische affiches* (Brussels: IBM Belgium, 1981).

Dustin, Jo; de Braekeleer, Catherine; Van Malderen, Luc: *Parade, 25 ans de sérigraphie* (La Louvière: Centre de la gravure et de l'image imprimée de la Communauté française de Belgique, 1998).

Engelen, Leen, *Cinema Leuven: een studie naar de Belgische filmaffiche aan de hand de collectie van het Leuvens Stadsarchief* (Leuven: Peeters, 2012).

Établissements Plantin, *Catalogue de caractères de la fonderie de caractères 'Plantin'* (Brussels: Établissements Plantin, 1955).

Établissements Plantin, *Les Établissements Plantin et ce que l'on y fait...* (Brussels: Plantin, 1961)

Établissements Plantin, *Les Établissements Plantin fournissent les caractères, machines et outillage pour les arts graphiques* (Brussels: Établissements Plantin, no date).

Établissements Plantin, *Letterproeven* (Brussels: Établissements Plantin, no date).

Établissements Plantin, *Moderne letters voor het vergulden* (Brussels: Établissements Plantin, no date).

Établissements Plantin, *Plantin: un caractère moderne inspiré des traditions Plantiniennes* (Brussels: Établissements Plantin, ca. 1925).

Federinov, Bertrand; Delattre, Marie-Blanche, *Micheline de Bellefroid, 1927–2008* (Mariemont: Musée Royal de Mariemont, 2011).

Fiszman, Gilles; La maison de l'image, *Autobiographisme: Gilles Fiszman, 50 ans de communication et de design graphiques* (Brussels: Seed Factory, 2014).

Floré, Fredie; Goubert, Ko; Lund, Irène; Serulus, Katarina; Van Regenmortel, Eva, *Vormgevingserfgoed in Vlaanderen na 1945* (Ghent: Art Paper Editions, 2016).

Folon, Jean-Michel; Glaser, Milton, *Affiches de Folon* (Paris: Chêne, 1978).

Forshaw, Alex; Ainsworth, Alain, *Brussels Art Nouveau: Architecture & Design* (Greensboro: Unicorn Press, 2016).

Gastmans, André, *Mark Severin graphiste/grafisch ontwerper/graphic designer* (Sint-Martens-Latem: De Dijle, 1993).

Géradin, Sara; Poinas, Claire, *Congo: kolonisatie/ dekolonisatie: De geschiedenis in documenten* (Tervuren: Koninklijk Museum voor Midden-Afrika, 2012).

Goffin, Josse; Baudoux, Vincent; Oleffe, Michel; Meuleman, Katrien, *Inventaire Josse Goffin* (Paris: Racine, 2010).

Groensteen, Thierry; Meulen, Ever, *Verve. Een verzameling tekeningen die Ever Meulen maakte tijdens de periode 1988–2005* (Amsterdam: Oog & Blik, 2006).

Grypdonck, A., *Inleiding bij de opening van de tentoonstelling Collectie Paul Ibou van creatieve en alternatieve boek-vorm-realisaties* (Leuven: Stichting Boek, 1983).

Gyselen, Gaby, *Jeanine Behaeghel* (Bruges: Stichting Kunstboek, 1993).

Gyselinckx, François, *Nieuwjaarsbrieven van de Moretussen* (Antwerp: Vrienden van het Museum Plantin-Moretus/ Prentenkabinet vzw, 2013).

Hannoset, Corneille, *Met de handen, of wat de machine niet kan maken: een proeve tot valorisatie van de manuele functie* (Brussels: Vereniging voor tentoonstellingen van het Paleis voor Schone Kunsten / Ghent: Snoeck-Ducaju & Zoon / Crédit communal de Belgique, 1981).

Hannoset, Corneille, *Taptoe* (Brussels: Éditions d'art Laconti, 1989).

Hannoset, Corneille, *Voyages Chroniques* (Gerpinnes: Éditions Tandem, 1997).

Hespeel, Jan; Sabbe, Randoald, *Graphic Mic-Mac* (Ghent: Jan&Randoald, 2008).

Hillebrand, Henri, *Graphic Designers in Europe 4: Franco Grignani, Heinz Edelmann, Jacques Richez, Celestino Piatti* (Fribourg: Office du Livre, 1973).

Hollis, Richard, *Henry van de Velde: The Artist as Designer* (London: Occasional Papers, 2019).

Hubert, Émile, Charles, Alphonse, *Historique de l'association libre des compositeurs & imprimeurs typographes de Bruxelles* (Brussels: Weissenbruch, 1892).

Huyghebaert, Pierre, *Prix Fernand Baudin 2011: prijs voor de best verzorgde boeken uit Brussel en Wallonië* (Brussels: Prix Fernand Baudin Prijs, 2012).

Huys, Paul; Daenens, Lieven; De Buck, Saskia, *Affichekunst in Oost-Vlaanderen* (Ghent: Museum voor Sierkunst en Vormgeving, 1984).

Ibou, Paul, *Activa 33: art & design concept* (Zandhoven: Interecho, 1987).

Ibou, Paul, *Art-Symbols 1: International collection of symbols and logos of art & design exhibitions, museums, galleries and cultural manifestations, designed by famous artists and leading designers worldwide* (Zandhoven: Interecho, 1992).

Ibou, Paul, *Banking Symbols: Collection 1* (Zandhoven: Interecho Press, 1990).

Ibou, Paul, *Banking Symbols: Collection 2* (Zandhoven: Interecho Press, 1991).

Ibou, Paul, *Book design* (Nijlen: Paul Ibou, 1978).

Ibou, Paul, *Collectie Paul Ibou: van creatie ten alternatieve boek-vorm-realisaties* (Diepenbeek: Limburgs Universitair Centrum, 1983).

Ibou, Paul, *Creatief Jaarboek: Vorm in Vlaanderen* (Zandhoven: Interecho, 1984).

Ibou, Paul, *Famous Animal Symbols: Volume 1* (Zandhoven: Groep Interecho vzw, 1991).

Ibou, Paul, *Famous Animal Symbols: Volume 2* (Zandhoven: Groep Interecho vzw, 1992).

Ibou, Paul, *Handboek-huisstijl Universitaire Instelling Antwerpen* (Antwerp: Paul Ibou, 1979).

Ibou, Paul, *Iboubook Activa 25: Paul Ibou: design & art* (Nijlen: Paul Ibou, 1974).

Ibou, Paul, *Logo Book 3: een verzameling emblemen en merken uit België* (Zandhoven: Interecho, 1990).

Ibou, Paul, *Logobook: 200 Trademarks and symbols* (Zandhoven: Interecho, 1990).

Ibou, Paul, *Paul Ibou: Overzichtstentoonstelling* (Antwerp: Archief en Museum voor het Vlaamse Cultuurleven, 1976).

Ibou, Paul, *Quadri-structures* (Nijlen: Paul Ibou, 1975).

Ibou, Paul; Aerts, Eddie; Cambré, Paul; Staal, Liliane, *Logobook: een verzameling emblemen en merken uit Vlaanderen, België* (Zandhoven: Interecho, 1986).

Kockelbergh, Iris, *Henri Cassiers, 1858-1944* (Brussels: Éditions Pandora, 1994).

Kuenzli, Katherine, *Henry van de Velde: Designing Modernism* (New Haven: Yale University Press, 2019).

Lamarche, Caroline; Middendorp, Jan, *Stad van letters, cahier X: Caroline Lamarche en Clotilde Olyff* (Antwerp: ABC2004, 2005).

Lambrecht, Wim, *They Shoot Typo, Don't They?* (Ghent: Grafische Cel, Sint-Lucas Beeldende Kunst Gent, 2012).

Lampaert, Herman, *Epitome Typographica* (Brussels: Erasmushuis, 2009).

Lampaert, Herman, *Startblok* (Brussels: Herman Lampaert, 1996).

Lampaert, Herman, *Waar kan een grafisch vormgever goed voor zijn?* (Brussels: Herman Lampaert, 1972).

Lane, John A., *Early Type Specimens in the Plantin-Moretus Museum* (New Castle Delaware: Oak Knoll Press, 2004).

Lane, John A.; Lommen, Mathieu, *Letterproeven van Nederlandse gieterijen / Dutch typefounders specimens* (Amsterdam: De Buitenkant, 1998).

Laurent, Denis, *Made in Belgium: Design Book* (Brussels: Huis voor Kunst- en Restauratieambacht, 2001).

Lebeer, Louis, *Het mooie Vlaamsche boek* (Antwerp: Museum Plantijn-Moretus, 1931).

Lebrun, André, *De officiële Belgische affiche van Cassiers tot Folon 1830-1984* (Brussels: Generale Bankmaatschappij, 1985).

Lucas, Robert; Scheerlinck, Karl, *Affichekunst* (Ghent: Openbaar Kunstbezit in Vlaanderen, 1995).

Lucas, Robert; Scheerlinck, Karl, *Antwerpen lonkt…: Culturele en toeristische affiches van 1940 tot nu uit de collectie van het Letterenhuis* (Antwerp: AMVC, Letterenhuis, 2005).

Mantels, Ruben, *Torens van boeken* (Veurne: Hannibal, 2020).

Marcy, Gérard; Adrien, Yves, *Affiches Marci: 1880-1970* (Brussels: Gérard Marcy, 2000).

Massin; Olyff, Michel, *Conversation avec Michel Olyff* (Gerpinnes: Éditions Tandem, 2006).

May, Néame, *353 Dessins de May Néame à la Bibliothèque Royale Albert I* (Brussels: Roche, 1969).

Mercier, Jacques; Scheerlinck, Karl, *Made in Belgium. Un siècle d'affiches belges* (Doornik: La Renaissance du Livre, 2003).

Meulen, Ever, *Conversation avec Vincent Baudoux* (Gerpinnes: Éditions Tandem, 2002).

Meuris, Jacques, *Affiches de spectacles en Belgique Francophone* (La Louvière: Centre Culturel de La Louvière, 1983).

Middendorp, Jan, *Twaalf vergeten, verdwenen, ongepubliceerde en grotendeels onclassificeerbare alfabetten* (Antwerp: De Ponsoen, 2003).

Minguet, Philippe; Sauvage, Claire; Lebrun, André; e.a., *L'affiche en Wallonie. A travers les collections du Musée de la Vie Wallonne* (Liège: Musée de la Vie Wallonne, 1980).

Mombaerts, Marc; De Mont, Wim, *De best verzorgde boeken van 2009* (Berchem: Vlaamse Uitgevers Vereniging, 2009).

Morrens, Paul; Willemse, Hans, *Panamarenko: Posters* (Ghent: Ludion, 2008).

Néama, May, *353 tekeningen van May Néama in de Koninklijke Bibliotheek Albert I* (Brussels: Roche, 1969).

Neirinckx, Pieter, *Affiches op het spoor: spoorwegaffiches in België 1883-1985* (Tielt: Lannoo, 2007).

Now, Yellow; Gevaert, Yves, *4 éditeurs / 4 publishers* (Mariemont: Musée Royal de Mariemont, 2007).

Oostens-Wittamer, Yolande, *De Belgische affiche 1892-1914* (Brussels: Koninklijke Bibliotheek Albert I, 1975).

Palmieri, Brooke S., *Women Against Imperialism; A catalogue* (London: Publication Studio / Camp Books, 2019).

Pas, Johan, *Artists Publications: The Belgian Contribution* (London: Koenig Books, 2017).

Pas, Johan, *Beeldenstorm in een spiegelzaal: Het ICC en de actuele kunst 1970-1990* (Leuven: Lannoo, 2005).

Pas, Johan, *Beroepsdocumenten aan hun samenhang onttrokken: een aspect van het Belgisch conceptualisme belicht via drukwerk,..., uit de verzameling van Johan Pas* (Antwerp: S&S 2014).

Pas, Johan, *Dear ICC - aspecten van de actuele kunst in België 1970-1985, 18.12.04 - 27.02.05* (Antwerp: M HKA, 2004).

Pas, Johan, *Een andere avant-garde: documenten uit het archief van galerie De Zwarte Panter, 1968-2008* (Tielt: Lannoo, 2008).

Pas, Wim; Pas, Greet, *Biografisch lexicon plastische kunst in België: schilders, beeldhouwers, grafici 1830-2000* (Antwerp: De Gulden Roos, 2000).

Peeters, Jan Evarist, *Letterkennis en letterkeus* (Ghent: KOLV, 1956).

Peeters, Jan, *Algemene historisch gefundeerde grafische esthetica* (Ghent: Higro, 1979).

Perquy, Julius, Laurent, Maria, *La typographie à Bruxelles au début du XXe siècle* (Brussels: Oscar Schepens & Cie, 1904).

Picqué, Charles; Du Four, Francis, *Campagnes électorales: Systèmes électoraux et techniques de persuasion* (Brussels: Crédit Communal de Belgique, 1977).

Poncelet, Carol, Bareau, Michel, *Lucien de Roeck: du plomb à la plume* (Brussels: Fondation Lucien de Roeck & Bibliotheca Wittockiana, 1998).

Pouillard, Veronique, *C'est du belge, Dit is Belgisch: The history of Advertising in Belgium* (Brussels: Labor, 2004).

Poulain, Norbert; Caese, Georgette; De Buck, Saskia, *Tentoonstelling farmaceutische reclame uit de jaren dertig (Ghent, Witte Zaal, 28.02.1983 - 17.03.1983)* (Ghent: Interbellum, 1983).

Puttaert Hugo; Poynor, Rick; Cleeren, Steven, *Think in Colour* (Ghent: MER. Paper Kunsthalle, 2014).

Remiche, Jean; Minguet, Philippe, *L'affiche en Wallonie: A travers les collections du Musée de la vie Wallonne* (Liège: Massoz, 1980).

Renoy, Georges, *Brussel onder Leopold I: 25 jaar porseleinkaarten 1840-1865* (Brussels: Gemeentekrediet, 1979).

Richez, Jacques, *L'Art d'art graphique, appliqué à la Publicité* (Brussels: Ed. Comptables, Commerciales et Financières, 1972).

Richez, Jacques, *Texte & prétextes: 35 ans de réflexion(s) sur le graphisme* (Brussels: Présence et action culturelles, 1980).

Robert, Jan; Vanhecke, Johan, *Velodromen: fietsaffiches uit het Letterenhuis* (Antwerp: Letterenhuis, 2020).

Roque, Georges, *Ceci n'est pas un Magritte: essai sur Magritte et la publicité* (Paris: Flammarion, 1983).

Rosart, Jacques-Francois; Baudin, Fernand; Hoeflake, Netty, *The Type Specimen of Jacques-Francois Rosart, Brussels, 1768: a Facsimile* (Amsterdam: Van Gendt, 1973).

Scheerlinck, Karl, *Affichekunst aan zee: Een eeuw Belgische Kustaffiches* (Bruges: Uitgeverij Van De Wiele, 2003).

Scheerlinck, Karl, *Alfred Ost 1884-1945: affiches/posters: oeuvrecatalogus* (Mechelen: Cultureel centrum, 1997).

Scheerlinck, Karl, *De affiches van Alfred Ost* (Antwerp: City Antwerp, 1995).

Scheerlinck, Karl, *Filmaffiches van Julien 't Felt (1874-1933)* (Antwerp: Provinciaal Museum voor Fotografie, 1995).

Scheerlinck, Karl, *Jenever en likeur: Affiches die blijven hangen* (Veurne: Hannibal, 2016).

Scheerlinck, Karl, *Kom nog eens af! 150 jaar affiches voor de Zoo* (Antwerp: Koninklijke Maatschappij voor Dierkunde van Antwerpen, 1993).

Scheerlinck, Karl, *Marfurt: Affiches voor jenever en likeur* (Hasselt: Nationaal Jenevermuseum, 2002).

Scheerlinck, Karl, *Terug naar school! Wervingsaffiches voor het onderwijs van Herman Verbaere* (Ypres, 2007).

Scheerlinck, Karl, *Woord in Beeld in het Belgische Affiche* (Sint Niklaas: Stedelijke Musea, 2005).

Scheerlinck, Karl; De Laet, Peter, *Vlaamse theateraffiches tijdens het interbellum* (Bruges: Van de Wiele, 2010).

Scheerlinck, Karl; Lucas, Robert, *58 affiches voor Expo 58* (Brussels: Plaizier, 2008).

Scheerlinck, Karl; Lucas, Robert, *Antwerpen geplakt: Vooroorlogse Antwerpse affichekunst* (Antwerp: Archief en Museum voor het Vlaamse Cultuurleven, 1993).

Scheerlinck, Karl; Terry, Caroline, *Papieren herauten: culturele affiches te Antwerpen (1880-1914) in kunsthistorisch perspectief* (Antwerp: City Antwerp, 1991).

Scheerlinck, Karl; Weill, Alain, *Folon: Les affiches* (Paris: Les Cahiers Dessinés, 2020).

Schoonbroodt, Benoît, *Privat Livemont: entre tradition et modernité au coeur de l'art nouveau 1861-1936* (Brussels: Racine, 2007).

Schwilden, Tristan, *Magritte livre l'image : Affiches, publicités et illustrations de 1918 à 1966* (Brussels: Galerie Bortier, 1998).

Serneels, Piet, *Piet Serneels graficus, 1919-1982: retrospectieve tentoonstelling* (Antwerp: VRIKA, 1983).

Serulus, Katarina, *Design and politics: the public promotion of industrial design in postwar Belgium (1950-1986)* (Leuven: Leuven University Press, 2018).

Serulus, Katarina, *Design Promotion in Belgium in the 1960s: National Interests and European Ambition* (São Paulo: Blucher, 2012).

Serulus, Katarina, *Designing the night: graphic design of Belgian club culture, 1970-2000* (Brussels: Design Museum Brussels, 2019).

Serulus, Katarina; Gimeno-Martínez, Javier, *Panorama: Een Geschiedenis van Modern Design in België* (Brussels: Design Museum, 2017).

Setola, Geert; Pohlen, Joep, *Letterfontein* (Roermond: Fontana, 1994-96).

Simons, Ludo, *Eugène de Bock* (Antwerp: Archief en museum voor het Vlaamse cultuurleven, 1989).

Simons, Ludo, *Geschiedenis van de uitgeverij in Vlaanderen (I & II)* (Tielt: Lannoo, 1984-87).

Simons, Ludo, *Het boek in Vlaanderen sinds 1800: een cultuurgeschiedenis* (Tielt: Lannoo, 2013).

Specht, Stephanie; Angelos, Aya; Moens, Hanna, *Stephanie Specht: Notes Forms* (Antwerp: Specht Studio, 2020).

Stallaerts, Rik; De Hert, Robbe, *Binnenkort in deze zaal. Kroniek van de Belgische filmaffiche* (Ghent: Ludion, 1995).

Stuyck, Raymond, *De winners: gesprekken met suksesmensen* (Antwerp: Brito, 1972).

Sunier, Coline; Mazé, Charles, *Dossier Fernand Baudin: Prix des plus beaux livres à Bruxelles et en Wallonie* (Brussels: Prix Fernand Baudin, 2013).

Teigeler, Piet; Vossen, Misjel, *Rob Buytaert: Vormgever in opdracht* (Antwerp: 't Elzenveld, 1991).

Terlinden, Charles, *La révolution belge de 1830 racontée par les affiches* (Schaarbeek: Richez, 1903).

Toussaint, Christiane; Defourny, Michel, *Josse Goffin* (Saint-Hubert: Service de la Diffusion et de l'Animation Culturelles de la Province de Luxembourg, 1994).

Valcke, Johan; Lampaert, Herman; Lapinne, Christinne, *In Koeien van Letters. 50 jaar grafische vormgeving in Vlaanderen* (Brussels: Vlaams Instituut voor Zelfstandig Ondernemen / Ghent: Museum voor Sierkunst & Vormgeving, 1997).

Valcke, Johan; Luyssaert, Bie; Vranken, Inge, *Iconen van design in Vlaanderen* (Brussels: Vlaams Parlement, 2003).

Van Assche, Hilda; Baeyens, Richard; Cockx-Indestege, Elly, *Vlaamse bibliofiele uitgaven 1930-1980* (Brussels: VEV Komitee Brussel, 1980).

Van den Broeck, Christian, *Who is Peter De Greef?* (Geraardsbergen: Belgatone, 2012).

Van den Eede, Louis, *In de schaduw van Sint-Lucas: enkele overwegingen bij het begrip 'typografisch erfgoed'* (Place of publication not known: De Ponsoen, 2008).

Van Goethem, Julie, *L'affiche fait la force ! De kunstaffiches van de Belgische wereld-tentoonstellingen (1885-1913)* (Ghent: Universiteit Gent, 2019).

Van Haute, Katrien, *Jos Léonard en de ontstaansgeschiedenis van het grafisch ontwerp in België (1918-1936)* (Leuven: K.U.Leuven, Faculteit Letteren, 2009, PhD thesis).

Van Malderen, Luc, *Luc Van Malderen* (Kasterlee: self-published, 1994).

Van Malderen, Luc, *Luc Van Malderen, Conversation avec Diane Hennebert* (Gerpinnes: Éditions Tandem, 1990).

Vandamme, Luc, *May Néama (1917-2007). Medailles, postzegels en bankbiljetten* (Zolder: Limburgse Commissie voor Numismatiek, 2019).

Vandeweyer, Luc; Scheerlinck, Karl; e.a., *100 jaar IJzerbedevaarten in affiches, 1920-2020* (Antwerp: Peristyle, 2021).

Vanschoonbeek, Rudy; Delsaerdt, Pierre, *De best verzorgde boeken van 2008* (Berchem: Vlaamse Uitgevers Vereniging, 2008).

Van Ypersele de Strihou, Adelin, *L'Affiche de Toulouse-Lautrec a nos jours* (Brussels: Palais des Beaux-Arts, 1957).

Velter, Johan, *De best verzorgde boeken van 2004* (Berchem: Vlaamse Uitgevers Vereniging, 2005).

Vermeulen, Jan, *Anderhalve eeuw boektypografie (1818-1965) in Amerika, Engeland, Frankrijk, Duitsland, Zwitserland, Italië, België en Nederland* (Nijmegen: Thieme, 1965).

Verstockt, Mark, *Bookdesign* (Antwerp: Provinciaal Hoger Instituut voor Toegepaste Typografie, 1987).

Verstockt, Mark, *De genesis van de vorm: van chaos tot geometrie* (Antwerp: Standaard, 1982).

Verstockt, Mark, *The Genesis of Form: From Chaos to Geometry* (London: Muller, Blond & White, 1987)

Verstockt, Mark, *Verstockt, 1970-75 : objekten, beelden, projekten, video tapes, collages, tekeningen, boeken, montages, drukken, lay-out, vormgeving, teksten* (Antwerp: Mercatorfonds, 1975)

Vervliet, Hendrik Désiré Louis, *5000 jaar geschiedenis van het boek* (Brussels: Arcades, 1972).

Vervliet, Hendrik Désiré Louis, *Ameet Tavernier: lettersteker* (Antwerp: Algemene Drukkerijen Lloyd Anversois, 1961).

Vervliet, Hendrik Désiré Louis, *De Garamondletters van Christoffel Plantin* (Antwerp: Stad Antwerpen, 1965).

Vervliet, Hendrik Désiré Louis, *Humanisme en typografie: de introductie van de romein en cursief in de Nederlanden (1483-ca.1540)* (Hilversum: Verloren, 1986).

Vervliet, Hendrik Désiré Louis, *Jan Lettersnijder: Antwerps drukker en graveur* (Brussels: Paleis der Academiën, 1964).

Vervliet, Hendrik Désiré Louis, *Maarten de Keyser: belangrijk Antwerps drukker* (Brussels: Paleis der Academiën, 1964).

Vervliet, Hendrik Désiré Louis, *Sixteenth-century printing types of the Low Countries* (Amsterdam: Menno Hertzberger, 1968).

Vervliet, Hendrik Désiré Louis; Pelckmans, Albert; Middendorp, Jan; De Vylder, Antoon; De Nave, Francine, *Magistraal: meesters van het Plantin genootschap 1951-1974* (Antwerp: Museum Plantin Moretus, 2007).

Vijver, Van de, Lies; Dupont, Guy; Winkel, Vande, Roel, *Gent filmstad: cinema's en filmaffiches, 1938-1961* (Antwerpen: Houtekiet, 2021).

Vints, Luc, *Leo Meurrens: Leuvens Graficus* (Leuven: KADOC-KU Leuven, 2017).

Vossen, Misjel; Mombaerts, Marc, *Goed voor druk* (Ghent: Academia Press, 1995).

Wells, James M.; Handover, P.M.; Blanchard, G.; Vox, Maximilien; Schaauer, Dr. G.K.; Rotzler, Dr. Willy; Riva, Franco; Baudin, Fernand; Ovink, Prof.Dr. G.W., *One and Half Centuries Book Typography, 1815-1965 in America, England, France, Germany, Switzerland, Italy, Belgium and The Netherlands* (Nijmegen: G.J. Thieme, 1965).

Magazine articles

Adriaens-Pannier, Anne, 'Tijd- en Strijdschriften van de Avant-Garde in België 1917-1929', *Avant-Garde in België*, 1992, pp.162-223.

Amstutz, Walter, 'Julian Key', *Who's Who in Graphic Art*, 1962.

Auwelaert, Patrick, 'Een boek is een huis: hedendaagse Vlaamse boekarchitectuur', *Kunsttijdschrift Vlaanderen*, 2011, 338, pp.257-99.

Avermaete, Roger, 'L'arte pubblicitario in Belgio', *Suggestione pubblicitaria*, 1951, 8, pp.47-56.

Baudin, Fernand, 'La formation et l'évolution typographiques de Henry van de Velde (1863-1957)', *Quarendo*, 1971-72, Volume 1: Issue 4, pp.264-81.

Bergmeir, Wolfgang, 'Paul Ibou (BEL)', *Novum Gebrauchsgraphik*, 1989, pp.44-49.

Blanchard, Gérard, 'Fernand Baudin, La typographie au tableau noir', *Communication et Languages*, 1984, 60, p.120.

Block, Jane, 'Boekdesign bij Les Vingt. Het werk van Lemmen, van de Velde en Van Rysselberghe tijdens het fin de siècle', *Les Vingt en de avant-garde in België. Prenten, tekeningen en boeken. ca. 1890*, 1992, pp.73–98.

Bosschem, Willy, 'Affiche: eigentijdse flitsen', *Vlaanderen*, jaargang 16, 1967, p.9.

Bosschem, Willy; Setola, Willy; Vansevenant, Roger; Sarlet, Werner, 'Affiche, Vlaams werk', *Vlaanderen*, 1967, 16, p.340–48.

Brams, Koen, 'Over een opvallende affiche met gemengde kleuren: Interview met Rik Lemaitre', *De Witte Raaf*, 2015, 173.

Claeys, Guinevere, 'Paul Ibou, verzamelaar van vormen', *De Standaard*, 2018, pp.26–31.

Cloostermans, Mark, 'De best verzorgde boeken 1996–2002 te zien in de KBC-toren', *De Standaard*, 2005.

Crombez, Thomas; De Bondt, Sara; Hautekiet, Tom; Puttaert, Hugo; Van Haute, Katrien en Rogiers, Bas, 'MADE IN BELGIUM: Een debat over de geschiedenis van grafisch ontwerp', 2018.

De Baerdemaeker, Jo, 'Belgium: Typographic News – Fernand Baudin (1918-2005)', *Reports of the country delegates 2004/2005. Association Typographique Internationale*, 2005, p.11.

De Baerdemaeker, Jo, 'Times New Belgian: de nieuwste leestechnologie met eeuwenoude Belgische letters', *De Tijd*, 2021.

De Pooter, David, 'Paul Ibou wordt tachtig, een ontmoeting met een multi-kunstenaar', *The Art Couch*, 2019, pp.58–61.

De Vulture, Roland, 'Paul Ibou "25": grafisch vormgever, boekontwerper-typograaf, beeldend kunstenaar', *Grafiek*, 1979, 118, pp.6–14.

Degrande, Geert, 'Paul Ibou koestert de verwondering', *Impact*, 1999, 3, pp.24–31.

Des Cressonnières, Josine; Stiefenhofer, Jean-Jacques, 'Dossier: Het Design Centre: tien jaar onderweg', *A+*, 1974, 9-10, pp.18–40.

De Kock, Cathérine, 'Een oeuvre met grote O', *De Standaard*, 10 January 2015.

Dierick, Phyllis; Lindemans, Katelijne, 'De uitnodigingskaartjes van de solotentoonstelling van Raoul De Keyser van 1965 tot 2013: Een onderzoeksverslag', 2014.

Dooreman, Gert, 'Wat vindt u van het Vlaamse Logo?', *De Standaard*, 15 July 2013.

Dubois, Jacques; Edeline, Francis; Klinkenberg, Jean-Marie; Minguet, Philippe, 'La Chafetière est sur la table', *Communication et Languages*, 1976, p.29.

Duchesne, Jean-Patrick, 'Roger Potier, de l'écriture au style', *Revue Art&Fact*, 1980, 2, pp.147–55.

Emergy, G., 'Enige Belgische aanplakbiljetten', *Grafisch Tijdschrift*, 1963, p.12.

Emiel, Bergen, 'De weerklank van het Bauhaus in de Belgische tijdschriften', *Bauhaus, ICSAC-Cahier*, 1987, pp.331–40.

'Fiche-Design: Buytaert', *Infordesign*, 1967, 14, p.13.

'Fiche-Design: Corneille Hannoset', *Infordesign*, 1967, 15, p.15.

'Fiche-Design: Hendrickx Alfred', *Infordesign*, 1967, 15, p.9.

'Fiche-Design: Herman Lampaert', *Infordesign*, 1967, 19, pp.19–20.

'Fiche-Design: Paul Ibou', *Infordesign*, 1967, 16-17, p.11.

'Fiche-Design: Luc Vanmalderen', *Infordesign*, 1967, 18, p.17.

Fontier, Jaak, 'Paul Ibou, design als kunstuiting', *Ons Erfdeel*, 1980, pp.757–59.

Gasser, Manuel, 'Josse Goffin', *Graphis*, 1976, p.183.

Guégan, Bertrand, 'Belgique', *Arts et Métiers Graphiques*, 1931, 26, p.14.

Hecq, Geneviève, 'Papieren geschiedenis: 100 jaar affiches', *Femmes d'Aujourd'hui / Het Rijk der Vrouw*, 1974, 1541.

Holcher, Eberhard, 'Jacques Richez', *Gebrauchsgraphik*, 1960, 11.

Hudek, Antony, 'L'Humour Coloré de Sara De Bondt', *EDGAR / Ecole supérieure d'art et de désign Le Havre-Rouen*, 2011.

Ibou, Paul, 'Avant-Garde pioneers in creativity & sculpture from "the Bauhaus"', *Sculpture*, 2007, 2, pp.78–79.

Ibou, Paul, 'De geschiedenis van het design in België', *Tijdschrift van de Belgische dienst voor buitenlandse handel*, 1990, p.3.

Ibou, Paul, 'Graphic designer of commercial artist', *Vlaanderen*, 1967, 95, pp.315–18.

Ibou, Paul, 'Quo Vadis. Has Design Tomorrow Still a Future?', *17 Biennale Brno '96*, 1996, pp.10–19.

Jacobs, Erna; Willekens, Emiel; Lampaert, Herman; De Schutter, Carl; De Vijlder, Antoon; Wouters, Antoon, 'Tien, met een Plantin-Moretuspenning bekroonde boeken', *Plantin-Moretus prijs*, 1992.

Jacobs, Erna; Binnenweg, Bram; Delaere, Boudewijn; De Schutter, Carl; Lampaert, Herman; Willekens, Emiel, 'Tien, met een Plantin-Moretuspenning bekroonde boeken', *Plantin-Moretus prijs*, 1993.

'Julian Key: Kwaliteitsaffiches', *Spoornieuws NMBS*, 1982, 1, pp.14–15.

Karel Van Oss, 'Josse Goffin, Julian Key, Jacques Richez, Charles Rohonyi', *Claxon*, 1971, 22.

L'Agence Vanypeco, '25 ans de creation au service de la Foire Internationale de Bruxelles', *Présence de Bruxelles*, 1970, 93.

Lambrecht, Luk, 'Filiep Tacq: Boeken moet je voelen', *De Morgen*, 2011.

Lewis, Angharad, 'Sara De Bondt profile', *Grafik*, 2007, pp.42–53.

Lucas, Robert, 'Martha van Coppenolle: Archief van een boekillustrator', *Zuurvrij*, 2010, 26, p.98.

Lucas, Robert, 'Waar reclame en poëzie elkaar vinden, Julian Key', *Zuurvrij*, 2010, 19.

Lutteraan, Johannes, 'Een affiche moet als een verkeerslicht zijn, maar te veel kleuren werken verwarrend', *Revue der Reclame*, 1968, 23.

Lutteraan, Johannes, 'Woorden moeten alleen zeggen wat niet kan uitgebeeld worden', *Revue der Reclame*, 1967, 5.

Maertens, Christophe, 'Expo Gert Dooreman in bib Wevelgem: "Als Ordnung dan toch muß sein, dan liefst die van Dooreman"', *Het Laatste Nieuws*, 10 December 2021.

Masaru, Katsumie, 'Graphic design in Belgium', *Graphic Design*, 1971, 4.

Ohchi, Hiroshi, 'Jacques Richez, A.G.I.', *Idea*, 1960, 43.

Olyff, Michel, 'Questions graphiques : Enjeux et contraintes', *Bulletin de la Classe des Beaux-Arts*, 2001, 7-12.

Ongenae, Cathérine, 'Grafisch Vormgever Gert Dooreman, Ik ben een overtuigde antisnob', *Knack*, 2015.

Oosterlinck, Christian, 'Vlaamse pioniers: Ibou, Olyff, Lampaert en Buytaert', *Kwintessens*, 2018, 4, pp.2–12.

Parmentier, Magali; Olyff, Michel, 'Michel Olyff : Hand en tekeningen', *De Facto*, 2000, 22, pp.100-03.

Pil, Lut, 'Het boek herdacht: Geoffrey Brusatto, Ruth Loos en Ellen Bilterest over hun Doctoraat in de Kunsten', *Kwintessens*, 2012, 3, pp.47-55.

Ponot, René, 'Les XXIIes Rencontres graphiques internationales de Lure', *Communication et Languages*, 1974, 24, pp.126-27.

Poulain, Norbert, 'Illustratrices uit het interbellum: Jenny Teeuwen, Elsa Van Hagendoren, Elza Severin', *Interbellum*, 2008, 28, p.11.

Poynor, Rick, 'Ten Things I Know about Belgian Graphic Design', *Kwintessens*, 2009, 4, pp.61-70.

Puttaert, Hugo, '20 jaar grafische vormgeving in Kwintessens', *Kwintessens* 4, 2011.

Puttaert, Hugo, 'Gilles Fiszman. De Kracht van de nuance', *Addmagazine*, 2005, issue 2, pp.32-35.

Puttaert, Hugo, 'Kaleidoscopically Irregular', *Kwintessens*, 2011, 4, unpaginated.

Puttaert, Hugo, 'Luk Mestdagh. Een beminnelijke onruststoker', *Addmagazine*, 2006, 3, p.22-24.

Puttaert, Hugo, 'Michel Olyff – Een beeld als beeltenis', *Addmagazine*, 2007, pp.32-37.

Richaudeau, François, 'Cinq siècles de typographie: Fernand Baudin L'Effet Gutenberg', *Communication et Languages*, 1995, p.103.

Richez, Jacques, 'Aspects nouveaux de l'art publicitaire belge', *Graphis*, 1969, 144.

Richez, Jacques, 'Au nom des graphistes les plus mal employés du monde', 1975, 2, p.36.

Richez, Jacques, 'Belgian Graphic Designers', *Idea*, 1969, 96.

Richez, Jacques, 'Belgian Poster and Cover Designs', *Graphis*, 1950, 29, pp.62-67.

Richez, Jacques, 'Fonction économique et rôle social de l'affiche en Wallonie', *Dossiers du CACEF*, 1976-77, 43-44.

Richez, Jacques, 'Graphic Design in Belgium', *Graphic Design*, 1971, 41.

Richez, Jacques, 'Recent Belgian Graphic Design', *Graphis*, 1969/1970, 144, pp.290-309.

Robert, Jan, 'Suiker tussen de rubrieken. Clausaffiches in het Letterenhuis', *Zuurvrij*, 2017, 33, pp.72-84.

Rohonyi, Charles, 'Graphic Design in Belgium', *Novum Gebrauchsgraphik*, 1971, 9 pp.12-29.

Rohonyi, Charles, 'Jacques Richez', *Novum Gebrauchsgraphik*, 1952, 2, pp.44-51.

Rohonyi, Charles 'Josse Goffin', *Novum Gebrauchsgraphik*, 1977, 2.

Rohonyi, Charles, 'Luc Van Malderen', *Novum Gebrauchsgraphik*, 1973, 4.

Rohonyi, Charles, 'Sophie Bertout & Sami Alouf, Bruxelles', *Novum Gebrauchsgraphik*, 1977, pp.22-28.

Rohonyi, Charles, 'The Advertising of the Belgian National Theatre', *Novum Gebrauchsgraphik*, 1971, 3, pp.52-56.

Rohonyi, Charles, 'Yvon Adam', *Novum Gebrauchsgraphik*, 1978, 10.

Scheerlinck, Karl, 'Affiches als promotiemiddel voor de stad Antwerpen en het opmerkelijke debuut van Lucien De Roeck, 60 jaar geleden', *Interbellum*, 1994, 5, pp.8-15.

Scheerlinck, Karl, 'Dromen van papier: Affiches uit de collectie van de Nationale Loterij', *Openbaar Kunstbezit Vlaanderen*, 2015, 1, pp.31-39.

Scheerlinck, Karl, 'Kroniek van kunsten en letteren. De affiche en de lithografie', *De Volksgazet*, 1934, p.11.

Scheerlinck, Karl, 'Red Star Line Museum. Mensen en migratie', *Openbaar Kunstbezit Vlaanderen*, 2013, 5.

Severin, Mark F., 'Graphic Art in Belgium', *The Penrose Annual*, 1959, pp.30-35.

Sterckx, Pierre, 'Julian Key: l'homme du Chat Noir', *Connaissance des Arts*, 1974, 3.

Sterckx, Pierre, 'Le clown et l'affiche', *Clés pour les Arts*, 1973, 38.

Stiefenhofer, Jean-Jacques, 'Pleidooi voor goed design (of betere konsumenten)', *Esso magazine*, 1973, 1, p.34.

Stiefenhofer, Jean-Jacques, 'Promoteurs de Design du monde entier, unissez-vous', *A-PLUS*, 1974, 9, pp.38-39.

Valcke, Johan, 'In het zog van de Bauhaus', *OKV*, 1997, 12.

Van Dijck, Peter, 'Solitaire kasteelheer', *Gentleman*, 2008, 10, pp.112-16.

Van Haute, Katrien, 'Het Belgische tijdschrift Grafiek en de katholieke interpretatie van de modernistische typografie tijdens de jaren dertig en veertig', *Tijdschrift voor mediageschiedenis*, 2016, 19, pp.1-18.

Van Haute, Katrien, 'Het prille Belgische grafisch ontwerp door de ogen van Arts et Métiers graphiques', *Arts et metiers graphiques: Kunst en grafische vormgeving in het interbellum*, 2015, pp.45-55.

Van Haute, Katrien, 'Grafisch design van Paul Ibou', *Grafisch Nieuws*, 2018, 68.

Van Haute, Katrien, 'The Indépendant, a Typeface as Period Document', *Quaerendo*, 2008, 38, pp.46-69.

Van Malderen, Luc, 'Belgium, Who's Who of European designers', *Idea*, 1972.

Van Malderen, Luc; Richez, Jacques, 'Un problème, l'affiche en Belgique', *Clés pour les Arts*, 1970, 4, pp.17-18.

Vandermeerschen, Rafaël, 'Design is nog assepoes in ons gezegend landje', *Spectator*, 1975, 34, pp.21-25.

Vincent Baudoux, 'Monsieur Julien Keymolen dit Julian Key', *Clés pour les Arts*, 1973, 38.

Walters, John, 'Sara De Bondt: A certain smile', *Eye*, 2011, 80.

Whittet, G.S., 'Jubilee for a Poster Impresario', *Art & Industry*, 1957, 373.

Willard, Joris, 'Computer graphics van Paul Ibou', *Grafiek*, 1988, 3, pp.2-3.

Magazines

La chronique graphique : revue mensuelle des arts et industries du livre et des branches connexes, Brussels: Société belge d'imprimerie, 1929-64.

Addmagazine, Brussels: Papyrus, 2005-10.

Gebrauchsgraphik: International Advertising Art, München: F. Bruckmann, 1924-71.

Grafiek, Ghent: Kunstdrukschool Sint-Lucas, 1936-2000.

Infordesign, Brussels: Kumps, 1964-71.

La Réclame, 1911-14.

Publirep. Organe technique de la publicité, 1921-31.

Vendre, 1923-71.

Vorm In Vlaanderen, Antwerp, 1981-82.

Photographers

Jo De Baerdemaeker 26, 28, 30

Albert Bayidikila (Inforcongo) 52

Hans G. Conrad 244 (left)

J. Costa (Inforcongo) 51 (bottom)

Michael Delausnay 128, 138, 152, 158, 191 (top), 192, 193, 196–97, 202, 211–13, 218–23, 250

J. Geleyns 141, 142, 148, 151

Corneille Hannoset 195

Katrien Van Haute 10–13, 17–20, 22, 23

C. Lamote (Inforcongo) 51 (top), 53

bibi Lonfils 70

Michel Olyff 63 (left)

Michael Penck 244 (right)

Royal Museum of Fine Arts Antwerp 207

Jacques Thomas 63 (right)

Kris Vercruysse 49

visionandfactory (Christophe Clarijs and Elke Scholliers) 201 (top and bottom)

Image credits

Boudewijn Delaere Archive
73, 126 (all), 128

Catapult, Antwerp
167 (top right), 202 (all)

CIVA, Brussels
36 (bottom)

Collection Annik Honoré
77, 78

Collection Archives et Musée de la Littérature, Brussels
189, 191 (top), 195 (all)

Collection Bart Gijsens
83 (bottom), 84

Collection Bruno Bulté
79 (bottom left and right)

Collection Centre de la Gravure et de l'Image imprimée, La Louvière
67, 129

Collection Ceuleers & Van de Velde
184 (bottom left and right), 191 (top), 192, 193, 196 (all), 197

Collection La Démence
87

Collection Fuse Club Brussels
85 (flyer for 'Ça Mousse')

Collection Jo De Baerdemaeker
30 (top and bottom)

Collection Paul Ibou
206, 208, 210 (all), 212-13

Collection Paul Sterck
81 (top and bottom)

Collection Peter Decuypere
86

Collection Philippe Motteux
76, 82 (top and bottom), 85 (all images apart from the flyer for 'Ça Mousse')

Collection Sara De Bondt
55 (bottom left), 69, 116, 117, 138, 147, 152, 158, 183 (bottom), 184 (top), 186-87, 220

Collection Vlaams Architectuurinstituut, Antwerp
252-53

Design Museum Gent
120

Ecole nationale supérieure des arts visuels de La Cambe, Brussels
38, 39

FIBAC, Berchem
15 (bottom right)

Ghent University Library
123, 127, 130, 131, 132, 133, 136, 143, 155, 160, 173, 241

Herman Lampaert Archive
140

HfG-Archiv / Museum Ulm
244 (right)

Industriemuseum, Ghent
32, 33

Institut d'histoire ouvrière, économique et sociale (IHOES), Seraing
228 (top right)

Institute of Social History (AMSAB), Ghent
68 (left and right), 148, 175

Jean-Jacques Stiefenhofer Archive
245-51, 255

Kunstenbibliotheek, Ghent
61 (right)

Letterenhuis, Antwerp
13, 45 (left), 66, 115, 118 (all), 119, 121 (all), 122, 124 (all), 137, 144-45, 146 (all), 150, 153, 154, 164 (bottom left and right), 165 (bottom left and right), 215

Liberas Archive, Ghent
114

Loterijmuseum, Brussels
48 (top left and right)

Lucien De Roeck Foundation
36 (top), 41 (bottom right), 231 (both), 232, 233, 234, 235, 236 (all), 237, 238 (both), 239 (all)

Michel Olyff Archive
226, 227, 228 (all apart from top right), 229

Mondelez Belgium, Mechelen
48 (bottom left and right)

Musea Brugge, Bruges
168

Private Collection
211 (top and bottom), 218, 219, 221, 222, 223

Pol Martens - Brugge in affiches
165 (top left and right), 166 (right)

Rencontres internationales de Lure, Lurs
63 (all)

René Magritte Museum - Museum of Abstract Art, Jette, Brussels
15 (top left)

Royal Library of Belgium, Brussels
26 (top and bottom), 28 (top and bottom)

Royal Museum for Central Africa (KMMA), Tervuren
41 (bottom left), 42-43, 45 (middle and right), 47, 50 (top and bottom), 51 (top and bottom), 52 (left and right), 53, 54 (all), 56, 57, 58

Royal Museums of Fine Arts of Belgium, Brussels
141, 142, 149, 151

Royal Museum of Fine Arts Antwerp
207 (all)

S+S Alouf Archive
156, 157

Stedelijk Prentenkabinet, Antwerp
12 (bottom), 15 (top right), 18 (top), 22 (bottom)

University Library Moretus Plantin, Namur
11, 12 (top), 17, 18 (bottom), 19, 20, 22 (top), 23

Acknowledgements

Special thanks to the authors and designers for their contributions and allowing me to reproduce their work.

Thank you to PhD supervisors Helena De Preester for her unwavering support, to Luc Derycke for his steadfast guidance, and to doctoral committee members Ruth Blacksell and Armand Mevis for their always constructive feedback.

I could not have edited this book without the unfailing support of the following people, to whom I extend my thanks: Suzy Castermans, David Depestel, Wim De Temmerman, Ronny Duquenne, Herlinde Van Langenhove, and Katrien Vuylsteke Vanfleteren at KASK – School of Arts; Evelien Bracke, Katrien Laporte, and Eva Van Regenmortel at Design Museum Gent; Sofie De Caigny and Katarina Serulus at Flanders Architecture Institute.

I would also like to warmly thank Koen Brams, Bambi Ceuppens, Thomas Crombez, Annie Gentils, Steven Jacobs, Herman Lampaert, Johan Pas, Stéphane de Schrevel, Benedict Vandaele, and Jeroen Wille for their research input, as well as Michael Delausnay, Sarah Horn, Stef Van Oevelen, and Kris Vercruysse for documenting the work included in this book. I am grateful to Michael Marriott for designing the furniture and Simon van der Zande for editing the videos in the exhibition *Off the Grid*.

Without the support of Jan De Bondt and Lieve Vercruysse, this publication would not exist (nor would I, for that matter).

But above all, thank you to Antony Hudek for his crucial input and boundless encouragement in the process of making this book, which is dedicated to him.

Index

A
Abdulla, Danah 41
Academy for Industrial Design, Eindhoven 95, 244
Académie Royale des Beaux-Arts 80, 182
AfricaMuseum *see* Royal Museum for Central Africa, Tervuren
Albers, Josef 208, 216
Albert I 47
Alechinsky, Pierre 183, 184, 185, 225, 232
Alkaselser 80, 88
Allard, Eugeen 21
Alliance Graphique Internationale 63, 181, 227
Alliance Typographique Internationale 68
Alouf-Bertot, Sophie 75
Alouf, Sami 75, 90
American Institute of Graphic Arts 71
AMSAB *see* Institute of Social History, Antwerp
Angus, Peggy 55
Ansari, Ahmed 41
Antiqua 25, 37
Antler-Subway Records 82
Antwerp City of Culture 93, 199
Antwerp Zoo 105
Aplus 109
Apple 106
Architecture 184, 189
Art Deco 52, 56
Art Director's Annual 102
Art Nouveau 45, 59
Association for Advertising Studies 23
Association Internationale Africaine 44
Atelier d'Expression Libre 65
Atelier Populaire 65
Ateliers du Marais 183, 225, 226
Au Vieux Saint Martin 64
Ausloos & Payot 115
Avril, François 230
Axion Design Partnership 177

B
Bacon, Francis 101
De Baerdemaeker, Jo 24, 258, 265
Bailleux, César 210, 222
Balasse, Thierry 80
Baudin, Fernand 31, 63, 68, 72, 90, 111, 116, 118, 256, 258, 260, 261, 262, 263, 264, 268
Baudson, Pierre 64, 72
Bauhaus 37, 90, 183, 199, 200
Bayer, Herbert 216
Bayidikila, Albert 52
Behaeghel, Jeanine 72, 163, 164, 165, 166, 168, 169, 170, 177, 259
Belgian Chamber of Graphic Designers 60, 62, 65, 72, 94, 95, 101, 108
Belgian Institute Graphic Design 71, 172-73, 174-75, 240-41 *see* Belgisch Instituut Grafisch Ontwerp
Belgische Radio- en Televisieomroep 105
Belovo 199
Benoît, Peter 59
Berger, Patrick 82
Van den Bergh, Joseph 47
Berthet, Philippe 230
Bertot, Lou 90
Bill, Max 88, 216, 246, 268
Binneweg, Herbert 119
Blauvelt, Andrew 88
Blondé Printing 199
Bodoni 37
De Boeck, Francine 65, 72
De Bondt, Sara 40, 60, 89, 162, 204, 258
Bonzai 82
Van den Boom, Raoul 105
Borgers, Marc 76, 79
Bos, Ben 227
Boss Paints 199
Van den Bossche, Phillip 23
BOZAR *see* Palais des Beaux-Arts, Brussels
Breker, Walter 170, 199
Van Brempt, P. 45
Van der Brempt, Stanislas 243
Breughel the Younger, Pieter 251
Van den Brink, Hans Maarten 254
British Petroleum 105
Brody, Neville 199
Brodzki, Constantin 55, 183, 184, 185, 189, 190, 194
Broodthaers, Marcel 183, 185, 189, 190, 192, 194
Brownjohn, Robert 55
Brueghel the Elder, Jan 251
Bruges Shipping Company 199
Brussels World Fair of 1935 48, 49
Bulté, Bruno 79, 80
Buñuel, Luis 109
Burroughs, William S. 79
Buschmann, Joseph-Ernest 29, 35, 37
Buytaert, Rob 101, 121, 122, 177, 199, 256, 262, 263, 268

C
Cabaret Voltaire 79, 80
La Cambre 3, 35, 37, 79, 90, 93, 98, 102, 109, 111, 183, 184, 225, 226, 231, 232, 237
Canotier 80, 82, 88
Cassandre 231
Catapult 199
Cauchie, Bernard 80
Centre for Fine Arts *see* Palais des Beaux-Arts, Brussels
CERA Bank 106
Ceuleers, Jan 182
Chaland, Yves 230
Church of St John the Evangelist 46
Citroën 2CV 185
Clarks International 106
Clément 26
Club Français du Livre 192
Cobra 183, 226
De Coene 101
Colonial Lottery 47, 48, 49, 50, 51, 52, 53, 54, 55, 56, 59, 61, 62, 63, 64, 66, 68, 71, 73
Colpaert, Rika 217
Le Congo Illustré 44
Congolese National Movement for the Liberation of Congo 56
Conrad & Joniau 26
Conrad, Patrick 26
Van Coppenolle, Hélène 105, 123, 256
Van Coppenolle, Martha 124, 256, 263
Coppens, Thierry 87
Le Corbusier 109
Coster, Jocelyne 78, 79
Côte d'Or 48
Cotteleer, Anton 230
Courrier d'Afrique 51
Courtoit, Elza 256
Cox, Jan 225
Craet Burssens, Frida 120
Des Cressonnières, Josine 61, 71, 97, 249
Creuze, Serge 183
Crouwel, Wim 203, 226, 227
Cube Art 108
Curtis, Ian 79

D
Darche, Jacques 192
Deceukelier, Marleen 173
Declercq, Bart 82
Degouy, Nelly 125
Dejonck, Frans 136
Delaere, Boudewijn 37, 61, 72, 75, 126, 127, 128, 166, 177, 232, 257, 259, 263, 266, 268
Delahaut, Jo 216, 258
Delaunay, Sonia 90
Delcoigne, Anne 175
Delemer 26
La Demence 87, 88
Denaeyer-Van Poelvoorde, Colette 65, 66
Denaeyer, Roland 65, 66, 68, 72, 129
Design and Art Direction 71
Design Centre 61, 62, 71, 75, 90, 97, 111, 112, 249
Design Museum Brussels 75
Design Museum Gent 7, 23, 89, 113
Design Vlaanderen 71, 97, 199

Design-Team 62, 95, 97, 143, 199, 203
Devries, Herman 216
Didot, Jules 26
Didot, Pierre 26
Die Keure 199
Disco Futura 80, 82
Dockx, Nico 217, 230
De Does, Bram 112
Dratz, Jean 47, 48
Dumont 25, 26
Dustin, Jo 65, 129, 259
Duval, Michel 79

E
Echo & The Bunnymen 79
L'Echo de Bruxelles 26
École supérieure des Arts Saint-Luc 93
Ecran du Séminaire des Arts 185
Edition der Spiegel 216
Van Eelen, Alice 243
Eisenbrand, Jochen 75, 88
Elizabeth Arden 90
Elle 190
Elno, Karel 62, 72, 95, 244
Elskamp, Max 37
eMDé see Deceukelier, Marleen
Établissements Plantin 25, 29, 49
Ethnographic Museum, Antwerp 251
Europa Prize 106
Europalia 106, 130, 225, 251
Expo 58 35, 55, 56, 61, 98, 185, 231, 232
EXPRMNTL 184

F
Facetten van de jonge Vlaamse kunst 14
Fauna Pavilion 55, 56, 185
Federation of Designers 71
Filliou, Robert 216
First Things First 66
Fiszman, Gilles 63, 64, 75, 177, 178, 179, 180, 181, 210, 218, 227, 259, 264
Flanders Fashion Institute 71
Flemish Community 108, 178
Folon, Jean-Michel 130, 232, 259, 260, 261
Fonderie et Gravure Typographiques A & F Vanderborght 29
Fonderie et Imprimerie Normale 26

Fonderie Typographique Carabin-Schildknecht 25, 29, 231, 232, 234, 235, 236, 238, 239, 243
Fonderie Typographique Maison Van Loey-Nouri 29
FontFont 199
FontShop 199, 203
Foudriat 26
Fournier 29
42/60 65, 72
François, André 25, 26, 181, 230
French Community 178
Front 242 79
Froshaug, Anthony 170
Frutiger 93
Futura 37, 80, 93, 98

G
Galerie Aujourd'hui 185
Galerie Taptoe 185
Gando 26
Garamond 37, 98
Garland, Ken 66
Gazet van Antwerpen 199
La Gazzetta dello Sport 31
Geersens, Fernand 37, 183
Van Gendt 31
Generale Bank 62
Gerstner, Karl 216
De Ghelderode, Michel 10
Giampietro, Rob 52, 59
Gigli, Aldo 80, 82
Gilbert, J. 45
Gill, Eric 109
Gilles, Raymond 63, 75, 80, 177, 227, 244, 248
Goddyn, Servaes 63
Godenne Foundation 10, 16
Godenne, Willy 10, 12, 13, 14, 16, 19, 23
Goepfert, Hermann 216
Goffin, Josse 177
Gonnissen, Adriaan 23
Goossens-Bara, Jacques 80
Goris, Fons 246
Grafische Vormgevers Vlaanderen 72, 108
Graphic Design 61
Graphis 61, 62, 94, 102
Grapus 178
De Groot, Frans 248
De Groot, Johannes 29
Guderian, Dietmar 173
Gulden Sporen 98
Gysin, Brion 79

H
De Haan, Anton 199
Haesaerts, Luc 109
D'Haese, Reinhoud 185, 225
D'Haese, Roel 185
De Hallen 98
Hankar, Paul 44
Hannoset, Corneille 55, 59, 63, 72, 75, 109, 177, 182, 183, 184, 185, 189, 190, 192, 194, 256
Harris, Silvia 41, 59
Hartung, Charles-Jacques 25, 29
Van Haute, Katrien 8, 23, 49, 258
Heck, Kati 254
Van Hecke, Willem 105
Heideland 98
Helvetica 93, 95, 102
Henrion, Henri Kay 227
Hens, Robert 45
Hepworth, Barbara 216
Hergé 237
Hermans, Gerard 109
Herreman, Lieven 200
De Heusch, Luc 225
Heyvaert, Pierre 216
Hochschule für Gestaltung, Ulm 243, 244, 246, 248, 254
Van Hoecke, Sony 173
Hoeflake, Netty 31
Hoet, Jan 173
Van Hoeydonck, Paul 210, 221
Hollis, Richard 34, 59
Honoré, Annik 79
Hoozee, Robert 251
Horta, Victor 44, 45
Hostettler, Rudolf 111
House of Graphic Designers 64
hugOKÉ 131, 256
Huidevettershuis 170
Hulet, Philippe 177
Hürrig, Manfred 132

I
IBM 199
Ibou, Paul 55, 72, 105, 132, 134, 166, 177, 205, 206, 208, 209, 210, 214, 215, 216, 217, 221, 256, 257, 259, 260, 262, 263, 264
IDEA 61, 94
Imprimarium 25, 29
L'Indépendance 56, 59
Indépendant 37, 49, 51, 52, 53, 59
L'indispensable 111
Infordesign 61
Information and Documentation Centre of Belgian Congo and Rwanda-Urundi 52, 53
Innovation 101
Institut Supérieur des Arts Décoratifs see La Cambre
Institute for Industrial Design 248
Institute of Social History, Antwerp 251
Integrated Conference 176, 198, 224
Interieur 98, 101
International Council of Graphic Design Associations 62, 63, 227
International Day of Graphic Design 65
Itterbeek, Philippe 80

J
J. Gatz 199
J. Gatz Paper 199
Jazz Middelheim 241
Jewish Museum of Belgium 177
Jorn, Asger 185, 225
Jossa, Idriz 82
Joy Division 76, 78, 79, 88

K
Kandinsky, Wassily 9
KASK School of Arts, Ghent 40, 60, 162, 204
Katsumie, Masaru 61
Key, Julian 75, 137, 177, 226, 256, 258, 262, 263, 264
Keymolen, Julien 226 see Key, Julian
De Keyser, Raoul 173
King Baudouin Foundation 199
Klacik 79, 80, 88
Kneebone, Peter 227
Koninklijk Ballet Vlaanderen 106
Koninklijke Musea voor Schone Kunsten van België, Brussels see Musées royaux des Beaux-Arts de Belgique, Brussels
De Korre 163
Korrekelder 170
Van Krimpen, Hubert 105, 112
KU Leuven 23, 72, 74

Kunst- en Kultuurverbond 248
Kwintessens 199, 200

L
Laban 106
Lambrechts, Joost 25
Lampaert, Herman 14, 23, 71, 72, 138, 139, 140, 170, 258, 259, 260, 262, 263, 266, 267, 270
Lannoo 98, 101, 109
Leaf Brands 106
Leblanc, Walter 216
Ledoux, Jacques 184, 185
Lemmen, Georges 25, 37, 263
Léonard, Jos 10, 11, 12, 13, 14, 15, 16, 18, 19, 20, 21, 22, 23
'T Leerhuys 170
Leopold II 41, 44, 45, 46, 47, 48, 59
Letraset 65, 102
Letterenhuis 72
Lindemans, Gorik 256, 263
Lithos 52, 59
Van Loey, Henri 25, 29, 31
Lonfils, bibi 111
Van Loock, Anne-Judith 75
Loterie Coloniale 47, 48
Loterie Nationale 225
Louis XIV 102
Louis XV 102
Lumumba, Patrice 56

M
Maaltecenter 199
MAD 71
Van de Maele, Walter 248
Mafundikwa, Saki 23, 59
Magritte, René 182
Van Malderen, Luc 90, 141, 142, 236, 259, 262, 263
Maison de la Culture, Namur 225
Malevich, Kazimir 9
Mansion, Colard 25
Mansy, G. 18, 19
Manzoni, Piero 185
Mara, Pol 216
Marfurt, Leo 105
Marie-Claire 190
Marlborough Graphics 216
MAS 53, 59
Masereel, Frans 105, 254
Mecanorma 102
Van Mechelen, Louis 109
Meer en Beter 21, 23
Melatre, Thierry 80

Van Melle 109, 111
Mestdagh, Luk 72, 95, 106, 143, 164, 166, 170, 173, 177, 199, 200, 203, 214, 256, 264, 270
MetaDesign 203
Meyers, Jean-Michel 41, 230, 272
Michaeledes, Michael 216
Middelheim Biennial 106, 123, 132, 205
Middelheim Museum, Antwerp 254
Ministry of Health Pavilion 55
Minne, Joris 35, 109, 231, 251, 254
Mirano Continental 80, 88
Mme Sabine 53, 54
Moedwil, Jan 37
Moerman, Mr 111
Le Monde 31
Mondriaan, Piet 9
More, Thomas 25, 41, 254
Moretus Plantin University Library, Namur 10
Morris, William 37
Mouvement Géographique 44, 59
De Mulder, Walter 109
Mulkers, Urbain 144
Müller-Brockmann, Josef 226
Multi-Art 106, 205, 209, 210, 214, 215, 216, 217, 221, 270
Munari, Bruno 106
Munro, Silas 41
Musée Lapidaire 189
Musées royaux des Beaux-Arts de Belgique, Brussels see Royal Museums of Fine Arts of Belgium, Brussels
Museum for Fine Arts, Ghent 251
Museum of Modern Art, New York 79, 189
Museum Plantin-Moretus, Antwerp 14, 216, 256, 259, 260, 263
Van Muysewinkel 111

N
National Bank 199
National Higher Institute for Architecture and Urban Planning, Antwerp 248
National Institute for Radio Broadcast 231

Néama, May 144, 256, 258, 260, 262
Neuland 52, 59
New Beat Fashion 82, 83
Nietzsche, Friedrich 25
Nippon Shuppan Hanbai 108
Nos Images 49, 51, 52, 59
Novum Gebrauchsgraphik 94, 102
NRC Handelsblad 31
Nutricia 105

O
De Oesterput 105
Off the Grid 9, 23, 71, 89, 113, 259
Olyff, Hubert 225
Olyff, Michel 37, 61, 63, 64, 65, 66, 68, 72, 75, 94, 109, 146, 183, 203, 225, 226, 227, 228, 229, 232, 236, 257, 258, 259, 260, 263, 264, 268, 270
Ons Erfdeel 170
Ost, Jacqueline 55, 147, 169, 177, 261, 270
Van Ostaijen, Paul 25, 254
Overberghe, Cel 216

P
Pauwels, Hilde 242, 272
Le Palace 80, 82
Palais des Beaux-Arts, Brussels 90, 178, 184, 185, 231, 248
Pan American Airways 55
Pans, Frans 148
Paper Art 106, 210, 214
Pas, Johan 217, 259, 261
Pasture, André 148, 257
Pater, Ruben 52
Patmos 98
Paulus, Camille 217
Peeters, Jozef 25, 150, 256, 258, 259, 261, 270
Peignot 231
Pennequin 26
Permeke, Constant 102, 105
PetraShoe 109
Photogravure De Schutter 95, 105
Pinochet, Augusto 175
Plan K 76, 78, 79, 88
Plantin, Christophe 25
Platteborze, Wim 258
POUR 79
Printing Museum, Brussels 25
Privat-Livemont, Henri 45

Prix de Jeune Peinture 106
Projekt 61
La Proue 109
Provincial and Intercommunal Drinking Water Company Antwerp 246
Provinciale Hogeschool Limburg 199
Provincie Antwerpen 106
Provincie West-Vlaanderen 101
Van Poppel 105
Puttaert, Hugo 176, 224, 229, 258, 261, 263, 264

R
Raacke, Peter 246, 254
Radio Belgique 37
Radio Congo Belge 53, 54
Rekto-Verso Club 65
Rencontres Internationales de Lure 63, 225
Renner, Paul 37
Reusens, Geert 243
Richez, Jacques 55, 61, 62, 63, 72, 75, 151, 152, 177, 258, 260, 261, 262, 263, 264, 271
Rijksmuseum, Amsterdam 11
De Roeck, Lucien 25, 35, 37, 41, 55, 98, 109, 177, 226, 230, 231, 232, 234, 235, 236, 237, 238, 239
Rohonyi, Charles 62, 94, 108
Rolland, Marco 80
De Roos, Sjoerd 109
Rosart, Jacques-François 25, 31
Rosart, Matthias 25
Rossi, Cat 75, 88
Royal Library of Belgium 25
Royal Museum for Central Africa, Tervuren 45, 59, 56
Royal Museum of Fine Arts, Antwerp 214, 251
Royal Museums of Fine Arts of Belgium, Brussels 64, 101, 225, 266
Royon, Louis 41
Ryckaert, Pierre 52, 59

S
Sabca 243
Sabena 243, 244
Saey, Angelina 87
Sagmeister, Stefan 227
Saint Laurent Gallery 190
Sandberg, Willem 216
Savignac, Raymond 226

Schockaert, Guy 63, 111
Schuurmans 101
Section 25 79
Seed Factory 177
Serneels, Piet 105, 153, 261
Serulus, Katarina 72, 74, 88, 258
Service for Productivity Enhancement 249
Servranckx, Victor 10
Setola, Albert 72, 154, 163, 170
Setola, Geert 72, 155
Severin, Mark 62
Severin, Elza 256
Shell International 105, 199
De Sikkel 98
Simple Minds 80
Sint Lucas Antwerpen 176, 198, 199, 224, 230, 234
Sint-Lucas Ghent 98, 109
Sint-Lukas, Léopoldville 51
Slothouber & Graatsma 210, 223
S.M.A.K. 173
Snoeck 111
Le Soir 190
Soomers, Frie 241
S+S Alouf 90, 156, 157, 266, 271
Staal, Liliane-Emma 105, 204, 205, 206, 208, 209, 210, 214, 216, 217, 260, 271
Staatliche Kunstakademie für Bildende Künste 163
De Standaard 16, 170, 262, 263
Stanley, Henry Morton 45
Sterck, Paul 80
Stiefenhofer, Fernand 243
Stiefenhofer, Jean-Jacques 75, 242, 243, 246
De Stijl 90
Strebelle, Olivier 225
Studio 54 80
Studio Novio 14, 15
Szukalski, Albert 214, 218

T
Talking Letterheads 71
Tejada, Ramon 41
Théâtre du Parvis 65
Théâtre National 178
The Cure 80
The Guardian 31
The New York Times 31
Theodore Lejeune 26
The Printer's Terms 111
This is... 7

Thybaert & De Graaf 21, 22, 23
Tigra 87
Tomaszewski, Henryk 178
Total Design 97, 203
Transito 51
Tschichold, Jan 14, 51, 109
Tuymans, Luc 101, 173
Twombly, Cy 185
Type an Sich 199
Typo Belgiëque 3, 24, 25, 29, 31
Typografische Monatsblätter 111

U
Uhuru 56
Ultima 108
UNESCO 45, 106, 227
Université Libre de Bruxelles 178, 225
University of Antwerp 56, 74
University of Reading 24
D'Ursel, Henri 109
Utopia 25

V
Valcke, Johan 72, 112, 170
Van, Alec 82
Vanderborght Frères 19
Vanderborght, Michel-Joseph 19, 25, 26, 29
Vandercam, Serge 185
Vantongerloo, Georges 182
Vaultier-Bonnard 26
Van de Velde, Henry 25, 35, 37, 44, 49, 59, 109, 170, 231, 232
Van de Velde, Wannes 37, 45, 105
Van der Velden, Hilde 63
Venturi, Robert 109
Vercruysse, Jan 173
Vereeniging voor Reklamestudie 23
Verhelst, Rudi 95, 199, 143
Verheyen, Jef 106, 208, 210, 214, 216, 217, 271
Verlant, Gilles 80
Verstockt, Mark 158, 216, 262
De Vigne, Claire 225
Villers, Bernard 65
Vista 61
Vitra Design Museum 75, 88
VIZO 71, 72, 97, 170
Vorm in Vlaanderen 108
Vrije Universiteit, Amsterdam 74

De Vuyst, Gaspard 109
De Vylder, Antoon 95, 199

W
Wabbes, Jules 230
Wagemans, Frank 230
Wallonie Design 71
Warneton 249
Wauters, Alphonse-Jules 44
Waxmann, Michel 65, 159
Weemaels 26
Weemaes, Margot 256
Wide White Space 190, 192
Willem I 25, 26
Wissing, Benno 112
Van Wolsschaten, Jan Baptiste 29
Woluwe Shopping Centre 90
Women's Technical Academy of Hainaut, Saint-Ghislain 234
World Commercial Design 61
Wyckaert, Maurice 185

Z
Zwart, Piet 200

Colophon

Off the Grid: Histories of Belgian graphic design

Edited and designed by Sara De Bondt

Interviews with Sophie Alouf-Bertot, Rob Buytaert,
Boudewijn Delaere, Paul Ibou, and Herman Lampaert

Essays by Jo De Baerdemaeker, Belgian Institute Graphic Design,
Sara De Bondt, Jan Ceuleers, Katrien Van Haute, Richard Hollis,
Jean-Michel Meyers, Hilde Pauwels, Hugo Puttaert, and Katarina Serulus

Published by Occasional Papers

Copy-editing by Heyvaert & Jansen and Antony Hudek
Proofreading by Melissa Larner
Translations from Dutch to English by Heyvaert & Jansen
Printed by die Keure

Cover: Jeanine Behaeghel, illustration for Kattestoet Ieper, 1966
Back cover: Paul Ibou, logo for Multi-Art, 1969

Typefaces: Or Lemmen (based on George Lemmen's Antiqua)
Jumbo Mumbo NF (based on Joan Collette and Jos Dufour's Indépendant)
Gerstner Programm FSL

© 2022 the contributors and Occasional Papers

All rights reserved. No part of this publication may be reproduced,
stored in a retrieval system or transmitted, in any form or by any means mechanical,
photocopying or otherwise, without prior permission in writing from the publisher.

Occasional Papers has made every effort to trace copyright holders,
but if any have been overlooked, we will be pleased to make the
necessary accreditations at the first opportunity.

occasionalpapers.org
ISBN 978-0-9954730-8-9

Supported by KASK – School of Arts Ghent, Design Museum Gent, and Flanders Architecture Institute
Financed by the HOGENT Research Fund for the Arts